THE ESSENTIAL
PAUL RAMSEY

THE ESSENTIAL
PAUL RAMSEY
A COLLECTION

PAUL RAMSEY

EDITED BY
WILLIAM WERPEHOWSKI AND
STEPHEN D. CROCCO

Yale University Press
New Haven and London

"Reference Points in Deciding about Abortion" is reprinted by permission of the
publishers from *The Morality of Abortion: Legal and Historical Perspectives*, ed.
John T. Noonan, Cambridge, Mass.: Harvard University Press, copyright © 1970 by
the President and Fellows of Harvard College.

"The Biblical Norm of Righteousness" is reprinted by permission from
Interpretation: A Journal of Bible and Theology 24 (1970): 419–29.

Set in Trump type by The Composing Room of Michigan, Inc., Grand Rapids,
Michigan. Printed in the United States of America by BookCrafters, Inc., Chelsea,
Michigan.

Library of Congress Cataloging-in-Publication Data

Ramsey, Paul.
   The essential Paul Ramsey : a collection / edited by William Werpehowski and
Stephen D. Crocco.
     p.   cm.
   Includes bibliographical references (p. xxx–xxx) and index.
   ISBN 0-300-05815-2

   1. Christian ethics—Protestant authors.   I. Werpehowski, William.
II. Crocco,   Stephen D.   III. Title.
BJ1251.R284   1994
241'.092—dc20   93-35449

A catalogue record for this book is available from the British Library.

The paper in this book meets the guidelines for permanence and durability of the
Committee on Production Guidelines for Book Longevity of the Council on Library
Resources.

10 9 8 7 6 5 4 3 2 1

Contents

INTRODUCTION

In his remarks at a memorial service for Paul Ramsey held at Princeton University in April 1988, the philosopher and bioethicist Leon Kass concluded: "I continue to learn from Paul, and I can still hear him laugh." For those in attendance, the words delivered comfort and insight. Ramsey's death earlier that year left colleagues and students in Christian ethics without that intellectually demanding, sometimes exasperating but nonetheless *amused* personal presence who contributed so much to common explorations. Even beyond the power of his writings there was, in Gilbert Meilaender's recollection, "the *viva voce*—the man, who was well nigh omnipresent at meetings and conferences. People wrestled with his writings because they came to see first hand the mind that was at work in them"[1] That Kass could still hear him laugh reflected the hope that Ramsey's voice and the example it set might yet mark a standard of involved inquiry for all who shared his work and concerns.

Of course, Kass was also referring to the remarkable published achievements of a scholar who everywhere insisted that Christian ethics maintain theological integrity and precision. As James Gustafson noted in 1984: "In North American Paul Ramsey has been a towering and forceful figure for almost four decades; his writing has forced persons with alternative views to come to grips with his thought, and had a deep impact on a younger generation of authors. He has been a persistent critic of moral fads, a steadfast proponent of

1. Gilbert Meilaender to William Werpehowski, undated letter.

the Christian ethics of love, and a vigorous participant in debates about public policy and medical ethics."[2]

Ramsey attributed much of his productivity to the fact that he spent his career in one place. After two years of teaching at Garrett Biblical Institute, he spent nearly forty-five years in Princeton, New Jersey. He was called to the nascent Department of Religion at Princeton University in 1944, and it was in Princeton that Ramsey and his wife, Effie Register, raised their three daughters, Marcia (b. 1944), Janet, and Jennifer (both b. 1946). When he retired from the faculty in 1982, Ramsey became a fellow at the Center of Theological Inquiry, adjacent to the Princeton Seminary campus. He was buried in the Princeton Cemetery in 1988.

Ramsey was born in Mendenhall, Mississippi, in 1913 to Rev. John William and Mamie McCay Ramsey. As a young Methodist graduate student with a degree from Millsaps College (B.S., 1935), Ramsey attended Yale Divinity School and the Yale Graduate School (B.D., 1940; Ph.D., 1943). His studies at Yale with H. Richard Niebuhr and the philosopher Charles W. Hendel prepared him for a teaching career in theological ethics and moral philosophy. Ramsey never thought much of his dissertation, "The Concept of Man in the Philosophy of Josiah Royce and Bernard Bosanquet," but it does illustrate his early interests in philosophical idealism. His first book, *Basic Christian Ethics* (1950), and the substantial introduction to Jonathan Edwards's *Freedom of the Will* (1957) illustrate this bent. Ramsey never lost his interest in or talent for metaethics, although he is best known for his work on moral problems.

Ramsey's opposition to situation ethics and his recovery of the just war tradition for Protestants kept him busy in the 1960s. His rich studies of Augustine and Barth bore fruit in *War and the Christian Conscience* (1961) and *Christian Ethics and the Sit-In* (1962). Ramsey spent the middle years of the decade as an opponent of situation ethics and the ecclesiastical endorsement of particular solutions to social problems. *Who Speaks for the Church?* (1967), *Deeds and Rules in Christian Ethics* (1967), and *The Just War* (1968) made for him enemies and friends wherever they were read. The Vietnam War occupied an enormous amount of Ramsey's attention, and his grudging support for U.S. policies in that war, along with his defense of a just nuclear deterrent, kept him in the heat of controversy.

---

2. *Ethics from a Theocentric Perspective*, vol. 2, *Ethics and Theology* (Chicago: Univ. of Chicago Press, 1984), p. 84.

In 1968 Ramsey turned his attention to medical ethics. He spent two semesters as the Joseph P. Kennedy Visiting Professor of Genetic Ethics at the Georgetown University School of Medicine, writing the lectures that would become *The Patient as Person* (1970). Ramsey explained that this position enabled him, "a Protestant Christian ethicist, to be located in the medical school faculty–not on its periphery–and to begin some serious study of the moral issues in medical research and practice."[3] *Fabricated Man* (1970), *The Ethics of Fetal Research* (1975), and *Ethics at the Edges of Life* (1978) grew out of these investigations.

With medical ethics behind him, Ramsey spent the last decade of his life editing Edwards's *Ethical Writings* (1989). He did so in part to settle an old obligation to the Edwards edition, but also because he was convinced that Edwards's theology of God might speak a good word to an age when a theology of everything but God was in fashion.

During his long tenure at Princeton, Ramsey struck up lasting relationships with his colleagues, many of his undergraduate majors, and his few graduate students. He delighted in reminding under-graduates in his lecture classes that they were incorrect in calling his southern oratory "preaching." His friendships carried over into a number of scholarly organizations. A long-time member of the Amer-ican Theological Society, the Society of Christian Ethics, and the Duodecim theological society, Ramsey welcomed their meetings as occasions to nurture the bonds which sustained him and the disci-pline of Christian ethics for four decades.

The editors believe that the examples of Ramsey's work collected in this volume present substantial opportunities for interested readers to learn, and to continue to learn, from him. Indeed, they may find in him "a companion *sans pareil*, who, on a second or third reading, will turn out to have anticipated all the moves by which they had thought they were advancing beyond his tuition."[4] The selec-tions range from general accounts of his "Christian ethics of love" to discussions of more specific issues concerning politics, medicine, and sexuality. This introduction, together with brief notes preceding each selection, orient the reader to some characteristic themes of his theological ethics.

---

3. *The Patient as Person: Exploration in Medical Ethics* (New Haven and London: Yale Univ. Press, 1970), p. xx.

4. Oliver O'Donovan, "Obituary: Paul Ramsey," *Studies in Christian Ethics* 1/1 (1988): 82–90.

THE PRIMACY OF NEIGHBOR-LOVE

In *Basic Christian Ethics*, Ramsey presented an account of the norm of love of neighbor that is founded on the authoritative pattern of God's action toward humanity in Jesus Christ. So derived, this norm of agape finds its rightful place "*on the ground floor* of [Christianity's] understanding of morality."[5] It defines for the Christian what is right, righteous, and obligatory.[6] While Ramsey's understanding of Christian love was refined and developed after *Basic Christian Ethics*, this statement of its meaning and justification characterized his thought throughout his career.

The basis for Ramsey's derivation of the norm of love is his conviction that "Biblical writers do not view ethics naturalistically as rooted in human nature or in the social environment, or abstractly in terms of some generalizations about human values. They view ethics theologically as rooted in the nature and activity of God."[7] Biblical understandings of the righteousness of God and the reign of this righteousness in the Kingdom of God in Jesus Christ constitute the two sources of Christian love. The former refers to God's "judgment and . . . steadfast faithfulness to the covenant he makes with men" and is expressed in a biblical pattern of divine activity that renders care to the vulnerable, deliverance to captives, and inclusive regard for aliens.[8] Biblical texts such as Exodus and the prophetic writings amply display this pattern. Persons faithful to God will measure their actions by it, as it is

> summed up in the principle: To each according to the measure of his real need, not because of anything human reason can discern inherent in the needy, but because his need alone is the measure of God's righteousness toward him. Such justice or righteousness is primarily neither "corrective" nor "distributive," as in the Greek view, but "redemptive," with special bias in favor of the helpless who can contribute nothing at all and are in fact "due" nothing.[9]

Jesus Christ decisively realizes the divine righteousness, which is expressed in the love for sinners. The supreme test of neighbor-love, Ramsey would later say, is not for the self to love the neighbor as

---

5. *Basic Christian Ethics* (New York: Scribner's, 1950), p. 115n.

6. Ramsey, *Deeds and Rules in Christian Ethics* (New York: Scribner's, 1967), p. 108.

7. *Basic Christian Ethics*, p. 1.

8. Ibid., pp. 2, 8–13.

9. Ibid., p. 14.

oneself (since self-love is too varying and often self-destructive), but to love the other in the manner of Christ's love for humanity.[10]

Yet Jesus' life and teachings also must be placed in connection with the apocalyptic expectation of the imminent arrival of the Kingdom of God. In particular, the content and meaning of Jesus' "strenuous" teachings appear to depend upon the anticipation of God's radical overcoming of the world in assertion of divine dominion; these include the prescriptions "to non-resisting, unclaiming love, overflowing good even for an enemy, unlimited forgiveness for every offense, giving to every need, unconditional lending to him who would borrow."[11] In these teachings unqualified and exclusive regard is urged for the single neighbor one may by chance meet, "because all neighbors except the one actually present were apocalyptically removed from view and taken care of by God."[12] Though he allows in the end that "The righteousness of God is one righteousness," Ramsey still takes this depiction of the inbreaking Kingdom of God as provisionally specifying a distinguishable biblical source for Christian love.

What does that depiction in its ethical aspects add to a view of agape to warrant even the provisional distinction? Ramsey points out that the continuing validity of Jesus' strenuous teachings depends upon culling from them the truth that remains effective *outside* their original context of kingdom expectation, where in fact "*there is always more than one neighbor.*"[13] Most textual evidence in *Basic Christian Ethics* suggests that the relevant truth involves an *intensification* of the injunction to attend exclusively to the needs of the neighbor, irrespective of self-regarding preferences for self *or* others.

> A chief problem in morals arises from the fact that the vast network of neighbor-claims tends to dim our perception of obligation and provides us with a too ready excuse for a lapse into concern for self. . . . Precisely the situation in which we need to be judged and transformed . . . is when, because of the multiplicity of neighbor-claims, we are tempted to defend the interests of self more than Christian love for even a single individual would allow.[14]

Above all, the biblical pattern is righteous regard for the well-being of human creatures for their own sake.

10. See selection 2.
11. *Basic Christian Ethics*, p. 24.
12. Ibid., p. 40.
13. Ibid., p. 42, author's emphasis.
14. Ibid., p. 43.

It follows for Ramsey that Christian love is focused without division or distraction upon the neighbor. No claims of self are to impede the sighting of neighbor-need, and no conditions are set as qualifications for moral regard. Attention to the full particularity of the other requires that the neighbor not be a mere extension of the self's partial desires for itself; the Christian is exhorted to discover the neighbor beneath friendliness or hostility, apart from enlightened self-interest or intentional concern for self-realization, and beyond the mixed motives associated with some "common good" that the self and other may reciprocally share.[15] Appeal to a general and universally applicable standard of worth as the basis of neighbor-love (for example, "the infinite, inherent value of human personality") is likewise rejected; since the self would meet the requirements of the standard, "such a doctrine would logically lead to subtracting from obligation as much as the just claims of self require." Another sort of condition of love, that one's own claims be included in the moral reckoning, would thereby find entry.

But after the leap to the neighbor's side has been accomplished, duties to oneself may be *derived* from neighbor-love. Not located on the ground floor of Christian ethics, attention to self remains both secondary and essential. The freedom of the Christian from selfish partiality is fully compatible with being bound to whatever concern for self is most needful for the neighbors who cross one's path. In fact, the scope of such mandated self-concern may be quite large. One must intend to cultivate the "givens" of natural talents and capacities. One should care for one's health and not be a burden on others. There may be grounds to refuse to sacrifice oneself to some persons for the sake of other neighbors for whom one is responsible, and similarly, to defend oneself against attack as a duty owed to others. Personal rights, or "conditions of life which a person must possess and exercise in order effectively to love his neighbor," ought to be asserted on one's own behalf—for the neighbor's sake.[16] The self-conscious intention to cultivate virtue for the neighbor's sake is quite fitting. And in his later work, Ramsey was even able to clarify how the self's resistance to exploitation may be required for the *exploiter's* own sake.[17] This approach affirms the freedom of Christian love. It also presupposes a distinction between (selfish) self-preference and the self's love of whatever she places his or her happi-

15. Ibid., p. 94–95, 102.
16. Ibid., pp. 176–77, 187.
17. See selection 10.

ness in—be that object the self or the neighbor. Hence there is a proper sense in which the Christian may *delight* in the project of neighbor-love and the duties to cultivate virtue and look after oneself that such a project calls forth.[18]

As Gene Outka has shown, Christian ethicists in this century have disagreed about the content of Christian love. Some have held that it involves an independent and unalterable regard for the well-being of the human creature as such. Others focus on some self-sacrifice, or on a love that elicits a loving, mutual response.[19] Six years after *Basic Christian Ethics*, Ramsey addressed the meaning of agape in Reinhold Niebuhr's work. Objecting to his constant use of *"sacrificial* love," Ramsey makes a point that he later counted as an important refinement in his own work: "Love is simply love, the genuine article; and it intends the good of the beloved one and not the response of mutuality; it intends the good of the other and not its own actual self-sacrifice or suffering. It is the *neighbor*, and not mutuality or heedlessness or sacrifice or suffering, who stands ever before the eyes of love."[20] Agape may and does issue in community, but "among-you-ness" as such is not its primary purpose. Agape is self-giving in its motive "steadfastly to affirm the well-being of another"; but the act of self-sacrifice is required "only when the occasion warrants it in terms of actually advancing the neighbor's good."[21] These claims are at the heart of Ramsey's later writings, whether he is discussing just war theory, resistance for racial equality, or care for the dying.[22]

LOVE TRANSFORMING NATURAL JUSTICE

Besides the development just mentioned, Ramsey extended and improved his theological ethics of love in at least three ways after *Basic Christian Ethics*. One concerned his conclusion that the idea of *faithfulness* stands as "the single univocal biblical concept in terms of which the meaning of 'love' in Jesus' twofold commandment has to

18. See Ramsey's discussion of Edwards in selection 3.

19. Gene Outka, *Agape: An Ethical Analysis* (New Haven and London: Yale Univ. Press, 1972), passim.

20. *Nine Modern Moralists* (Englewood Cliffs, N.J.: Prentice-Hall, 1962), p. 183. Cf. Ramsey, "A Letter to James Gustafson," *Journal of Religious Ethics* 13/1 (Spring 1985): 75.

21. *Nine Modern Moralists*, p. 172.

22. See William Werpehowski, "Christian Love and Covenant Faithfulness," *Journal of Religious Ethics* 19/2 (Fall 1991): 103–32.

be understood."[23] Earlier he was reluctant to admit that any single notion would do. Second, there was fuller appreciation of how moral rules can express the work of Christian love. Third, Ramsey made better sense of the relation between Christian love and the "natural" moral law (or justice) that may be discerned in human judgments apart from explicit faith in the revealed Christian story of God, Israel, and Christ. The last two themes, in reverse order, make up this and the next section. The first will occupy us, in different ways, for the balance of the essay.

Ramsey credits his greater clarity concerning agape and natural morality to H. Richard Niebuhr's observation that he had adopted a stance of "Christ transforming natural law" in *Basic Christian Ethics*. The general argument that follows up on this observation may be found in Ramsey's *Nine Modern Moralists*.

The crucial question was this: Christian disciples may well govern their lives by conforming to agape; but how do they relate to forms of moral insight ("natural law") that seem available to Christians and non-Christians alike, and that serve to organize human life in various ways at some distance from the Christian church and the Christian story? Alternatively, the question has to do with thinking through the connections and distinctions between moral requirements that explicitly express God's redemptive righteousness ("Christian love") and requirements that shape and guide human beings considered in their common status as *creatures*—creatures who, while "fallen" into moral error and sin, may still testify to God's good creation by seeking good lives in communal settings, such as the family and the *polis*, in a variety of more or less fitting ways ("natural justice"). Ramsey frames his answer by contrasting it with two strategies of evasion.

> The chief problem for Christian social ethics is how we are to understand the relation between the law of nature and the righteousness of the covenant. There are two ways, and only two ways, of avoiding this problem. Ethics may, on the one hand, remain wholly within the "Egypt" of the natural law, deriving the standard for man solely from man and from the structures immanent in human society. This is the path taken by every humanistic ethic. Christian ethical theory may, on the other hand, pass wholly into "Exodus," taking note only of the demands upon men who live in the immediate presence of God and ignoring the fact that they still live within the ordered forms of *some* natural community which is based, in part at least,

23. *Nine Modern Moralists*, p. 129.

upon agreement as to inherent principles based on creation. This is the path sometimes taken by the ethics of Protestantism with its radical doctrines of sin and grace.[24]

Instead, Christian ethics must devise a "dynamic ethic of redemption which does not simply build upon yet does not destroy the ethics of creation"; the first option gives too much authority to natural justice, the second too little. Positively put, the work of love must be free to confirm some norms of justice, but also to "manifest a dynamic, redirecting, and transforming influence upon the apparently given necessities of the orders of society and upon any of the standards of natural justice which may commend themselves to the minds of men."[25] Ramsey commends H. Richard Niebuhr's stress on the Incarnation of the Word who has entered into "a human culture that has never been without his ordering action"; thus moral wisdom may be sought and accepted wherever it is given in the world, so long as it is held liable to transformation by Christian love.[26]

Powerful examples of this approach may be found whenever Ramsey works within the framework of Karl Barth's claim that creation is the "external basis" of covenant and covenant is the "internal basis" of creation. The works of creation, including the realities of sexual differentiation, human embodiment, and individual freedom, need to be honored and protected in the world, especially in the case of the weak. They are conditions of creaturely flourishing in relationships of covenant fidelity or "fellow humanity," whereby persons live with and for one another as social beings who, as such, reflect God's being for humanity. "Covenant" is the "inner meaning" of these conditions. Relationships among human creatures in the contexts of marriage, medicine, economics, citizenship, and the like may be ceaselessly transformed, however, by the work of faithful Christian love. Love protects property rights, rights to consent to medical experimentation, and norms that prohibit direct killing of dying patients, because these rights and norms secure the well-being of creatures who are made for covenant. But love might also redirect and invigorate these structures of human relationship, so that in them human persons may become more caring, more solicitous, and more personally loyal to the vulnerable.[27]

24. Ibid., p. 224.
25. Ibid., pp. 235–36, 254–58.
26. See Gilbert Meilaender, "'Love's Casuistry': Paul Ramsey on Caring for the Terminally Ill," *Journal of Religious Ethics* 19/2 (Fall 1991): 133–56.
27. See selections 9, 10, 13, 14, 15.

Thus the ethics of creation is given a relatively independent status in the light of the work of God; it sets terms to which the order of Christian love, reaching down to it, must respond. Love does good work for the good of the neighbor when it sustains the external conditions of covenant, "affirming and confirming justice and fundamental rights as first and also required of a Christian by the saving love of Christ"; but love may go on "elevating, transforming, definitely shaping, and fashioning what justice may mean, if possible, more in the direction of the requirements of charity." New possibilities for fellow humanity are always considered *beyond* a minimal ascription of rights, and *toward* the realization of the fullness of human need in fellow humanity which agape discerns. All of this is accounted for *along with* love's critical freedom; "the order of justice reaches up to the order of charity, submitting to its final review every judgment and proposed action based only on what 'nature itself teaches' or what society and its present laws require."[28] Agape is first and last faithful to persons in their need. It keeps faith with them both in their being as creatures and with their possibilities for fulfillment in loyal relationships with one another.

THE IMPORTANCE OF PRINCIPLES

Basic Christian Ethics stressed the freedom of agape from legalism and the codes of social convention. Agape is "free from" rules in these ways because it is utterly "free for" the neighbor in his or her genuine need. Rules and conventions may or may not serve the neighbor, and hence may or may not meet love's stern demands.[29] However, considered attention to this form of "positive liberty" led Ramsey to see that moral rules or principles may fittingly embody and fulfill neighbor love in any Christian social ethic worthy of the name.

To be sure, there is nothing inconsistent about endorsing a rule such as "never directly attack noncombatants in wartime" in the name of the freedom of Christian love. If a careful assessment of the values and human needs at stake leads to the conclusion that the practice of war thus regulated is most faithful to the well-being of neighbors whose lives sit in the balance, well and good. Simply to deny this in the name of agape's "freedom from law" risks creation of a new legalism of "freedom." But there was more to the matter than

28. *Christian Ethics and the Sit-In* (New York: Association Press, 1961), pp. 124–28.

29. See selection 1.

this. Ramsey discerned a link between the character of God's fidelity to humanity and a Christian ethics that stands faithful to God in part by keeping covenant with the neighbor.

> A position we might call "pure or general rule agapism" would seem to be entailed in any conviction that in Jesus Christ the righteousness of God and the mystery of the ages, the meaning of creation, of mature manhood, and the destination of man toward unfailing covenant with God and with fellowman, have been made manifest. An unbinding love would seem the least likely conclusion one would reach if he seriously regarded the freedom of God's love in binding Himself to the world as the model for all covenants between men. . . . Love seems to have only a dissolving or relativizing power when the *freedom of agape* is taken to mean love's *inability* to bind itself one way and not another or in no way except in acts that are the immediate response of one person's depth to another's depth.[30]

Given the likelihood of some regularity and continuity in human needs, relationships, and the social institutions bearing on human well-being in particular communities, agape may well start with *people*, not rules, and find that people are loved well through recourse to rules that have a general validity.

In addition, the debate over "situation ethics" that took place in America in the 1960s appeared to identify an antilegalistic interpretation of agape with a utilitarian mode of moral decision making. At least Joseph Fletcher, the author of *Situation Ethics*, held this view: "As the love ethic searches seriously for a social policy it must form a coalition with utilitarianism. It takes over from Mill the strategic principle of 'the greatest good of the greatest number.'"[31] But this principle, at least when applied isolated case by isolated case (and in this sense "in the situation"), notoriously subordinates the needs of particular persons to the good of "the greater number" affected by this or that social policy. The *neighbor* is to be loved, not to be counted as a piece of "well-being" in the group among other personally undifferentiated factors of "well-being." The neighbor is a *creature*, made for covenant-partnership with God and one's fellow; to absorb him or her into the collective through utilitarian calculation is to abandon his or her genuine good by failing to revere the separateness of his or her life, since that is itself an external condition of such partnership.

Ramsey marshaled other arguments on behalf of his commitment

---

30. *Deeds and Rules in Christian Ethics*, pp. 127–28.
31. *Situation Ethics* (Philadelphia: Westminster, 1966), p. 95.

to the "in-principled" character of Christian love, but these two will suffice for our purposes.[32] It remains to note the sorts of principles that Ramsey would affirm and employ in his work. Two are of crucial importance. *Rules of practice* are norms that define and regulate roles and behaviors within a particular moral relationship or institution. The norm of agape is applied to the love-embodying character of the practice itself; rules here are "rules of the game."[33] That promises are to be kept is a classic example, and Ramsey refers to it often. "If, to the question 'Why did you do that?' a person replies, 'Because I promised,' that is clear and sufficient evidence that he understands the nature of promise-keeping as a rule of practice, which as a Christian he justifies because *that* is what love requires *as a practice*."[34] Exceptions are not justified within the practice itself, although agape may work to change the rules of the game. In that case as before, however, one justifies an action by appeal to the practice itself.

Ramsey would often question whether exceptions, or liberty to make them, should be built into some moral practice itself. Should physicians or experimenters adopt a policy of remaining *open* to suspending a requirement of informed consent for patients and experimental subjects in cases where great good and minimal harm will be done? Should doctors allow that in the rare cases where dying patients are in insurmountable pain, they may act to kill them directly? In the first example, the ethicist must look to the consequences of the practice in enabling an error in judgment, especially in light of severe pressures on healers and scientists to "make progress" and "get results." In the second example, even *if* the isolated *act* could be justified by Christian love, attention to the *practice* of medicine invites an inquiry about whether physicians shaped by the practice would find their commitment to heal and care eroded or corrupted by their new license to kill. Ramsey suggests that these considerations indicate a negative judgment about the exceptions in question.[35]

In both instances the projected general social consequences of the practice in question play a significant role in the moral reckoning. Agape's efficacy requires that it be interpreted in part to embrace rule-utilitarian calculations. Ramsey never wanted to disavow the propri-

---

32. See especially Ramsey's remarks on eschatology and an ethics of means in *Fabricated Man: The Ethics of Genetic Control* (New Haven and London: Yale Univ. Press, 1970), pp. 22–32.
33. See selection 2.
34. *Deeds and Rules in Christian Ethics*, p. 138.
35. See selection 14 and *The Patient as Person*, pp. 157–64.

ety of this interpretation, but he became concerned to sharpen theologically his treatment of promises, marriage vows, commitments to "do no harm," and the like. "We must . . . *distinguish significantly*, if not entirely separate, 'canons of loyalty'" from rules of practice having primarily utilitarian justification. . . . There is need throughout our Christian ethical reflection to distinguish a merely *practice* conception of the promising-game or the marriage-game and all the other covenants of life with life in which men are engaged from a thoroughly *performative* conception of all these faithfulness-claims upon men."[36]

What is the point here? "Canons of loyalty" refer to a sort of "rule" based on a "performative" account of moral relationships. In Ramsey's usage, they may be justified with reference to a "practice conception," but their meaning is not exhausted by it. Indeed, the latter is subordinate to the primary injunction that moral agents in their communities above all else *demonstrate faithfulness* to one another. These demonstrations are "performances" correlative to the "divine performance" of steadfast love that norms Christian action and graciously constitutes the human creature. Thus moral requirements conceived as "canons of loyalty" do not utterly depend on the consequence-features of acts or policies, even if they are also not independent of them. They but figure in the process by which Christians come more and more to grasp the meaning of faithfulness. The claims and occasions of faithfulness constitute the relevant moral features of any action or relationship, and attention to consequences serves the quest to discern what makes for fidelity. In this light, calculations of consequences are constrained by the demand to keep covenant with the neighbor—practices that build in exceptions to rules, or openness to exceptions fail if in that way they fail to underwrite covenant loyalty.[37]

Along this path Ramsey was led to a Christian defense of exceptionless moral rules. The principle of discrimination with which we began this section—the prohibition on direct attack of noncombatants in wartime—is a rule of this kind.[38] With it and others, Ramsey's ordering of a rule utilitarian "practice conception" to the demand to be faithful to the neighbor deftly improved his ethics; for he was thereby able to use the *effects* of policies and practices on social

36. "The Case of the Curious Exception," in Gene H. Outka and Paul Ramsey, eds., *Norm and Context in Christian Ethics* (New York: Scribner's, 1968), p. 120n.

37. See selections 14, 15, 16.

38. See selections 5, 6, 8.

values in order to "build a floor under the individual fellow man by minimum faithfulness-rules or canons of loyalty to him that are unexceptionable."[39] The neighbor's good, and not the good overall or the good of practices generally, remains paramount.

REALISM

Ramsey's writings on war and politics, as well as his sustained attention to the need to protect persons most liable to exploitation and abuse, reflect a stance toward the human condition that takes the human tendency to evil very seriously. Often this stance led him to stress the limited way that moral ideals and aspirations can be realized in a world still fraught with the sinful self-assertion of individuals and groups. This stance has a conventional name, and it is "Christian realism"; but some features of Ramsey's realism were not so conventional at all—if, that is to say, Reinhold Niebuhr's Christian ethic stands as paradigm.

In a letter to Sid Macauley of the Christian Medical Society, Ramsey writes of Niebuhr's contribution to the erosion of the early pacifism of his student days at Millsaps College.

> I was among the thousands of ministers and young people who, as World War II approached, were pacifists. Also at Millsaps we were socialists, inter-racialists, and opponents of intercollegiate football as a brutal sport. I remember when back teaching at Millsaps, 1937–1939, after two years at Yale Divinity School, making a speech at a rally from the steps of one of the buildings and reading a telegram I had sent to President Roosevelt to stay out of the war (the occasion, I believe, was Hitler's move into Poland; but it might have been some other event).
>
> It was against this ethos, of course, that Reinhold Niebuhr set his face . . . His shattering book *Moral Man and Immoral Society* was published, I believe, in 1936, the year after I graduated from college. *The Nature and Destiny of Man* came later, and of course, that began to eat away at the foundations of the position I then held.[40]

Prominent themes of Niebuhr's work—the suspicion of Christian sentimentalism, the stress on the inevitability of inordinate self-assertion and "ideological taint" among collectives, the need to balance power with power in the pursuit of the historical ideals of justice and equality, and the idea that the self-transcending human spirit,

39. *Deeds and Rules in Christian Ethics*, p. 133.
40. Quoted by D. Stephen Long, *Paul Ramsey; Reflections on Christian Ethics, 1935–1989*, forthcoming.

shorn of the pretense of the purity of motive, may yet help to secure a more tolerable common life—all find their place near the center of Ramsey's thought.

Yet Ramsey wanted "to propose an extension within" Niebuhr's Christian realism. Proximately the revision concerned showing that "there was more to be said about justice in war than was articulated in Niebuhr's sense of the ambiguities of politics and his greater/lesser evil doctrine on the use of force. That more is the principle of discrimination," the absolute immunity of noncombatants from direct attack.[41] There may be something coy (if also deeply respectful) about calling this an "extension within" Niebuhr's standpoint; for in fact the move can reasonably appear to be a critical revision of Niebuhr in two related ways. First, in Ramsey's hands the principle of discrimination is an implication of the faithfulness of Christian love. We have here not so much a case of justice *approximating* the "impossible possibility" of self-sacrificing *agape* (the Niebuhrian account) as we have an instance of love properly *applied* transforming natural justice! Second, to hold that discrimination is an exceptionless moral rule counters Niebuhr's tendency to rely on consequentialist assessments that lead to the doing of the lesser evil. The latter procedure could in principle undermine the former status, since it is compatible with overriding the principle in the name of preventing a greater evil from occurring.

Nevertheless, Niebuhr's concern to meet human sin honestly and without naive illusion does find a sort of extension in Ramsey's ethics. He can be understood to see prohibitions like discrimination to be supported by the intractable tendency of human persons to take advantage of one another. The prohibitions "protect us from harms which cut deeply into our physical and psychical well-being. . . . [They] make sense only in a world where such effects of sin usually threaten."[42] If faithfulness to the neighbor is a prime imperative, then the concepts and categories of Christian ethics ought to fit the demand. Too much talk of approximation and ambiguity hurts the cause.

In any case, Ramsey's realism was not limited to talk of war. He

41. Ramsey, *The Just War* (New York: Scribner's, 1968), p. 260. See also David Attwood, *Paul Ramsey's Political Ethics* (Lanham, Md.: Rowman and Littlefield, 1992), pp. 42ff.

42. Gene Outka, "The Protestant Tradition and Exceptionless Moral Norms," in Donald G. MacCarthy, ed., *Moral Theology Today: Certitudes and Doubts* (St. Louis: Pope John Center, 1984), p. 160.

was especially fond of applying to other cases the Niebuhrian dictum "Man's capacity for justice makes democracy possible; man's propensity for injustice makes democracy necessary." So we have Ramsey arguing that the human capacity for fidelity makes marriage possible, and that the human capacity for infidelity makes marriage necessary.[43] And then there was, in connection with medical ethics, the dictum "Man's capacity to become joint adventurers in a common cause makes the consensual relation possible; man's propensity to overreach his joint adventurer even in a good cause makes consent necessary."[44] The discussions of marriage and consent carried Niebuhr forward while improving upon him. Especially significant was the way in which Ramsey actually *paid theological attention* to the first half of the formula. He had a modest but effective anthropology at work which presented the creature as made for covenant with his or her fellows, and he played this out without giving way on the deep-seated resources for human betrayal.

We cannot here and now recover or reclaim the "viva voce"; we can only remember it. Still, there are features of Ramsey's written corpus that do direct us to the manner of the man at work. A brief word, then, about the *style* and *scope* of Ramsey's Christian ethics.

The style was based on the love of careful argument and the conviction that precision in our language and conceptions of ethics is a great good for the Christian community and the world. Ramsey believed that mistakes in language gave way to mistakes in thought, and that mistakes in thought could lead to the most horrible practices.[45] These concerns were not abstract. On the contrary, they were the result of the exemplary loyalty that a scholar might display toward one's craft, its history, and current practitioners. Whether he was doggedly and boisterously engaged in debate with opponents, or subjecting himself as a good editor to the writings and thought of Jonathan Edwards (an activity that occupied some fifteen years of his career),[46] the test he set for himself was the same as that which he announced on the first page of *Nine Modern Moralists*: "The highest tribute one can pay any thinker, or any body of writing, is to wrestle with it; and this may be the best way to bring out the innermost and most vital meaning of what any man has said. I trust that in this

43. See selection 2 and Ramsey's *One Flesh* (Bramcote, Nottingham: Grove, 1975).
44. See selection 14.
45. See especially selection 6.
46. For an example of his Edwards scholarship, see selection 3.

wrestling I have nowhere simply commanded an issue to be gone, or have ignored the real meaning or strength of an idea or point of view in rejecting or reformulating it."

Ramsey's insistent questioning of his fellows in Christian ethics, and the sometimes maddening complexity and detail of his moral analysis, reflect this effort to honor his colleagues and "to make his writing a continuation of many conversations in which he had, with the help of others, begun to wrap his mind around a question."[47] He could be combative, and he sometimes seemed overwhelming; but there was an infectious joy he took in conversation. It was, above all, against the grain of the man to be dismissive.

Ramsey also remained ready to question and criticize himself. He once wrote to Stanley Hauerwas that "every word I have every written has been written to *myself*. I have always been exploring the meaning in practice of the Christian faith—for myself. I have wanted to know *which way* to go if I ever wanted to depart from it."[48] A controversial supporter of the Vietnam War, Ramsey admitted later that he was too long in judging its immorality. Once a defender of the "bluff" in nuclear deterrence policies, Ramsey conceded that he erred.[49] His development regarding the meaning of Christian love, and the intellectual movement through "rules of practice" to "canons of loyalty," discussed above, afford other examples of self-correction. His "thorough and prolonged probing"[50] into the meaning of Christian love—finding the proper language and moral concepts to express it, bringing it down to cases, reaching back and rethinking its sense in relation to his teachers (Augustine, Edwards, the Niebuhrs, Barth)—carried at its best a thoroughgoing and impartial honesty.

Finally, and as the selections in this book attest, Paul Ramsey believed that "Christian discernments" can legitimately be presented as "public ethics."[51] Taking the world to be God's world in the particular sense of the first chapter of the Gospel of John, a world enlightened in its entirety and from the outset by the Word made flesh, Ramsey held fast to a vision of love permeating and transforming renderings of justice in the wider affairs of human persons. But this account, like that of the meaning of love, was subject to qualification and critical elaboration. He worried about how churches ad-

---

47. Meilaender, " 'Love's Casuistry,' " p. 135.
48. Ramsey to Hauerwas, Aug. 4, 1978 (Perkins Library, Duke University).
49. See selection 8.
50. Meilaender, " 'Love's Casuistry,' " p. 134.
51. Ibid., p. 136.

dressed issues of public policy; they should neither coerce the consciences of individual Christians nor let the character of public debate dictate the terms of a distinctively Christian witness.[52] And his interest in lending Christian support to the general moral ethos of human culture did not overrun his sensitivity to "an enduring tension between loyalty to Christ and our responsibilities in a less than ideal world." He acknowledged

> a dialectic between the motif of withdrawal from the evil of the less than perfect structures of the world and the motif of shaping or reshaping society so as to maintain better the human dwelling place. There is movement toward perfection of discipleship, which entails selective (perhaps radical) withdrawal, and there is movement toward engagement, which entails selective (perhaps deep) involvement. Indeed, we are called to *do both*, to be in the world but not of it.[53]

These words from Paul Ramsey's last book show forth again the "thorough and prolonged probing" that so much defined his work. They are words that spring from the Christian tradition. They were written as part of a lively dialogue with a colleague (Stanley Hauerwas). They intimate a nuanced revision of the author's own position. In all of these ways, they keep the conversation of Christian ethics going.[54] The editors hope that this volume of readings will contribute to the same task.

The editors acknowledge a debt of gratitude to the many persons who contributed to the publication of this volume. We thank Jeffrey Stout, who first encouraged us to take on this project. Paul Ramsey's daughter, Marcia Wood, deserves our gratitude for helping us to cut through the thicket of copyrights and permissions. Thanks go to Stanley Hauerwas, D. Stephen Long, Gilbert Meilaender, Oliver O'Donovan, Gene Outka, and Edmund Santurri for various reasons. Kevin Long, Barbara McFarland, and Philip Sanders assisted with the preparation of the bibliography. The staff of the Special Collections Library at Duke University and Charles Grench and the staff of Yale

52. See Ramsey, *Who Speaks for the Church?* (Nashville and New York: Abingdon, 1967) and *Speak up for Just War or Pacifism* (University Park and London: Pennsylvania State Univ. Press, 1988). See also Philip Turner, "Social Advocacy as a Moral Issue in Itself," *Journal of Religious Ethics* 19/2 (Fall 1991): 157–82.

53. *Speak Up for Just War or Pacifism*, p. 142.

54. Cf. Kenneth Vaux, ed., *Covenants of Life: Contemporary Medical Ethics in Light of the Thought of Paul Ramsey* (forthcoming). The editors learned of this manuscript at the time of the publication of this volume. The manuscript contains a number of essays on Ramsey's thought, as well as a substantial response by Ramsey.

University Press were unfailingly helpful. Our wives, Anne McGuire and Mary Wilson Crocco, contributed their time and talents to the volume. Our families took a break from Paul Ramsey to welcome James William Werpehowski and Glory Magdalena Crocco into the world on June 16, 1992. Readers of Ramsey will know the significance of dedicating this book to these individual pearls of equal price.

WILLIAM WERPEHOWSKI
STEPHEN D. CROCCO

1

WHAT THE CHRISTIAN DOES WITHOUT A CODE

In *Basic Christian Ethics* (1950), which he called an "essay in the Christological ethics of the Reformation," Paul Ramsey sought both to explicate the source and meaning of the injunction to love the neighbor, and to demonstrate how that injunction has its proper place "on the ground floor" of Christianity's understanding of morality. A unique norm of activity drawn from the biblical pattern of God's redemptive work in Jesus Christ, agape fixes itself steadfastly on the neighbor's need; hence it surpasses any system of ethics that would authorize conduct on another basis. In the following selection we find Ramsey developing this point in connection with Christianity's challenge to "legalism." (From *Basic Christian Ethics*, pp. 74–90)

Concerning Jesus' teaching on the inwardness of real purity or defilement, the gospel of Mark makes editorial comment, "Thus he declared all foods clean" (Mark 7:19). Jesus, however, on that occasion was dealing only with the questions of ritual handwashing; he himself never abrogated the food laws of the Jews. This was the work of St. Paul, who extended the principles manifested by Jesus mainly in connection with sabbath observance and ceremonial cleanliness to cover also the law of clean and unclean meats and the rite of circumcision.

> If with Christ you died to the elemental spirits of the universe, why do you live as if you still belonged to the world? Why do you submit to regulations, Do not Handle, Do not taste, Do not touch (referring to things which all perish as they are used), according to human precepts and doctrines? These have indeed an appearance of wisdom in promoting rigor of devotion and self-abasement and severity to the body, but they are of no value in checking the indulgence of the flesh. (Col. 2:20–23)

1

Except for Paul, Christian liberty from Jewish legalism might not have gone so far, and only after the success of his polemic against a more conservative and more Jewish interpretation of Christianity did the author of Mark's gospel, and other Christians like him, realize that Jesus had *in effect* if not in actuality "declared all foods clean" and circumcision unnecessary.

The letter to the Galatians was Paul's great declaration of Christian independence from legalism. Dispute now centered upon a powerful party of Jewish Christians who insisted that for a Gentile to become a Christian he must first of all become a Jew by undergoing circumcision and submitting to food laws and other requirements of Torah. In answer to those who wanted to judaize Christian ethics by *enforcing* circumcision, Paul notably did not impose a new law *forbidding* it. Instead, he went beyond any form of law, declaring that "in Christ Jesus neither circumcision nor uncircumcision is of any avail, but faith working through love" (Gal. 5:6).

Notice the far-reaching consequence of this position. St. Paul advanced significantly beyond the actual views of Jesus by nullifying laws which in all likelihood Jesus never thought of questioning, yet his ethical perspective and reasons for doing so were essentially the same as Jesus'. This means that it is of little importance for Christian ethics to know exactly what part of the law Jesus or Paul actually rejected and which laws they still retained. Their rejection of particular laws which happened to engage their attention, propelled as it was by a radically new understanding of morality, cannot be limited to overcoming this or that historical form of law. In principle every form of legalism was nullified by them from the beginning. If Paul might go beyond Jesus, Christians of a later day may go beyond Paul if in any respect Paul still considered Jewish law binding as law. Paul himself sees quite clearly that the standpoint from which circumcision and food laws are rightly declared no longer of any avail also overturns more universal rules for distinguishing good from bad, worthy from unworthy, persons. "There is neither Jew nor Greek, there is neither slave nor free, there is neither male nor female; for you are all one in Christ Jesus" (Gal. 3:28). The business of Christian ethics, therefore, does not consist in following literally the selection of rules from Torah made by Jesus or Paul. It consists rather in employing their spirit of freedom in relation to the existing morality of custom and law born anew and bred in every man.

"There is obviously a great deal written in the Old Testament as divine law which no Christian can regard as binding upon himself unless he ceases to be a Christian." How shall permanently valid teachings be discovered in the Bible and separated from the "great deal" that is no longer binding, without recourse to some third rule or set of rules and without importing into Christian ethics some sub-Christian philosophical principle? Christian regard for the worth of human life cannot be grounded in the commandment not to kill (or in the Stoic notion of a divine spark in every human being), nor can Christian marriage be derived from the continuing validity of the seventh commandment *as a law* (or from a self-sufficient order of creation in which monogamous marriage is clearly written), not even with the support of a secondary *rule* that these rules are superior to all the rest. Brunner is correct in saying that, "When we wish to know what is just in the state, in economics, in society, marriage and the family, we receive no help from the Decalogue"—certainly not in its primitive meaning—"but can only attach, to its commandments what we have learned in other ways."[1] His error is in the primacy he assigns to the "law of nature," a sub-Christian source of insight, in correcting the defects of scriptural and other actual codes of law.

There are those in every age who insist that for a person to become a Christian he must first of all become respectable by submitting to certain accepted social requirements. Yet obviously a great deal in any code of gentlemanly respectability no Christian can regard as binding upon himself unless he ceases to be a Christian. How, again, shall discrimination be made without simply revising the rules of conventional respectability or having too early recourse to some principle of philosophical ethic itself a modern Torah? "In Christ Jesus neither 'respectability' nor lack of respectability, neither conventional nor unconventional behavior, is of any avail." With this as a starting point, we shall inquire whether from "faith working through love," and from this alone, an entirely Christocentric ethic can be elaborated. Interpreting scripture by scripture, this is the question: Is there any principle in scripture itself whereby we may leave aside the "great deal written there as divine law which no Christian can regard as binding upon himself unless he ceases to be a Christian"?

The ethics of Paul, indeed Christian ethics generally, seems always in peril of opening the floodgates of anarchy and license in the name of freedom from law. In order to avoid this danger, Christian ethics has frequently been placed in the protective custody of certain

1. Emil Brunner, *Justice and the Social Order* (New York: Harpers, 1945), pp. 123, 122.

supposed ways for making ethical distinctions more forceful. Surrounded by a guard of Judaism, Aristotelianism, Stoicism, or, in recent times, personalistic idealism, "faith working through love" proves less disturbing to prevailing ethical conceptions and directions are laid down in advance for deciding what is permitted and what not. Nevertheless, in contrast to these forms of coalition ethics, the answer St. Paul himself gave to this issue is beyond doubt more distinctive of Christianity.

In 1 Corinthians Paul had occasion to defend his position against a party of Christian libertines who came upon him in an opposite direction from the Jewish Christians. These libertines were extreme antilegalists or antinomians who believed Christian liberty to be quite without regulation. "All things are lawful for me," all things are now permitted, the slogan of this faction, Paul quotes several times in course of refuting it.

Paul counters with the theme, All things are lawful for me, all things are now permitted, *which Christian love permits.* " 'All things are lawful,' but not all things are helpful. 'All things are lawful,' but not all things build up. Let no one seek his own good, but the good of his neighbor" (1 Cor. 10:23,24). For Paul there is a clear connection between love and doing good works. Paul's principle may be formulated as, "Love and do as you *then* please"; this by no means implies simply, "Do as you please"; for by definition Christian love will be pleased only by doing what the neighbor needs. In place of rules for conduct, instead of "the law" which Christianity entirely finishes, comes not irregularity but self-regulation, and not merely the self-regulation of free, autonomous individuals but the self-regulation of persons unconditionally bound to their neighbors by obedient "faith working through love."

Although the practical problems with which Paul deals in this letter to the church at Corinth are those of a bygone day, as long as he sticks to teaching only what he understands love will teach them, he gives imperishable ethical instruction. Only when he appeals in sub-Christian fashion to what "nature itself teaches" does Paul adopt parochial standards about women's hairdress and such matters (1 Cor. 11:14). The wonder is that Paul was so thoroughly emancipated from his Jewish background as not to appeal to Torah, or that under pressure of advising in church administration he did not "lay down the law," his own law or that which "nature itself teaches," more than he does. His exhortations generally have authority only as love's directions, and hold in view the needs and "edification" or "building up" of others. Christian love will not be limited by any previously existing regulation drawn from what society or "surely nature itself" teaches; it will not conform to preconceptions about right and wrong or conventional codes of conduct with which authorities on good and evil happen to be prepossessed.

Nevertheless, such love, far from being directionless, lays down its own directions, internal self-regulations conformable only to the needs of neighbor. While love itself never submits to external rule and does not proportion its benefaction according to some rule, it never becomes unruly, since the needs of other persons are the rule of love and quickly teach such love what to do. Serving the needs and claims of others requires discrimination and maximum self-control, yet giving the name of duty solely to the needs of neighbor has already led quite beyond law as a primary source of discriminating insight and as power regulating behavior. What should be done or not done in a particular instance, what is good or bad, right or wrong, what is better or worse than something else, what are "degrees of value"—these things in Christian ethics are not known in advance or derived from some preconceived code. They are derived *backward* by Christian love from what it apprehends to be the needs of others. Christian love which teaches the Christian what to do is itself *teachable* without restriction. Solicitous love elicits from a man conformity to its own requirements, and while these requirements vary with the neighbor's needs, they are also as inflexible and "total."

"Everything is lawful, everything is permitted which Christian love permits" also means "Everything is demanded which Christian love requires." The former is Christian liberty, the latter is slavery to Christ. The former, Christian leniency; the latter, Christian self-severity. Aristotelian "moderation" in all things strives to hit the "mean" between too much and too little; it is inflexible and immoderate about the principle of moderation. The religious ethic of St. Paul led him, in contrast, to become "all things to all men" (1 Cor. 9:22), a principle of accommodation which lays down its own regulation as to when much or little should be done without primary reference to any principle, even the principle of moderation, standing between a Christian man and doing everything for all men. By being immoderate about this one thing—namely, Christian care for the neighbor's needs—Christian ethics is *on principle* alternatively more lenient (more free from regulation) and more severe with itself (more subject to command) than any other ethic. Thus Paul sometimes became "as one under the law," at other times "as one outside the law" (1 Cor. 9:20,21).

Luther spoke of these two sides of the matter in his *Treatise on Christian Liberty*. The Christian, he said, is "perfectly free lord of all, subject to none." This is Christian leniency and flexibility in ethical behavior. "What love teaches" cannot be identified for all time and all historical or social circumstances with any particular program of action such as prohibition or socialism. In Christ Jesus, teetotalism is not of any avail, neither is the current informal regulation requiring a person to drink in order for him to be socially acceptable; socialism is of no avail, neither is private property an absolute; a rigid rule against taking life is not necessarily valid in all circumstances, as legalistic pacifism believes, neither, of course, is the opposite; forbidding card-playing or gardening on Sunday avails nothing, neither does the persuasion that a game of bridge is an indispensable right of man or that Sunday is the day a man has fully to himself.

Persons who desire rigid allegiance to certain programs for social reform, or the imposition of rules that will remove all doubt about how the individual should conduct himself, will have to go elsewhere than to Christian ethical theory. And they generally do: these are the fanatics for secular gospels and supernatural sanctions. Christian love, whose nature is to allow itself to be guided by the needs of others, changes its tactics as easily as it stands fast; it does either only on account of the quite unalterable strategy of accommodating itself to neighbor-needs. Indeed, only in contrast with this fundamental strategy does the work *law* receive decisive definition: that law which Christian ethics transcends and abrogates may be defined generally as *any* standard or principle which, for whatever good reasons, we do not allow to be breached even though the needs of others, when alone considered, require different actions from us.

A glance at the programs to which today both secular and religious groups are devoted leaves the impression that their inflexibility is more a vice than a virtue. They "have indeed an appearance of wisdom in promoting rigor of devotion and self-abasement and severity to the body, but they are of no value in checking the indulgence of the flesh" (Col. 2:23); they manifest, indeed, the mind of fleshly self-interest claiming to speak authoritatively on good and evil. These programs live on from pride in a position once taken, not from love sticking close to human needs which would long ago have altered them. On the surface and because of their numerous factions this seems especially true of left-wingers who live by opposing each other's proposals and avant-garde individuals who dearly love to be shocking. The same, however, is also true of Catholic opposition to birth control, the precise, almost murderous, practice of the principle that a mother ought to give her life for her child, and many a Protestant's legalistic championing of prohibition and total abstinence. What surely "nature itself teaches," what is taught by our own special enlightenment or intelligence, and indeed what love *once* taught must always be held suspect enough for critical reexamination in the light of present neighbor-needs and the means available for meeting them. Movements to reform human behavior as well as defenses of the status quo ante often gain prolonged life from "pride working through selfishness," while "faith working through love" would be a sensitive instrument responsively alert to change its doings with every real change in human affairs, always keeping itself abreast with changing needs. Such infinite willingness to learn springs from having our sensitivity to obligation in the actual situation confronting us quite freed from any slant in favor of self. Surely nature and grace both teach us that selfish partiality can best be protected under cover of some conventional ethical standard we are capable of performing easily and in which we can gain the authority of Pharisees.

Paul's way of declaring independence from law and from accepted customs stands in significant contrast to other so-called emancipated viewpoints that are more often met with. Intellectuals frequently act as if superior enlightenment give them unqualified right to act in a different manner from what, they condescendingly concede, must still be required of ignorant people. The Corinthian Christians knew the pagan deities were nonentities, images of them idols that had no real existence, being mere replicas of nothing. Some of them declared, "All of us possess knowledge" (1 Cor. 8:1), and then made a show of their freedom, ostentatiously buying meat from butcher shops next door to temples, meat which was known to have been previously offered to idols. No more than they did St. Paul believe such meat defiled: "We are no worse off if we do not eat, and no better off if we do" (1 Cor. 8:8). But he taught that love would not give them such freedom as they were claiming on account of superior enlightenment. Knowledge may have its privileges, but the violation of love is not one of them. Paul's theme, Love and *then* do as you please, has little in common with, Gain superior knowledge, and *then* do as you please. All things are now permitted which knowledge permits, leads to results decidedly different from those which follow from, All things are now permitted which Christian love permits. Love takes care not to offend others, while increasing knowledge does not necessarily decrease arrogance or lead to increased concern for "edification." "Therefore, if food is a cause of my brother's falling, I will never eat meat, lest I cause my brother to fall" (1 Cor. 8:13). This love-imposed restraint applied, of course, *only* to babes in Christ whose conscience may be wounded "when it is weak" (8:12), not at all to self-styled authorities who may take offense from observing some violation of their particular conception of good and evil.

On the other hand, religious people often believe that superior "spirituality" ought always freely to manifest itself in face of anything less spiritual. Some of the Corinthian Christians gave way to ecstatic seizures, speaking in tongues or unintelligible gibberish, they believed, under the impulse of the Holy Spirit. Now, just as St. Paul possessed the knowledge that an idol had no real existence, so also he did not doubt the possibility of real spiritual inspiration. He himself on occasion exercised the gift of tongues. But for him neither of these undeniable facts was basic for Christian liberty. He did not declare, Be certain you are divinely inspired and do as you *then* please, All things are lawful for me which the Spirit moves me to do, but rather: Love and do as you *then* please, All things are lawful but not all things are helpful. To be helpful the Spirit also gives the gift of interpreting unknown tongues, so that presumably a Christian speaking in tongues will, out of consideration for edification, pause awhile for the translation to be given.

> Therefore, he who speaks in a tongue should pray for the power to interpret. For if I pray in a tongue, my spirit prays but my mind is unfruitful. What am I to do? I will pray with the spirit and I will pray with the mind also; I will sing with the spirit and I will sing with the mind also. Otherwise, how can any one in the position of an outsider say the "Amen" to your thanksgiving when he does not know what you are saying? For you may give thanks well enough, but the other man is not edified. I thank God that I speak in tongues more than you all; nevertheless, in church I would rather speak five words with my mind, in order to instruct others, than ten thousand words in a tongue. (1 Cor. 14:13–19)

The Christian will also recognize that there is diversity of spiritual gifts, the mystery and ecstasy behind his own behavior giving him no special claim to divine inspiration in comparison with persons whose actions and emotions are less tempestuous. Indeed, for Paul, the *holy* Spirit may always be known by its quality, not by its strength; only the spirit of Christ is the true Spirit of God. "Therefore I want you to understand that no one speaking by the Spirit of God ever says 'Jesus be cursed!' and no one can say 'Jesus is Lord' except by the Holy Spirit" (1 Cor. 12:3). This also means that no one speaking by the Spirit of God ever says an unlovely thing. "If I speak in the tongues of men and of angels, but have not love, I am a noisy gong or a clanging cymbal" (1 Cor. 13:1). The sophisticated freedom of enlightened people and claims to independence of spiritual inspiration made by religious people are both put in halter by Paul's "still more excellent way" to freedom.

But may not human reason or conscience comprehend right and wrong from what "nature itself teaches"? If so, then it may be asserted that the rational, moral law known to all men gives them sufficient ground for freedom from "unjust" statutory laws and from oppressive social institutions and conventions. Perhaps here, and not in some special enlightenment or special inspiration, is to be found a basis for sound morality without specific rules and for every legitimate claim to freedom. Christian liberty, it may be affirmed, cannot transcend moral law known by practical reason and sensitive conscience.

The question arises whether Paul himself did not form a coalition with another, equally primary source of valid ethical insight by his appeal to the law written on the hearts or natural consciences of men generally.

> When Gentiles who have not the law do by nature what the law requires, they are a law to themselves, even though they do not have the law. They show that what the law requires is written on their hearts, while their conscience also bears witness and their conflicting thoughts accuse or perhaps excuse them on that day when, according to my gospel, God judges the secrets of men by Christ Jesus. (Rom. 2:14–16)

This passage has been made to bear the weight of an elaborate theory of "natural law," or right naturally and generally known to human reason or conscience. From man's native moral capacity Christian ethics might derive a system of definite and forceful precepts and prohibitions—in short, a law. At least, it may be asked, did not St. Paul and must not any acceptable view of ethics in some sense trust the promptings and warnings of conscience?

Whether or not there is actually a natural morality inscribed in every human heart, this much is certain: this law also Christian ethics transcends. The fact that such law is inward and indeed that God Himself wrote it there in his work of creating man would not alter its character as law or give this law primacy for the Christian. Paul believed that *God* actually revealed Torah to Moses no less certainly than he may have believed that God wrote His precepts and prohibitions on the heart, giving voice to human conscience. Divine origin either of the written law or of the natural law (the suggestions of conscience) was simply not decisive for Paul. Tracing law home to a moment of historical revelation in the past before Christ or to creation apparently did not altogether settle the issue he raises regarding present validity. Regardless of what God did through Moses in the past, what He has now done in Jesus Christ, and what He is doing, ought now to become the one and only center of man's existence before God. God has *now* showed thee, O man, what is good and what the Lord doth require of thee. Through decisive historical events and in a historical person making time A.D. quite different from time B.C., God *now* enters into covenant with man, overcoming, to speak of ethics only, all Do and Don't morality whether in the form of an external law *once* valid for the Jews or of an inward law *once* valid for the Gentiles. Man's ethical and religious orientation focuses on the Christ, necessarily turning away from the old Law, away also from the sovereign dictates of natural conscience. The primacy of either is overcome, both must be schooled by Christ. Code morality still finds a standing point in the words of Jeremiah, "I will put my *law* within them, and will write it on their hearts" (31:33); but his use of the future tense of the verb obviously refers to some source of instruction outside the normal, universal promptings of conscience. No looking backward in time toward God's activity in creation, no delving deep into rational human nature or the human heart (which in fact he believed inscrutable) fulfills Jeremiah's expectation, but looking toward that person from whom men may learn something they do not already know merely from capacities within themselves. Whether in the old Law or in the new covenant, God manifests His will in something objectively given to which man must conform rather than something conformable to man. Christian ethics is an ethics of perfection which cuts man to fit the pattern, not the pattern to fit man: how, then, can any major part of its fundamental content be drawn from man?

In striking fashion St. Augustine confirms the interpretation just given of Romans 2:14–16: these words of St. Paul's cannot be taken as ground for importing into the heart of Christian ethics a sub- or extra-Christian source of moral judgment. We must inquire with great care, St. Augustine remarks, precisely what sense it is in which the apostle attributes authenticity to the law written in natural conscience; this we must do

> *lest there should seem to be no certain difference in the new testament,* in that the Lord promised that He would write His laws in the hearts of His people, inasmuch as the Gentiles have this done for them naturally. This question therefore has to be sifted, arising as it does as one of no inconsiderable importance. For some may say, "If God distinguishes the New Testament from the Old by this circumstance, that in the old He wrote His law on tables but in the new He wrote them on men's hearts, *by what are the faithful of the new testament discriminated from the Gentiles,* which have the work of the law written on their hearts, whereby they do by nature the things of the law, *as if, forsooth, they were better than the ancient people, which received the law on tables, and before the new people, which has that conferred on it by the new testament which nature has already bestowed on them!"*[2]

Indeed, by what is Christian ethics to be distinguished from generally valid natural morality, if some theory of natural law becomes an authentic part and to any degree the *primary* foundation of Christian morality? This would amount to saying that the dictates of natural conscience and morality reasoned out in terms of the common good or some other philosophic norm (while these are doubtless better than an ancient, external code) are nonetheless "before the new people, which has that conferred on it by the new testament [i.e., by Christ] which nature" and reason have already bestowed upon others.

St. Augustine holds that by "the Gentiles" the apostle undoubtedly means only those Gentiles who have become Christian; these as well as former Jews have *now* had God's law written on their hearts by the new covenant; just as, in an earlier passage, St. Paul speaks of the gospel as "the power of God for salvation to every one who has faith, to the Jew first and also *to the Greek*" (Rom. 1:16). This is poor exegesis but good Christian ethics. Too often "natural law" theory has been validated in such fashion as to render the gospel ethic superfluous; Christian ethics has then nothing *distinctive* (and also *primary*) to say about morals that has not already been bestowed upon mankind by nature or philosophy. Undoubtedly it must be admitted that St. Paul actually refers to the voice of natural conscience, a God-given morality of nature, and not simply, as Augustine supposes, to the insights conscience gains when converted toward Christ. Beyond

---

2. *On the Spirit and the Letter*, Chap. 43, in Whitney J. Oates, ed., *Basic Writings of St. Augustine* (New York: Random House, 1949), 1:494 (italics mine).

question, then, he refers to a ground for morality natural to all men and within their competence as reasonable beings. *But this law also, he believed, Christian ethics transcends,* for all its vaunted inwardness or natural spontaneity and in spite of the fact that God Himself ordained it for the Gentiles along with special Torah for the Jews. What God has now ordained shifts morality from foundation in either of these ancient standards for righteousness.

When Paul wrote that "the law was our custodian until Christ came" (Gal. 3:24), he did not mean a division of function between inferior and superior teachers. The custodian in question did no teaching, he was a slave who conducted a young man through the bewildering streets of the city and turned him over to his one and only teacher. Whatever validity Paul assigns the law in his letter to the Romans, it never includes positive instruction in any aspect of Christian morality. Jesus Christ is the one and only teacher.

The same may be said for the validity allowed the promptings and warnings of conscience, or, in the doubtful possibility that Paul went so far, the quite secondary validity he found in a system of first principles of ethics known as natural law. They serve perhaps as custodians, performing even this function in extraordinarily self-contradictory fashion. These inner lawgivers make us acquainted with sin and awaken defiance in us; far from wanting to follow what the inner voice suggests, every man also wishes daringly to do otherwise and, "aroused by the law," bit in teeth, he often does otherwise (cf. Rom. 7). No law, not even an inner one, has positive moralizing power.

Moreover, it is insufficient to say that code morality written on tablets of the mind or on tables of stone has not enough control over will and action. The problem lies not only in willing what is good but also in knowing what is good among all existing customary regulations and among the equally numerous and diverse suggestions of conscience. Paul cared for the conscience of the weak who thought it wrong to eat meat offered to idols, but he by no means believed this scruple to be right. Instead of going to the voice of conscience for final instruction, the Christian, both he who is weak and still under regulation and he who is strong and not, needs to have his conscience instructed.

> A Turk who hath possessed himself with a false belief that it is unlawful for him to drink wine, if he do it, his conscience smites him for it; but though he keep many concubines, his conscience troubles him not, because his judgment is already defiled with a false opinion that it is lawful for him to do the one, and unlawful to do the other.

For conscience followeth judgment, doth not inform it. . . . So we confess also, that conscience is an excellent thing where it is rightly informed and enlightened: wherefore some of us have fitly compared it to the lanthorn [lantern], and the light of Christ to a candle; a lanthorn is useful when a clear candle burns and shines in it: but otherwise of no use. To the light of Christ then in the conscience, and not to man's natural conscience, it is that we continually commend men.[3]

The early Quaker theologian who wrote these words setting forth the doctrine of the supranatural light *within* the lantern of man's conscience needs to be supplemented only by reference to the decisive moment of light *for* conscience in the historical Christ to place him in entire agreement with St. Paul's view of a source of ethical knowledge transcending all law, a source outside the heart toward which the heart should turn.

Christian ethics, therefore, is not greatly concerned to prove that there is anything in our moral intuitions not derived from social training. It may be that we are what we are in our moral judgments because we have been where we have been and belonged to what we have belonged to. But Lord of both conscience and custom is Christ; he alone, standing without the law, has become the norm for selecting among the rules that surround us, he alone the one authentic teacher for conscience. Only love, and not special knowledge, inspiration, or clear conscience, liberates the Christian from bondage to the laws and conventions of society.

While love frees from the law, it binds a man even closer to the needs of others, even as Jesus Christ was bound; and precisely that which alone frees also binds. The possession of law—any law, as defined above—"puffs up" the man prepossessed with it. Conventional respectability puffs up the "gentleman" with self-importance. Acting according to "the principle of the thing" puffs up. Knowledge and wisdom puff up. Appreciation of high spiritual values puffs up. St. Paul realized long before Nietzsche that at least everyone considers himself an authority on good and evil, and no less than everyone desires to know that he is good. But love which is not puffed up does not leave men without a directive in life such as these other views supply. As Paul says, "Love builds up" (1 Cor. 8:1). Love builds up others, and so doing it also builds up its own unlegislated self-discipline in personal living. Variable as the neighbor's needs, love is

3. Robert Barclay, *Apology for the True Christian Divinity* (1676), in Eleanore Price Mather, ed., *Barclay in Brief*, Pendle Hill Historical Studies no. 3, p. 39.

constantly engaged in tearing down where need be, and again building up, directives as to how better the neighbor may be served.

Everything is quite lawful, *absolutely everything* is permitted which love permits, everything without a single exception. "Therefore let no one pass judgment on you in questions of food and drink or with regard to a festival or a new moon or a sabbath. . . . Why do you submit to regulations, Do not handle, Do not taste, Do not touch (referring to things which all perish as they are used), according to human precepts and doctrines?" (Col. 2:16,21). Turned around, however, this ethic becomes very grim, very grim indeed. *Absolutely everything* is commanded which love requires, absolutely everything without the slightest exception or softening. *Freedom from* the law belongs only to that individual who is *free for* reason of the most terrifying obligation. So Luther could turn to the other side of the matter and say that the Christian man is in bondage to all and subject to everyone, "a perfectly dutiful servant of all, subject to all." In a Christian outlook there is always inflexibility against difficult opposition or repeated rebuff which gives steadfastness in action on behalf of any need love discerns. With whatever is relevant to actual need, love changes its tactic; against what is irrelevant love stands firm. When all fellow-feeling and natural affection wither, when there are no grounds for love in the neighbor's apparent worth, when his response is not appreciative but the contrary, when "nature itself teaches" us to be repelled, when, in short, love that has only begun to be Christian would be destroyed by the enemy, a Christian in love believes against hope, even as was said of Abraham, the father of faith, "in hope he believed against hope" (Rom. 4:18). When otherwise there is no foundation or justification for love, a Christian loves on in faith; love never ends because it endures all things (1 Cor. 13:7,8). A Christian says "nevertheless" and "in spite of this" to every circumstance, persistently finding the works of love obligatory. The commands of love are as stringent as the needs of the world are urgent: sensing this, let any man *then* do as he pleases.

2

THE BIBLICAL NORM OF RIGHTEOUSNESS

Here Ramsey gives a detailed description of neighbor-love as a patterned form of witness to the character of God's righteousness, or to the nature of Christ's love for humanity. We also find positive endorsement of the ways in which moral rules properly express the work of agape. The supposed "antilegalism" of the preceding selection developed into a suspicion of that very stance—for the selfsame reason that the good of the neighbor is paramount. A Christian love that is truly free for the neighbor is free also for commending adherence to rules and principles when they serve him or her in the life of society. Ramsey shows how this may be so in connection with the moral institution of marriage. This essay appeared near the close of the "situation ethics debate" that occupied many Christian ethicists during the middle and late-1960s in America. (*Interpretation* 24/4 (1970): 419–24, 425–28, 429)

We must first understand the most essential thing our Christian faith has to say about morality and about the decisions we make. If anyone wanted to form his conscience and shape his life in accord with biblical ethics, what would this mean for the way he goes about making an ethical decision? The message of both the Old and the New Testament is that God means to mold human life into the action of God; human righteousness into God's righteousness; man's frequent faithlessness, or maybe his fragile faithfulness, into the faithfulness of God Himself. If this is the destiny toward which God is creating and bending His people, then we must ask: What does this entail for the choices we make? What kind of onlook should we have in forming our own consciences and lives?

There is a model which will quickly introduce us into the heart and soul of biblical ethics. This is essentially the same model for both Testaments, though couched in appropriately different language. In this way we can quickly tell how a man of the faith of the Old Testament and then how a person of the faith of the New Testament would (ideally and as such) go about answering any question of ethics that might be posed to him, and with what insights he would seek to win his way through any moral dilemma he faces.

"You shall make response before the LORD your God"—a member of the Old Testament people confesses—saying: " 'A wandering Aramean was my father' [he was a very unlikely fellow!], but the LORD called him and made something of him." If you believed that, it would have not a little to do with the way you deal with every human wayfarer or with the goodly number of wandering Arameans there are today. We are all wanderers in this life, aspiring no doubt to become wayfarers with a destiny somewhere; but still particularly apt to prey on other wanderers in all sorts of subtle and not-so-subtle ways unless we know the heart of a wanderer and God's special care for him.

Or: How should you treat a stranger? The sojourner or resident alien in the land of living? Ought we simply to require him to register once a year at the United States Post Office and let it go at that? Or perhaps we should figure out how much the man, though an alien, has contributed by his particular skills to the commonwealth and treat him accordingly. That would be distributive justice. Finally, we might argue that, after all, he is a *man*, and then we might evolve an ethic that tells us how a man should treat all men, and by them be treated. This would be a genuinely humanistic ethic, which is a fine, fine thing—and a more and more diminishing thing today.

But the Bible does not make man the measure. It does not in any of these ways derive from man himself the standard for man. Now this is the meaning of molding the actions of men into the action of God. If you want to know how to treat the stranger or the sojourner or alien in the land, according to the Old Testament, you would proceed to reason as follows: You know the heart of a stranger, since you too were strangers and sojourners in the land of Egypt; and the Lord your God acted rightly by you when He brought you up out of the predicament and so right-wised the dealings you may ever have with the littlest and unlikeliest people on this earth (Exod. 22:21 and 23:9). This is the source and at the same time the measure of human righteousness. Expressly excluded from the heart and soul of biblical ethics is the notion that we should deal with people only according to their merits, earned or unearned; or that we are simply to treat all men as their manhood intrinsically deserves. Not corrective justice or distributive justice or any other humanitarian standard is the measure, but a *contributory* justice, a helpful, redeeming, caring justice, since the day God began to form the consciences of men and to shape their lives to the measure of God's own righteousness that stooped to conquer wrong.

Deuteronomy 7:7f. shows man ceased to be the measure of the right and the good for man when that measure was taken by the divine righteousness. This is a standard at once far more bracing and far more merciful than any human requirement. It is God's own unswerving and redeeming love, His indefectible fidelity, beside which the faithfulness of men is as a morning mist that a mere wind drives away—not to mention the heat of the day and the animus of daily human affairs.

This tells us not of doubtful events of the long ago. It is, it always is, no matter how much we may say it, true that (as Martin Buber has written) "he who does not *himself* remember that God led *him* out of Egypt . . . is no longer a Jew."[1] And he who remembers of *himself* that God brought him up out of Egypt, and showed him *what justice means* to the heart of a sojourner, that man and that man alone remains or becomes a true Jew. No matter what may otherwise have been his racial or ethnic origins, he comes to define himself and his identity and his tasks in terms of the people of the Old Testament. He is joined with them in his own "internal history," even as a first-or second-generation Chinese or Italian can still say with Lincoln at Gettysburg: "Fourscore and seven years ago, *our fathers* brought forth on this continent a new nation . . . conceived in liberty and dedicated to the proposition . . . ." He who does not *himself* remember that eventful dedication of himself ceases to be an American. And whoever *himself* remembers that God rescued him while a sojourner from a land of bondage becomes and remains a true Jew. That is to say, he knows how to answer moral questions like How shall I treat an alien or a helpless, or an insignificant, needy person? He answers that question by reference to no human measurement, but by faith in the faithfulness and love of God manifest in his own life. By this he becomes what he is, and is what he is becoming. So likewise in his life for and with other men.

The model is the same for the New Testament. Right away we

---

1. "Der Pries," in *Der Fude,* October 1917, quoted in Will Herberg, ed., *The Writings of Martin Buber* (Meridian, 1956), p. 31 (italics added).

must eliminate the Golden Rule because, no matter how superior this may be to our ordinary behavior, it is a proverbial maxim that is to be found in folklore of almost every people. But what about the commandment "Thou shalt love thy neighbor as thyself"? This takes the measure of what we should do from every person's love of himself. Ordinarily it is a good rule of thumb to say that we ought to love another as unswervingly and indefectibly as we love ourselves; this is a good provisional standard for our own faithfulness and righteousness toward another person.

But then everything depends on how we love ourselves. If we are negligent and careless of ourselves, if we do not make the most of ourselves or do not wish always our own real good, if we perhaps hate and despise ourselves or even act out of some deep death-wish, then the commandment should read: You should certainly *not* love your neighbor as yourself. Thus, our love for ourselves cannot be taken as the final measure of the right thing to do. Just so, to tell a young man that he ought to treat every girl as he would wish his sister to be treated is only *sometimes* a helpful hint: Everything depends on how he want his sister to be treated. In regard to how people expect a young man nowadays to expect his sister to be respected, there has been considerable slippage in recent years, has there not? There is need for another test.

Therefore, the New Testament does not take from man himself the measure of what it means to be a mature or righteous man. Instead this standard is taken from the man Christ Jesus. Jesus' words "Love one another *as I have loved you!*" are the commandment, the model, the organizing principle of all New Testament ethics. So if you want to know what to do or how to treat someone in need of help—the ungodly sinner, or an enemy of yours—the way to begin is to ask, How did God treat me when He sent his only Son to the rescue? (Rom. 5:6–8,10).

Herein the Christian knows the claim that has been placed over human life. He who does not remember of *himself* that Jesus Christ saved him from the Egypt of sin and death ceases to be a Christian. And he who for himself remembers of himself that Jesus Christ actually saved him from the Egypt of sin and death becomes a man on exodus from any natural or human standard, a man whose conscience and life are destined to be formed in accordance with the saving righteousness and faithfulness of God. "Have this mind in you which was also in Christ Jesus" becomes the measure: "Love one another as I have loved you," one's ultimate commandment.

Now let us simply summarize these models, this pattern, this final norm of the Christian life, by using the words *Christian love* or *Christian charity*.

The next question to be asked is: What on earth does that entail? What, then, must we do? What directives for living can be implicated, produced, adduced, or amplified from Christian love?

In answer to that question we come to a fork in the road, a juncture at which a decision must be made between two ways to proceed; two major schools of thought, especially in Protestant ethics; two procedures for answering the question What does Christian love require us to do?

The first is called contextualism or situation ethics. According to this view, we determine what we should do in a particular situation simply by getting the facts of the situation very clear and then asking, What is the loving or the uniquely loving thing to do? We are to apply the law of love directly and separately, unique moment by moment, in each case with which we are confronted. The principle of situation ethics does not teach that we should do as we please; it says rather: Love, and do as you *then* please, according to whatever proves pleasing to the searching requirements of Christian love. Still, having said that, it must be noted that this view calls attention to the unique features of persons and of how different one situation is from another. We are to ask in every decision: What *singular* deed will prove to be most love-embodying or love-fulfilling?

The second view draws our attention to the similarities among situations; to the likeness of one person who bears a human countenance with every other person in his needs and claims; to the respects in which one marriage, for example, is like every other marriage. Since this is my own position, let us call this the correct view—correct because it says more while not denying the truth grasped by situation ethics in its stress on uniqueness and on the discontinuities in moral experience. According to this second approach, we may determine what we ought to do, not only by asking which singular action is the most loving, but also by asking which *principles* of action or *rules of practice* will prove to be generally most love-embodying or love-fulfilling. A person is not fully in earnest about the Christian moral life if he is so concerned about the Christian compassion expressed and exhibited in individual actions case by case that he neglects the Christian compassion that must needs be expressed and exhibited in societal *rules of practice*, in law, and in social institutions. In fact, there can be no such thing as Christian social ethics, or any social ethics at all, unless there are *practices* having general validity, unless there are moral institutions.

Now, situation ethics does not absolutely exclude moral principles or rules. But these are only rules of thumb, cautionary advice to be set aside promptly whenever in the discontinuities of moral experience love requires them to be set aside. These are only tactical directives to the players which tell them most of the time how they ought to play the moral game. These rules of thumb are like the rule "punt on fourth down" in the game of football. The imperative, punt on fourth down, will ordinarily be the way to play the game; but everyone knows that this tactical advice to the players (which holds true most of the time) ought certainly to be violated when the circumstances are such that your team has the ball on your opponents' fifteen-yard line and there is only one yard to go for a first down. This is the meaning of "circumstance ethics" today. It regards all principles of conduct and rules of practice as analogous to the tactical advice to the players. . . .

The crucial question is whether in morality there are only *tactical directives to the players*. Are there not also *rules of the game* itself? Are there any moral institutions? Are there any binding moral practices which the individual must adhere to if his is to be the best life he can live? Practices like the rule that prohibits more than eleven players on the field at the same time, or the rule defining "offside." Anyone who said, I think it would be best on the whole, or most fun-fulfilling, if in this instance I was allowed twelve players or a man offside, must be understood not to know the game he is playing or the meaning of a universally binding rule of the game. This is the nature of societal rules and institutions and of moral *practices*. Of course, at the end of the season one can ask whether the game could be improved by changing the rules; and in any society with regard to any moral institution one can ask whether there is a different *rule of practice* that would be more love-embodying and more fulfilling for all persons. But meantime, responsibility calls for individual actions falling within or under the rules of practice governing the society or the moral institution in question.

Thus if you ask a quarterback, Why don't you use twelve players? and he replies, Because we're playing football, that is evidence enough that he knows the nature of the game he's in and the meaning of its practice. Likewise, a person who responds to the question, Why are you in a hurry to pay him? by saying, Because I promised to pay him today—the one who makes *that* his terminal justification—is the man who alone knows the meaning of promise-keeping. Ask a man the question, Why don't you make love to Mary? If he replies, Because I'm married to Jane, he may correctly be supposed to understand the nature of marriage as a practice. If he says, I think it would be best on the whole and most love-fulfilling if in this instance I make love to Mary, the most charitable interpretation (even if his wife's name *is* Mary) would be that he meant to ask the meaning or *practice rules* governing the marriage game. He wanted to know what conjugal love requires.

If a person genuinely means to attach an exception-making criterion to his promises or to his marriage vow, if he means to live by a rule of practice which states that the marriage covenant holds, that promises should be kept except when by a direct appeal to what Christian love requires it would be better *not* to keep them, he had better say so, since the one he promises or his marriage partner (unless they are Fletcherites who have been briefed) will not understand it that way! If you promise a dying friend, no one else knowing, to take care of his children, *why should you do so* if two other children come along who are more intelligent and whose care and nurture by you would do more good? If a person means to get married for better, in health and in prosperity, and has some reservation about the worse, in sickness, poverty, and adversity, he had better say so, since one's partner will not understand it that way—unless he or she is a latter-day consequentialist whose marriage was in the first place a *bargain* founded upon a calculus of doing the most good on the whole. Thus, there are such things as fairness and justice, promises made, and marriage covenants established, concerning which one should do more than ask, Which unique situational decision or particular action would exhibit the most love? One must also ask, Which principles of action and societal rules of practice are most love-embodying and love-fulfilling?

Thus, Christian love entails certain principles or *rules of practice* governing crucial areas of human life in which each of us has decisions to make concerning his responsibility. Marriage is a chief illustration of this.

In regard to marriage, the question to be raised is, Whence comes the standard or ideal of permanent, lifelong partnership and the notion that the marriage covenant embraces "till death us do part"? Is anything other than this so contrary to the meaning of faithfulness that Christians must mean this in the exercise of their sexual powers and the practices of life, or else they go contrary to what a Christian responsive and responsible love requires?

What Paul says on the subject of marriage in Ephesians 5 repeats in every respect the model which we have seen to be the essence of New Testament ethics. There is a subordinate reference, but only a subordinate and quite provisional reference, to a person's love for himself as a way to tell how married partners should love one another. "Husbands should love their wives as their own bodies. He who loves his wife loves himself." But this is a good way to tell the meaning of married responsibility only on the premise which the apostle goes on to announce: "No man ever hates his own flesh, but nourishes and cherishes it." But one does not have to live very long in this embodied life of ours to learn that many a person hates his own flesh and fatally dishonors his own body, his own being. Such a person should not be told that he should love his wife as he loves his own body, as he unlovingly loves himself. To the contrary, he needs to find elsewhere the measure for the marriage partnership.

Secondly, the apostle did not fail to invoke the "one-flesh unity" that the Scriptures throughout tell us, and our Lord himself says, is the created nature of human wedlock. In fact, Paul boldly takes the verse about the marriage of Adam and Eve ("and the two shall become one flesh") and applies this to even the relation of harlotry. We are such ensouled bodies and embodied souls, he boldly asserts, that one cannot belong to a harlot in the unity of the flesh and still belong to Christ.

Nevertheless, this one-flesh, natural unity, God's creation that is in us, and the injunction to the married that they love one another as they love their own bodies, are ingredients or measures that Paul passes by on his way toward an ultimate norm. This ultimate measure is one that applies also to anyone who does not love himself rightly, who may even be a hater of his own flesh, in whom the one-flesh unity inscribed in the creation of man-womanhood may be distorted or obscured. "Husbands, love your wives," he writes, "as Christ loved the church and gave himself up for her." The marriage question, then, is a question of how Christ loved the church. This, indeed, is how a man *should* nourish and cherish his own fleshly embodied being if that is ever to be made the measure of how married partners are to love one another. Thus, the final measure for man is not taken from man, but from the extent and quality of Christ's own love for us; the claim and task laid upon marriage is not taken from marriages, but from the marriage covenant and union of Christ with his church. What does that mean? He gave himself up with a caring love, that the church might be consecrated, and presented "in splendor, without spot or wrinkle or any such thing, that she might be holy and without blemish."

This contrasts mightily with the current practice through which in this age wives and husbands daily give one another up because they have not a few wrinkles and many a blemish! It was married faithfulness cut to the measure of God's own faithfulness that opened the possibility of permanent, lifelong partnership as the meaning of the marriage covenant. It was the inseverability of Christ's covenant with us that, touching the covenants among men, made for the inseverability of the marriage bond. Because the final norm was "Love one another as I have loved you," the marriage relation was elevated and strengthened, as it were, up to the sticking point. Why so? Because among those who *themselves* remembered that Jesus Christ saved us from sin and from *death* it became an ideal, the task and requirement that marriage pledges should go so far as to embrace the loved one's dying in the words "till death us do part," as a replica—if but a faint replica—of the exodus from sin and death toward which men and women had been set in course.

. . . The attempt will no doubt continue to be made in the present age to remove the foundation of permanent marriage without bringing down the house. But a Christian can scarcely imagine that the task laid upon him is simply to decide every morning or anew in each unique situation whether or not on the whole it would be better and more love-fulfilling to remain married with the one with whom he originally set out on pilgrimage.

To the contrary, he will know that his love is not all it should be if he does this. He will know the perfection of conjugal love is to wish to grow old beside another. He will know this while still seeing very clearly the audacity of *being* married as he promised upon *getting* married. The marriage vow, taken in itself, constitutes an almost untenable wager. We count on the persistency of present feelings. We wager against the deteriorations of time, and venture constancy in the face of blemishes and wrinkles and all the ungracefulness connected with growing old, and in face of the disease and the mutual recriminations that spring simply from the fact that we are mortal.

Why do we do this? Because, just as we know the heart and needs of a stranger from God's care for us while we were yet strangers, we also know the heart and the need of a dying one from God's care for us who live always in the midst of death. This means that the perfection of love is a working knowledge of another as a creature of flesh and blood whose fate it is to live always in the valley of the shadow of death. The essence of a care-full love is respect for the shadow of death upon another human countenance, a sense of the griefs and grievances they bear because of the power of death that is in them, an awareness of the temptations to despair and estrangement because we and our loved ones exist from day to day in the shadow of the same shared, ambiguous destiny that Christ took on himself when for our sakes he became mortal man. This is why the marriage vow proposes provisionally to take hold of the shadow of death upon the human countenance and promises permanence "till death us do part." If this is not so, there is found in marriage no "helper" fit to the human condition; and, Christians believe, there is then no marriage that has been touched by God's perduring love.

3

SELF-LOVE, LOVE OF HAPPINESS, LOVE TO GOD AND TO NEIGHBOR

Ramsey's edition of Jonathan Edwards's *Freedom of the Will* was the inaugural volume in the Yale University Press edition *The Works of Jonathan Edwards*. In the late seventies, following more than two decades of groundbreaking work in political, medical, sexual, and legal ethics, Ramsey returned to Edwards, spending the last decade of his life editing his ethical writings. The following extract from the Editor's Introduction reveals something of Ramsey's considerable achievement. It also attends to some themes indicative of his own Christian ethic: the character of self-love and the meaning and conditions for the love of God. Note especially the employment of "typology" to render a Christocentric interpretation of the Golden Rule. (From *Ethical Writings*, vol. 8 of *The Works of Jonathan Edwards*, pp. 12–27)

In one of the "Miscellanies" Edwards asks the question whether each and every one of the desires of human hearts has become exorbitant as a consequence of the Fall. He answers no—because love of happiness (which necessarily means love of one's own happiness) cannot be too much. A cynic always wins the debate over whether all people are selfish by failing to distinguish between a blameworthy selfishness and the general human endowment to love happiness. Yet a love of happiness is evidently different from always finding that happiness in a narrow, confined love of self as if the self were all—in Ibsen's apt description of Peer Gynt, living in "a cask of self, stopped with a bung of self."

Contemporary ethicists often break apart these two meanings of self-love by speaking of the grammatically "ambiguous genitive" case in present-day English language usage in such expressions as "the love of God" or "the love of self." The love of God can mean either God's love to us or our love to God. The love of self can mean the self's love to itself only (or to an extended social ego), or it may mean the self's love of whatever the self loves, whether that is its love to itself as object, or its love to God or to neighbor, or its love of learning, beauty, sensual pleasure, or anything else.

Edwards does not employ this distinction between the objective and subjective genitive. Instead, he plays out the same analysis in terms of what can only be called the "ambiguous pronoun." A man's love of his own happiness, he writes, is "ambiguous . . . as the pronoun 'his own' is equivocal" and can be taken in "two very different senses." A self's love of its own happiness may simply mean the self's love of whatever is "grateful[1] and pleasing," more often than not found in other objects than the self *sole*.

Love of one's own happiness is "universal" in all, the same degree in all. To resolve the will and action of moral agents into nefarious self-love on the grounds that the propensity of will and action is our own happiness was for Edwards nonsense. That amounts to saying that there is something censurable in the fact that moral agents have wills, and differ from "stones and trees, which love nothing and hate nothing." Within the definition of self-love as love of one's own happiness, to put the question "whether all our love . . . don't arise from self-love" is an "impropriety and absurdity." For this is only to say,

> self-love is a man's liking, and being suited and pleased in that which he likes, and which pleases him; or that 'tis a man's loving what he loves. For whatever a man loves, that thing is grateful and pleasing to him, whether that be his own peculiar happiness, or the happiness of others. And if this be all that they mean by self-love, no wonder they suppose that all love may be resolved into self-love. For it is undoubtedly true that whatever a man loves, his love may be resolved into his loving what he loves—if that be proper speaking. If by self-love is meant nothing else but a man's loving what is grateful or pleasing to

1. JE uses "grateful" to qualify some object, relation, or event that is "pleasing to the mind or the senses; agreeable; acceptable; welcomed." Gratitude in the heart is directed to that which is objectively "grateful." The *Oxford English Dictionary* gives the following illustrations of this usage: "His coming was very grateful unto the king," 1656; "He is so far from being hateful, he is exceedingly grateful to the people of Rome," 1690; "In grateful sleep," 1725; "This is a doctrine grateful to scientific men who are afraid of being thought hostile to religion," 1867. JE's "grateful" finds in things or situations a pleasing quality; "gratitude" is in the heart's answerableness to the grateful. The work in this sense is suited to and frequently used in JE's proof that moral terms are founded "in the reason and nature of things," not in sentiment (*True Virtue*, Chap. 8).

him, and being averse to what is disagreeable, this is calling *that* "self-love" which is only a general capacity of loving, or hating; or a capacity of being either pleased or displeased: which is the same thing as a man's having a faculty of will.

The notion that men can fail to love their own happiness in whatever they find objectively "grateful" or pleasing amounts to the absurdity that they "incline to nothing and will nothing." This is one main theme running through Edwards's ethics: I have just been quoting from his treatment of it in *True Virtue*.[2]

Such "self-love taken in the most extensive sense" was already Edwards's analysis twenty-three years before *True Virtue* when he wrote Miscell. no. 530. LOVE TO GOD, SELF-LOVE (c. 1731–32), at twenty-nine years of age.[3] Again, some seventeen years before *True Virtue* was written, Edwards made the same point preaching on a text that uses the ambiguous pronoun, charity "seeketh not her own" (one of his famous 1738 series on 1 Cor. 13). That cannot possibly mean that a Christian spirit is contrary to all self-love, contrary to all love of one's own happiness. Love of one's own happiness is as necessary to man's nature "as a faculty of will is." To destroy that would be "to destroy the humanity." Thus in the seventh sermon of the charity

2. *True Virtue*, pp. 575–76. What makes an act to be "one's own" was the point of Edwards's *Freedom of the Will*; and the upshot for ethics and moral psychology was the same: "That act which is performed without inclination, without motive, without end, must be performed without any concern of the will. . . . If the soul in its act has no motive or end; then in that act . . . it seeks nothing, goes after nothing, exerts no inclination to anything; and this implies that in that act it desires nothing, and chooses nothing; so there is no act of choice in the case: and that is as much as to say, there is no act of will in the case." Jonathan Edwards, *Freedom of the Will*, ed. Paul Ramsey, in *The works of Jonathan Edwards* (New Haven: Yale Univ. Press, 1957), 1:333.

3. JE's language then was not as carefully honed as in his later works and his thought perhaps not so clear. Still, he wrote of "self-love taken in the most extensive sense" as "a man's love of his own pleasure and happiness . . . or rather, 'tis only a capacity of enjoyment or suffering. For to say a man loves his own happiness and pleasure, is only to say that he delights in what he delights [in]. . . . So that self-love is only a capacity of enjoying or taking delight in anything." Thus the young JE answered the question of this entry, "whether or no a man ought to love God more than himself." Self-love in "the most extensive sense" (i.e., a capacity of enjoying) and "love to God are not things properly to be compared one with another," "Proportionable to our love to God, is our disposition to delight in his good. Now our delight in God's good, can't be superior to our general capacity of delighting in anything; or which is the same thing, our delight in God's good can't be superior to our love to delight in general: for proportionably as we delight in God's good, so shall we love that delight." JE's generalization is that "the degree of delight in a particular thing, and the degree of love to pleasure or delight in general, ben't properly comparable one with another." But one reason given for this may be obscure: for the two "are not entirely distinct, but one enters into the nature of the other."

series, Edwards signals the importance of this question by affirming that the point "needs to be well stated; for the resolution of many scruples and doubts, which persons have, depends upon it."[4] The first step is to fix firmly in mind that what is censurable in self-love does not consist in love of our own happiness "being absolutely considered in too high a degree." Man cannot love happiness too much, if such love is viewed *simpliciter*. Such love is not "a thing liable to diminution or increase." It is "alike in all" because it belongs to the "nature of all intelligent beings" as necessary to their nature "as a faculty of will is." Love of one's happiness is without degree.

Such self-love our first parents had before the Fall, in high degree, in no degree too great; or better to say, simply in no degree, since it was a thing not to be compared. "Saints and sinners" in the life "love happiness alike, and have the same unalterable propensity to seek and desire happiness." Finally, in the redemption of creatures on earth, it would be an absurdity to suppose that happiness increases as the love of it decreases upon the infusion of love to God; or that the holy saints above are happy, but their *love* of happiness diminished as their holiness increased. The saints and angels in heaven love their own happiness. If this were not so, heaven "would be no happiness to them; for that which anyone does not love, he can enjoy no happiness in."

Here we have a correlation of the nature of the will with love, and of love with happiness, that cannot be other than "one's own" while it is willed and loved and enjoyed—a correlation matched only by that in Augustine.[5] Since will and love are alike in all, the meaning of inordinate self-love, to which a Christian spirit is contrary, cannot lie in too much love of one's happiness.

So far, we have one "principle" founded in human hearts. Edwards used the word *principle* in the sense of the Latin *principium* or the Greek *arché*. The word *principle* means a source or beginning or spring of disposition and action. But it also means the direction, shape, or contours of human hearts and lives, as in the root of our word *archetype*, or the *arché* or formative power of Plato's ideas, such as justice or beauty, or triangularity. So when the first verse of St. John's Gospel reads "In the beginning was the Word," that in Greek is *en arché* and in Latin *in principio*. The verse not only points to the source and beginning of all things, without whom "was not anything made that was made." These verses also tell us something about the

4. *Charity*, p. 255.

channel in which the whole creation runs, its shape, meaning, and direction.

A universal and ineradicable will and love of happiness, Edwards says in his sermon, makes the world go round. But that propensity of "intelligent willing perceiving" beings explains nothing specific. It does not explain why we find one particular object of love "grateful and pleasing" and not another. It does not explain the reason why such and such things become an agent's happiness, or why we *look on* others as ourselves, and so on their happiness as *our own*. Consider also Edwards's exclamation, "What can more properly be called love to any being, or any thing, than to place one's happiness in that thing?"[6] and his use of "placing" happiness to depict the goodness of Christ and of the saints in the charity sermons. An agent's general capacity to *place* his love of happiness anywhere or in any object, somewhere or in some object, and to *find* his own happiness therein, "can never be a reason why men's love is placed in such and such objects" and not in others. A "capacity of enjoying happiness, cannot be the reason why such and such things become his happiness."[7] The difference between Hitler and you and me, and between Mother Teresa and you and me, lies not in our common love of happiness, but rather in what each of us looks on as that in which our own happiness consists. We need other principles to explain why we creatures move the world the way we do.

5. In the same breath, a radical difference between JE and the Augustinian tradition must be pointed out. In that tradition, a telling response to the account of the Augustinian "Synthesis" in Anders Nygren's *Agape and Eros* (London: SPCK, 1953) would be to carve out a legitimate place for *creatures'* "need-love" to God—as did C. S. Lewis in *The Four Loves* (New York: Harcourt Brace Jovanovich, 1960). JE would not have limited himself to that rejoinder. His point was not the nature of *creatures'* wills and loves, but that of *any* intelligent willing perceiving being. That includes *God's* self-sufficient acts of will. He, too, must love his own happiness if he is different from sticks and stones, which will nothing. This is the problem of the first dissertation, why God willed to create any world at all.

6. *Charity*, p. 258. A principle *uniting* one person to another was JE's formulation of the meaning of "pure" or "absolute" benevolence. See Miscell. no. 530 and App. III. The older Edwards said essentially the same thing as the young Edwards when he wrote in the second dissertation, "To speak more accurately, it [true virtue] is that consent, propensity and union of heart to Being in general, that is immediately exercised in a general good will"; or, still more precisely, true virtue "primarily consists . . . simply considered; exciting 'absolute benevolence' (if I may so call it) to Being in general"; and "pure benevolence in its *first* exercise is nothing else but being's uniting, consent, or propensity to Being" (see *True Virtue*, pp. 540, 544, 546). In some respects, JE's earlier "*uniting* principle" was a better expression of his meaning than the work *union* in *True Virtue*, which is less connotative of continuous action.

7. *True Virtue*, p. 576.

Two questions then: What accounts for the fact that love to God, and glorifying Him and praising Him forever, become a human heart's delight? What accounts for the fact that amoral agent lights upon the happiness of another human being as that in which love of his own happiness is gratified? Edwards's answer to this twofold question (which is the question asked of us by the twofold love commandment) is that only some "compounded self-love" can be any further explanatory—that is, love of happiness compounded with some other principle laid in human hearts and lives. This notion of principles conjunctively explanatory of *particular* loves and *particular* joys was best expressed in Miscell. no. 530. Compounded self-love, Edwards wrote,

> arises from the necessary nature of a perceiving and willing being, whereby he loves his own pleasure or delight; but not from this alone, but it supposes also another principle, that determines the exercise of this principle, and makes that to become its object which otherwise cannot: *a certain principle uniting this person with another*, that causes the good of another to be its good. The first arises simply from his own being whereby that which agrees immediately and directly with his own being, is his good; the second arises also from a *principle uniting him to another being*, whereby the good of that other being does in a sort become his own[8]

Once more the mouth of the cynic must be stopped. The cynic is liable to say that love of our own happiness can be stretched to explain, by itself, every particular love. We secondarily and circuitously love another person because we first and primarily love our own specific happiness. All other-love is for our own sakes.[9]

---

8. Cf. n. 3 above.

9. This notion derives other-love from "a love to love our own [specific] happiness," i.e., from the self's love to self. In Miscell. no. 530 JE contrasted "compounded self-love" with what he called "simple mere self-love." He gave a somewhat confused account of the latter. On the one hand, "simple self-love" was so called "because it arises simply from . . . the nature of a perceiving willing being." With no more said, such simple self-love would be equivalent to that general capacity or universal meaning of self-love amply endorsed in this entry. On the other hand, "simple mere self-love" is "a man's own proper, single and separate good," and *this* selfishness is said always to be "what arises simply and necessarily from the nature of a perceiving willing being." Love to God can't be superior to the former, while superior to the latter, "love to God can and ought to be." "Simple self-love" is, to say the least, ambiguous.

Norman Fiering understands "simple self-love" to mean our love to "single and separate good" (*Jonathan Edwards's Moral Thought and Its British Context* [Chapel Hill: Univ. of North Carolina Press, 1981], p. 157), "in common language, selfishness" (p. 159). He is mistaken, however, in taking "compounded self-love" to be "in an intermediary position in Edwards's theory" (p. 157), a "necessary *balance* between self-

This may be the case in the world as it is, because of a principle of sin acting conjunctively with willing beings' love of their own happiness. Indeed, love to self or to some extensive "private system" is the principle treated at length in *True Virtue*, chap. 4, and in sermon seven. Still, another principle in the heart was, for Edwards, not a metaphysical impossibility: there is no contradiction in assuming that a human being *first* loves another and *then* finds or places his own happiness in the other's happiness, looks on that other's happiness as his own.[10]

Indeed, he argued in *True Virtue* that such a cynical location of a selfish system in the *nature* of the will (rather than in its corruption) is nonsense. That account makes the effect (our own happiness) "the cause of that of which it is the effect." It makes "our happiness, consisting in the happiness of the person beloved, . . . the cause of our love to that person." Plainly the truth must be the other way round: "Our love to the [other] person is the cause of our delighting, or [as an effect] being happy in his happiness. How comes our happiness to consist [particularly] in the happiness of such [persons] as we love, but our hearts being *first united to them* in affection, so that as it

---

love and social love" (p. 158; cf. p. 167), only "an enlarged sense of one's own good, which may include others to greater or less degree" (p. 159), consequent upon a line of reasoning later called "enlightened self-interest" (p. 160). All this is laid upon or arises from a hedonic/eudaemonic law (pp. 153, 157), which seems too pejorative a reference to self-love taken in JE's most extensive sense, or to the nature of any perceiving willing being's love of its own happiness. Fiering then must deem the charity sermons to be idiosyncratic among JE's works, forgetful of his "earlier differentiation [in Miscell. no. 510] of three types of love: simple, compounded and holy" (p. 172). Instances of Fiering's natural, compounded self-love or natural affection (pp. 158–59) allow inroads of "social love," which is love to others from an extended egotism. So he reads the several principles explanatory of the ordinary morality of perceiving willing creatures in *True Virtue* as, to say the least, too readily overwhelmed by the inroads of nefarious self-love. The other principles of natural morality are stripped of their variety, richness, and mutual support, if not altogether reduced to a single foundation in selfishness.

The alternative is that, when writing Miscell, no. 530 in his nineteenth year, JE already had in place his understanding of universal self-love as a general capacity of willing or delighting in anything, and that this is the meaning to be ascribed to "simple mere self-love." Without this reading, it is difficult to understand the corollary of this entry, that it is "impossible for any person to be willing to be perfectly and finally miserable for God's sake," or for him to love God supremely and have that be "further informative" of his own particular happiness. My reading of Miscell, no. 530 is consistent with JE's argument in *True Virtue*, that our hearts must first be united to others in affection; then their happiness becomes ours. See *True Virtue*, p. 577.

10. Such statements are true of regenerate creatures; there is no contradiction in saying so. On this meaning of metaphysical "necessity" and "possibility," see *True Virtue*, p. 579 and n. 4.

were, *we look on them as ourselves*, and so on their happiness as our own.[11]

So the question is, How comes the universal nature of a willing perceiving being, loving its own happiness, to be compounded with a principle of unitive love or truly virtuous benevolence and unalloyed goodwill toward another? In the familiar language of scripture, How come love to God and love to neighbor to be what our happiness consists in? How can we creatures, who are on earth and not in heaven, place our happiness in God's glory and look on another person's happiness as our very own? Only if, in truth, we are first made one with them in "pure" or "absolute" benevolence, Edwards answers.

We are approaching, with increasing celerity, the very center of Christian theology. On the relation to God and His creatures, first let us ask Edwards, in the simplest terms, Whence come any knowledge of God and any love of God?

In the twentieth century Karl Barth answered, "Only God can reveal knowledge of God." That statement, on simple inspection, clearly must be true. No one would think of denying it but for the fact that man is (as Plato said) that most religious of animals and (as Calvin taught) the human mind a veritable factory of approximate ideas about the ultimate nature of things.

Jonathan Edwards in the eighteenth century said *why* only God can reveal knowledge of God: because God's knowledge of himself *is the only knowledge of God there is.* I cannot get to know you, i.e., I cannot get to know anything about you that is of any importance to you or to me, unless you communicate yourself to me in words without dissimulation or in actions that are authentically yours. These remain your words and actions, though they resonate in my heart and life. If the word from you that I hear is not and does not remain yours in reality, or if my hearing is only some echo of your word, I will never know more than something *between* us, nor know any more than something *about* you, but never *you.* In self-disclosure, the word sent forth and the hearing of it are one. In like manner, knowledge of God cannot be knowledge about God or knowledge of Him from a distance.[12]

---

11. *True Virtue*, p. 577 (italics mine).

12. I use an analogy to end the use of versions of *analogia entis* in interpreting JE. See the merely negative theology afforded by proceeding from man's natural knowing (*True Virtue*, pp. 591–92). My analogy itself—to interpersonal self-disclosure and communication—is appropriate if there is no reality more "other" to us than another

So if there is knowledge of God communicated to any human understanding, this is God's very own knowledge of Himself, for that happens to be the only knowledge of God there is in heaven or on earth. If there is any love to God enkindled in any human will, this must be God's own love spread abroad in human hearts. If there are in human affections any happiness, joy, and delight in God, this must be God's own felicity communicated to us. These are the divine principles needed to "further inform" natural principles. When mingled and compounded with love of our own happiness, they direct and channel that love into love to God in particular, so that our greatest good and happiness consists in his glory.

We have now come upon expressions that look like "ambiguous genitives," but according to Edwards only seem so: the knowledge of God, the love of God. The two possible meanings of these expressions are not equivocal. Indeed, there are *not* two meanings. As a datum in our language, of course, "the knowledge of God" can mean either our knowledge of God or God's knowledge of Himself; but according to Edwards these two are but one and the same thing. If there is any such thing as a creature's knowledge of God, this must be the creature's participation in God's knowledge of Himself. "The love of God" grammatically can mean either our love of God or God's own love in Himself; but according to Edwards, these are but one and the same thing. If there is any such thing as a creature's love to God, this must be an infusion of God's own love.

The simple fact that in past times English-speaking people used both *of* and *s* in genitives bears out the foregoing interpretation of Edwards. They wrote and said, "the house of my father's" for "my father's house." Similarly, in Miscell. no. 1084 Edwards wrote that

---

person. So far, anthropomorphic language is not only proper in address to God but in any talk about God as well.

Our way of knowing the core of Christian truth is not by analogy, or by metaphors drawn from common experience. JE's types are not veils of heavenly archetypes; his natural types are types of Christ; his notion of participation is grounded in the communication of divine and human qualities in the person of Christ (*communicatio ideomatum*). Thus, JE wrote in his early twenties: "LOVE OF GOD, as it is in the divine nature, is not a passion, is not such a love as we feel; but by the incarnation [it] is really become passionate to his own, so that he loves them with such a sort of love as we have to him or to those we most dearly love. This was one great end of his incarnation, a merciful High Priest. So that now, when we delight ourselves at the thought of God's loving us, we need not have that alloy of our pleasure which our infirmity would otherwise cause, that though he loved us, yet we could not conceive of that love. Now this passionate love of Christ, by virtue of the union with the divine nature, is in a sort infinite" (Miscell. no. 2). See App. III, pp. 706–38 below.

John expressed "two ways of God's flowing forth and being communicated . . . viz. manifesting God's name and communicating His love; or in other words Christ being in the creature in the name, idea or knowledge of God being in them, and the Holy Spirit's being in them in the love of God's being in them."[13] Edwards himself punctuated that last line. He awkwardly (it seems to us) wrote "the love of God's being in them," where ordinarily he would write "love to God" or "divine love" dwelling in the heart. I suggest that his rare use here of the ambiguous genitive "the love of God," which is our usual practice today, followed by a possessive *s* ("the love of God's being in them"), reinforces the conclusion that, for Edwards, if an intelligent, willing perceiving creature is disposed and determined to love to God, this must be from partaking of the divine love. Edwards might also have punctuated the preceding phrase to read "Christ being in the creature in the name, idea or knowledge of God's being in them." No creature has a natural capacity to actualize in itself knowledge of or love to God; that is the common teaching of classical Christian theology. In evangelical Christianity in America this was, of course, and still should be, the meaning of being "born again."

Unique to Edwards is only the philosophical setting of this understanding of God and his creatures. Thus Edwards believed that "perceiving being only, is properly being"; minds, spirits only, are properly beings; to speak of material things as "beings" is to speak improperly. God "communicates Himself properly only to spirits; and they only are capable of being proper images of his excellency, for they only are properly beings. . . . Yet He communicates a sort of shadow or glimpse of His excellence to bodies which . . . are but the shadows of being, and *not real beings*."[14] In one of his notes on "the mind," Edwards asks us to make the following supposition: "Suppose that we received none of the sensible qualities of light, colors, etc. from the resisting parts of space (we will suppose it possible for resistance to be without them), and they were to appearance clear and pure, and all that we could possibly observe was only and merely resistance." Suppose, in other words, that we are hummingbirds bumping into the clear glass of a window pane. Then all we would observe of "solidity" would be "that certain parts of space . . . resist anything coming within them." We would never bump into matter.

13. Jesus' prayer was "I have declared unto them thy name . . . that the love wherewith thou hast loved me may be in them, and I in them" (John 17:26).
14. Miscell. no. 108, written c. 1724, at twenty-one years of age (italics mine).

All we would experience would be "impenetrability"; and all we need to suppose to account for the bump-up-againstness is some immediate *action* that prevents coming within various parts of space. We are stopped here and now, and not elsewhere or later. According to Edwards, God's immediate action accounts for the resistance bumped into whenever we encounter solid, impenetrable bodies. *No matter there.* Of course, it is natural for men to suppose that there is "some latent substance, or something that is altogether hid," which upholds every moment the solidity of created bodies. "All therefore agree that there is *something* that is there, and upholds these properties; and it is most true, there undoubtedly is. But men are wont to content themselves in saying merely that it is something; but that 'something' is *he by whom all things consist.*"[15]

This is the ontology into which Edwards set his understanding of God and His creatures. He is nothing if not ontological and theological or biblical at the same time. Here we have a sort of "scale of being." As surely as an archangel is further removed from nonentity than is a worm or a flea,[16] so spiritual beings—the only proper beings—are further removed from nonentity than bodies. To this we can now add that "*understanding* and *will* are *the highest kind of created existence,*" higher than merely perceiving being. Then to that we can add: understanding and will in exercise are higher in actuality than those faculties dormant. Finally "and certainly the most excellent *actual knowledge and will* that can be in the creature is the knowledge and the love of God.[17]

A being to whom has been imparted knowledge of God and love to God is the being of a creature furthest removed from nonentity. This was Edwards's interpretation of St. Paul's "If any man be in Christ, he is a new creature" (2 Cor. 5:17).

> The increasing knowledge of God in all elect creatures to all eternity is *an existence*, a *reality*, infinitely worthy to be in itself. . . . If *existence is more worthy than defect and nonentity*, and if any created existence is in itself worthy to be, *then this knowledge of God and His glory is worthy to be.* The existence of the created universe consists as much in it as in anything, yea, *it is one of the highest, most real and*

---

15. "The Mind," no. [61]. SUBSTANCE. Jonathan Edwards, *Scientific and Philosophical Writings*, ed. Wallace E. Anderson, in *The Works of Jonathan Edwards* (New Haven: Yale Univ. Press, 1980), 6:379–80 (italics mine). The scripture reference is to Col. 1:17, "And he is before all things and by him all things consist."

16. *True Virtue*, p. 546, n. 6.

17. *End of Creation*, p. 454 (italics mine).

substantial parts of all created existence; *most remote from nonentity* and defect."[18]

Thus, the "new creation" is the name, idea or knowledge of God's, being in human understanding; the love of God's, being in human wills, and the joy of God's, being in human affection. This was the original ultimate end God had in the creation of the World.

So Edwards in the eighteenth century joins Barth in the twentieth in the belief that it is not God whose existence needs proof, but rather the existence of anything other than God, any world at all, that needs explaining. Edwards's cosmic teleology was ultimately Christological; the work of redemption accounted for the history of the universe at large. God's end in the natural world was the end of the moral world, the end of the moral order was the end of the good part of the moral world, the end of the good part of the moral world was the end of the saints at their best, venting their souls in praise of God, and the end of the best part of the moral world at their best was what Jesus Christ sought as his last or ultimate end, in his "great request" in what we call his High Priestly prayer: "that they may have my joy fulfilled in themselves"; "that they all may be one; as thou Father, art in me, and I in thee, that they may be one in us . . . that they may be one, even as we are one" (John 17:31,21–22).[19] That was Edwards's ultimate answer to the question, Whence came knowledge of God to any human understanding, and whence any love to God? Since the being of that knowledge, love, and joy is existence most worthy of being, most remote from nonentity, the same was his answer to the perplexing question—if this be proper speaking—Why on earth there is any being outside of God himself.

"Divine love" in the heart also goes out to our fellow creatures. Characteristically, Edwards always spells out "Do unto others as you would that others do to you" by adding, "If you were in their circumstances and they in yours." That is, he spells out the Golden Rule to mean "swapping places" in order to tell what we should do. Moses' command "Thou shalt love thy neighbor as thyself" also puts you in your neighbor's place, and he in yours.

Modern moral philosophy calls this the "reversibility" test, crucial in Golden Rule arguments generative of specific moral conclu-

18. Miscell. no. 1225. END OF THE CREATION. GLORY OF GOD. This entry marked for use or when used.

19. For the progression rapidly sketched above, see JE's hermeneutical principles, his twelve "positions" on how *rightly* to ask scripture concerning the end for which God created the world. *End of Creation*, pp. 469–74.

sions, or verdicts concerning right or wrong. Since philosophers talk that way, it looks as if there can be a truly virtuous love of neighbor *without* divine love in the heart. Before letting ourselves be culture-bound to that view, however, consider the extraordinary conclusions Edwards drew from "swapping places." In his sermon on "Charity suffereth long and is kind," Edwards commented as follows on Jesus' parable, Luke 10:25–37: "If the Samaritan was neighbor to the Jew, his enemy, so the Jew was neighbor to the Samaritan; because neighborhood is a mutual relation equally predicable of both those between whom there is such a relation."[20] So Moses' "as thyself" entails love of alien or enemy neighbors no less than of those who are friendly. In the application of this sermon, Edwards reformulates "neighborliness" (in terms of Golden Rule reversibility) in words that in their extremity must include freely doing good to enemies no less than to friends, strangers, or the poor. "If others have a hearty good will to us," he wrote, "and there is a great deal of kindness, and they are ready to help us when we stand in need of help, and to that end are free to do for us, to labor for us, to give to us, to suffer for us, and help bear our burdens, and share with us in our calamities, are free and cheerful in it, and seem to be open-hearted and liberal in it, *this we approve of when we are the objects*; this we highly commend; . . . *we are not apt to think that they exceed their duty*."[21] While yet an enemy we would not think such beneficence exceeded the duties of neighborhood if we were the object helped. "Swapping places" requires that if *I* am hostile and an implacable enemy to someone, yet am in serious need of help, I ask myself whether I would approve or disapprove of aid kindly given me by my implacable enemy; and go now and do likewise to him.

Now that it truly extraordinary. Edwards assumes that people, whose only obvious "mutual relation equally predicable" is that of stranger, alien, venomous hostility, may also become sharers in an equally predicable mutual relation of neighborhood; and that then anyone can know quite well the right disposition and action due to a hateful enemy by imagining that we are in his place and he in ours when we see him suffering under great calamity. If we suffered similarly, we would not say *he* "exceeded his duty" by helping *us*. But the language of "duty" or obligation may be questioned here.

Not many of us are likely to believe that love of enemies (real

20. *Charity*, p. 210.
21. Ibid., p. 215 (italics mine).

enemies, not ideal or imaginary ones) is a duty. Indeed, it is reasonable to argue that the expression "the duties of charity" is a contradiction in terms. In the Roman Catholic tradition of ethics, "counsels of perfection" placed less strain on ordinary, reasonable people's conception of their bottom-line obligations. And in Lutheran and Reformed traditions, the first function of the example of Christ, the perfection of righteousness he taught, the "love one another as I have loved you" of John 13:34, was to cast people down in their own eyes so that they realize they have no health in them, and can do nothing but seek a Savior. Yet, as we have just seen, Edwards's shared neighborhood consists of moral roles, relations, and duties having extraordinarily elevated standards of bottom-line expectations, which he tries to show are entirely reasonable. His demonstration consists in a use of the reversibility test, which ordinarily aims at attaining an unbiased derivation to others of the self's natural inclinations and preferences. On its face that reasoning fails to reach the moral dispositions and actions Edwards commends. The reverse of love of self is not naturally love of enemies. How are we to explain the remarkable meaning Edwards finds in the "as thyself" of the Mosaic law? Does what he says really follow from a rational use of reversibility or Golden Rule arguments?

In his sermon on "seeketh not her own," Edwards wrestles with why Christ called "love one another as I have loved you" a new commandment in "rule and motive." This was a problem since he believed the *love*, the matter of the command, is the same as the old "as thyself"; the "substance" is the same but with "a new enforcement and light annexed," a "new rule and motive." What he says under these heads is all very puzzling. It explains nothing. No answer can be given to those who demand a "rational" explanation of how the rule of loving others as Christ has loved us only "more clearly" shows our obligation in respect to our neighbor. "In a further degree" hardly describes the remarkable meanings Edwards draws from the "swapping places" that Moses and modern moral philosophy command.[22] Reason alone teaches no such thing to be the meaning of virtuous benevolence.

Typology is the key to understanding Edwards on the sum of the moral law, Old and New. Typology, or figural interpretation, was the way Puritan exegetes held on to the narrative unity and truth of the

22. For JE's discussion of the "two chief and most remarkable descriptions which the Scripture gives us of a truly gracious love to our neighbor," see ibid., pp. 265–66.

whole of scripture, without either fundamentalist literalism or medieval allegorization. The story of Jonah, for example, was a marvelous type; its real but veiled meaning was unveiled and made manifest in the antitype, the entombment of Jesus Christ—who, risen from the dead, also reveals in the Great Commission (Mark 16:15) the true meaning and scope of preaching God's forgiveness to the Ninevites. The blessed land of Canaan, passing over Jordan into the promised land, Zion, Jerusalem were all remarkable types whose meaning will be fully manifest only in the future the New Testament promises God's people.

In like manner, the old commandment contains the new under a veil; the new is the old unveiled and made clear. Love of neighbor "as thyself" is a typical adumbration of the antitypical love to one another "as I have loved you." Therefore, I suggest, "swapping places" (with the remarkable meaning Edwards finds in that interchange) is a type whereby we substitute ourselves in the stead of others as Jesus Christ stood in ours. Or rather, substituting Jesus Christ in the stead of others (when *he* was in prison, etc. [Matt. 25:35–40], when *he* went down from Jerusalem to Jericho or up to Golgotha) "derives to others" our own position when we were dead by the roadside and the Good Samaritan freely shared with us in our own calamities. We are not apt *then* to think excessive duty was done them. I can conceive of no other grounds than these for deriving *to* myself *from* my implacable enemy succor for me when he catches me in distress, as the standard for what his implacable enemy should be and do toward him in disposition and in action in his calamities. Of course, there is the example of David who, after Saul became his "enemy continually," yet spared Saul's life when Saul was resting in a cave from pursuing him. But in this and other respects David was for Edwards a type of Christ.[23] Thus the gospel meaning of "pure benevolence" was contained in the old rule "as thyself"; and thus only is it discoverable by reversibility or Golden Rule arguments.

Given Puritan typology, it should surprise no one that Christ substituting himself for us gives the meaning to Golden Rule arguments; that the doctrine that Christ looked on our happiness as his own, placed his happiness in ours, placed his glory in our glorification with

23. 1 Sam. 24. On that occasion Saul's "conscientious" morality acknowledged true righteousness that was not his own. Both warriors safely at a distance from one another, Saul lifted up his voice and cried, "Thou art more righteous than I: for thou hast rewarded me good, whereas I have rewarded thee evil. . . . For if man find his enemy, will he let him go well away?" (vv. 17, 19).

him gives the meaning of pure benevolence to our neighbor; or that looking on others happiness as our own, placing or finding our own happiness in theirs is the manifest meaning of the "as thyself." For the matter of the old law, the meaning of swapping places, types out Jesus' taking our place. Truly virtuous love to neighbor, if there is any such goodwill in human hearts, must be love "so great as to be justly looked upon as a thorough union with them"; so great as the friendship of Christ for his people, which was a love "justly looked upon as making himself *one with them*, as is thoroughly assuming them into *union with himself*."[24] John 17:21–22 is the manifest, fully unveiled meaning of goodwill among men.

By this measure, we who do not reveal ourselves to one another without dissimulation and are not united in affection can hardly have virtuous and holy goodwill among us. It begins to look as if no one in this life has a native capacity for the first act of truly virtuous benevolence to our neighbors—as was said of love to God. A perfect conjunction of love of our own happiness consisting in their happiness must be the effect (and not the cause, nor we the cause) of our first being united with them.[25] There must be an assumption of their happiness into the will and love of our own happiness, as Christ assumed our own nature into his. Mostly, love of our happiness and of theirs runs on two tracks; or sometimes so, sometimes not; sometimes converging, sometimes diverging. Our wills and loves to happiness are compatibly similar—*homoiousios*, I am tempted to say. Still our own happiness does not consist in theirs. There remains an iota between us; my happiness is not *homoousios* with theirs, placed in theirs by our first being united in perfect affection.

In the Christian life, according to Edwards, the old creature has passed away, yet not perfectly; all things are made new, yet none perfectly.

24. Miscell. no. 483 (italics mine).
25. Cf. *True Virtue*, p. 577.

4

CHRISTIAN VOCATION AND RESISTANCE

If Christian love enjoins discovering the neighbor in every person, the question arises as to whether and how there may be a decision and preference among the needs of the many neighbors who cross one's path. In *Basic Christian Ethics* Ramsey argued that there are grounds in scripture and tradition for an ethic that prefers the victim rather than the perpetrator of injustice. Preference may even take the form of violent resistance. Ramsey relies in part on a distinction between a self-regarding use of resistance in self-defense and an other-regarding resistance on the *neighbor's* behalf and for his or her protection; but he even permits the possibility of a "vocational" defense of self justified derivatively from agape. Here we would find, then, another example of agape's eminently free and uncompromising commitment to the neighbor. (From *Basic Christian Ethics*, pp. 153–57, 166–84)

THE PROBLEM OF CHRISTOCENTRIC VOCATION

The Protestant Reformation abolished the medieval Catholic distinction between special religious merit and dignity attached to the role of the clergy and the inferior, though altogether necessary, function of ordinary lay Christians in the world. All vocations, said the Reformers, rank the same with God, none more sacred, none more secular than others, no matter how they are ranked by men. Of course, some callings are socially more pivotal than others, in that the vocations of many other individuals are subsumed under them; but the difference between monk or magistrate and gardener or garbage collector is an "official" distinction only, implying no real difference in merit or dignity before God. Therefore no individual, whatever his work may be, has any necessity for forsaking the responsibilities of his calling to go off on a crusade or to enter a monastery out of bad conscience about what he is now doing and under the illusion that he can be more perfect somewhere else.

> The Lord commands every one of us, in all the actions of life to regard his vocation. . . . He has appointed to all their particular duties in different spheres of life. . . . Every individual's line of life . . . is, as it were, a post assigned him by the Lord, that he may not wander about in uncertainty all his days. . . . Our life, therefore, will then be best regulated, when it is directed to this mark; since no one will be impelled by his own temerity to attempt more than is compatible with his calling, because he will know that it is unlawful to transgress the bounds assigned him. He that is in obscurity will lead a private life without discontent, so as not to desert the station in which God has placed him. It will also be no small alleviation of his cares, labours, troubles, and other burdens, when a man knows that in all these things he has God for his guide. The magistrate will execute his office with greater pleasure, the father of a family will confine himself to his duty with more satisfaction, and all, in their respective spheres of life, will bear and surmount the inconveniences, cares, disappointments, and anxieties which befall them, when they shall be persuaded that every individual has his burden laid upon him by God. Hence also will arise peculiar consolation, since there will be no employment so mean and sordid (provided we follow our vocation) as not to appear truly respectable, and be deemed highly important in the sight of God.[1]

Martin Luther likewise wanted everybody to be somebody in the eyes of God even though this meant that no one would be anybody by comparison with each other.

> What you do in your house is worth as much as if you did it up in heaven for our Lord God. For what we do in our calling here on earth in accordance with His word and command He counts as if it were done in heaven for Him. . . . Therefore we should accustom ourselves to think of our position and work as sacred and well-pleasing to God, not on account of the position and the work, but on account of the word and the faith from which the obedience and the work flow. No Christian should despise his position and life if he is living in accordance with the word of God, but should say, "I believe in Jesus Christ, and do as the ten commandments teach, and pray that our dear Lord may help me thus to do." That is a right holy life, and cannot be made holier even if one fast himself to death. . . . It looks like a great thing when a monk renounces everything and goes into a cloister, carries on a life of

---

1. John Calvin, *Institutes of the Christian Religion*, III, x, 6, in H. T. Kerr, Jr., ed., *A Compend of the Institutes of the Christian Religion* (Westminster, 1939), p. 107.

asceticism, fasts, watches, prays, etc. . . . . On the other hand, it looks like a small thing when a maid cooks and cleans and does other housework. But because God's command is there, even such a small work must be praised as a service to God far surpassing the holiness and asceticism of all monks and nuns. For here there is no command of God. But there God's command is fulfilled, that one should honour father and mother and help in the care of the home.[2]

All this is familiar. Less has been said so clearly of how a Christian's duty in some secular calling stands in relation to Christian love, which should be normative for everything he does. Granted that a theocentric or a law-/or decalogue-centered theory of vocation may very well be formulated, how can there be a *Christocentric* vocation without withdrawing an individual quite completely from actual tasks in the world?

Count Leo Tolstoy, Russian novelist, Christian idealist, and opponent of all government, understood to the full the essential meaning of nonresisting Christian love in the respect that such love has absolutely no *selfish* reason for preferring one person to another. He defined Christian love as "a preference for others over oneself," with the immediate implication that before a man can love he must "cease from preferring some people to others *for his own personal welfare.*"[3] For a Christian the activity of love does not

> proceed in any definite order with the demands of his strongest love presenting themselves first, those of a feebler love next, and so on. The demands of love present themselves *constantly* and *simultaneously* and *without any order.* Here is a hungry old man for whom I have a little love and who has come to ask for food which I am keeping for the supper of my much-loved children: how am I to weigh the present demand of a feebler love against the future demand of a stronger?[4]

Tolstoy not only seems to comprehend clearly the essential nature of unclaiming, nonresisting, nonpreferential love for neighbor, but also his deep suspicion of introducing any other sort of preferences into the activity of love sprang from considerations which Christian ethics must judge quite correct. Any sort of preference among neighbors so easily turns again into care for them only in the sequence and degree called for by self-love.

2. *Works, V,* 102; IV, 341; V, 100. Quoted by A. C. McGiffert in *Protestant Thought Before Kant* (New York: Scribner's, 1911), p. 33.
3. Leo Tolstoy, *On Life,* xxiv, trans. Aylmer Maude, Oxford World's Classics ed., pp. 102, 103 (italics mine).
4. Ibid., xxiii, p. 97 (italics mine).

If I admit that a freezing child may remain unclothed because my children may some day need the clothes I am asked to give, then I may also resist other demands of love out of consideration for my future children. . . .

If a man may reject the present demands of a feebler love for the sake of the future demands of a greater love, is it not evident that such a man, even if he wished it with all his might, will never be able to judge to what extent he may reject present demands in favour of future demands; and therefore, not being able to decide that question, *will always choose the manifestations of love which please him best—* that is, he will yield not to the demands of love but to the demands of his personality. If a man decides that it is better for him to resist the demands of a present very feeble love for the sake of a future greater love *he deceives himself and others and loves no one but himself.*

Future love does not exist. Love is a present activity only.[5]

Tolstoy's views are at many points actually a paraphrase of the Sermon on the Mount and other of Jesus' strenuous teachings which we have seen are an eschatological stimulus making us well acquainted with the pure and perfect will of God. Jesus said, "If any one comes to me and does not *hate* his own father and mother and wife and children and brothers and sisters, yes, and even his own life, he cannot be my disciple" (Luke 14:26); and to a would-be disciple who wanted first to wait until his father was dead and buried, he laid down the condition, "Follow me, and leave the dead to bury their own dead" (Matt. 8:22). What then becomes of vocational obligation to one's own family? How can nonpreferential love *prefer* some persons to others so far as must be the case within the actual lines of any vocation? How can non-resisting love take upon itself any responsibility for public protection or in support of just social reform through the vocation of legislator, judge, sheriff, hangman, or soldier? How can the strenuous teachings of Jesus come into actual practice? How can the ferment of ideal perfectionism in Christian ethics provide foundation for any actual calling except by outright or thinly disguised compromise? These questions have now to be answered. . . .

A PREFERENTIAL ETHICS OF PROTECTION AND THE TEACHINGS OF JESUS

Unless the instance in which Jesus fled from the territory of Herod Antipas in order to avoid arrest (Luke 13:33) was a case of his saving his life for a better accounting and a more promising opportunity for

5. Ibid., pp. 97–98 (italics mine).

sacrifice in Jerusalem, an explicit manifestation of "duties to him-self" can hardly be expected within the short closing period of Jesus' lifetime, to which our knowledge of him is largely limited. Neverthe-less, neighbor-centered preferential love and a Christian ethic of pro-tection do have their beginning in him, in spite of the effect of apoca-lypticism in expelling concern for the permanent organization of justice and making men well acquainted with the pure will of God in the case of a single neighbor.

To see this, we need not bandy proof-texts back and forth or engage in St. Augustine's hair-splitting exegesis on the saying "If any one strikes you on the right cheek, turn to him the other also" (Matt. 5:39). This teaching, Augustine reasoned, involved only a case of insult, not of assault; for, assuming a greater number of right-handed assailants in the world, their blows would normally be delivered to an opponent's left cheek. A blow upon the *right* cheek, which Jesus talked about, would most likely be struck by the *back* of the hand; this is as if a glove were thrown in the face; we need only conclude, then, that in case a Christian is *insulted* he turns the other cheek and avoids *unnecessary* conflict. This interpretation, or any other which seeks to moderate the extremity of Jesus' requirement, cannot be correct, because Jesus spoke this saying merely as an illustration of his strenuous teaching "Do not resist one who is evil," than which nothing could be more severe. In case of attack *or* insult from "one who is evil" turning the other cheek can be the only possible meaning of nonresisting love.

Nevertheless—and this is to understand, not to lessen, the requirement—Jesus deals only with the simplest moral situation in which blows may be struck, the case of one person in relation to but one other. He does not here undertake to say how men, who them-selves ought not to resist at all or by any means whatever when they themselves alone receive the blows, ought to act in more complex cases where nonresistance would in practice mean turning another person's face to the blows of an oppressor. We are not at all uncertain what Jesus' ethic was in bilateral, two-party situations. When his life alone was concerned Jesus turned the other cheek, when smitten he smote not again, and he died quite without defending himself.

Yet without distorting the text, the beginnings of a multilateral ethics of protection, certainly a multilateral neighbor-centered pref-erential love, may be found in Jesus' own attitudes and example. On occasion he showed indignation, even wrath, over injustice, using vitriolic words as weapons against the devourers of widows' houses

(Luke 20:47). He was unsparing in his condemnation of the complacency of Israel's religious leaders. Indeed, a great Jewish scholar, while attributing real originality to the teachings of Jesus, raises serious objection against the consistency of Jesus' practice:

> I would not cavil with the view that Jesus is to be regarded as the first great Jewish teacher to frame such a sentence as: "Love your enemies, do good to them who hate you, bless them that curse you, and pray for them who ill-treat you" (Luke 6:27,28). Yet how much more telling his injunction would have been if we had *a single story* about his doing good to, and praying for, a single Rabbi or Pharisee! One grain of practice is worth a pound of theory. . . . But no such deed is ascribed to Jesus in the Gospels. Towards his enemies, towards those who did not believe in him, whether individuals, groups, or cities (Matthew 11:20–24), only denunciation and bitter words! The injunctions are beautiful, but how much more beautiful would have been a *fulfillment* of those injunctions by Jesus himself.[6]

Jesus' prayer on the cross that God forgive his executioners (Luke 23:24) might be cited in reply, and here and there a friendly conversation with an inquiring scribe, or the act of healing the daughter of Jairus, a ruler of the synagogue. Moreover, some responsibility for anti-Jewish sentiment in the gospels must be laid at the door of later controversy between Christians and Jews. Still, in the last analysis, the only answer to the charge that Jesus did not always display an attitude toward his opponents consonant with the main body of his own teachings must grant the fact yet deny the interpretation given. When it was a question of injustice done to persons other than himself, especially when he confronted the huge burden of fossilized religion fastened upon the people of the land, Jesus did not remain at his ease lifting up their faces to additional blows or supporting by silence their compulsion to go a second mile. Although his words were, "Do not resist *one* who is evil," Jesus did not even draw out very explicitly the distinction between resisting *evil* yet not resisting the evil-*doer*, between condemning "the system" and denouncing people who support it, which Christians often insist was his meaning. The evil and the one who does it are in any actual situation bound so closely together that a person who, in one-one relationship to an enemy-neighbor, wishes not to resist the evildoer can find no way of resisting evil; and a person in multilateral relationships with more

6. C.G. Montefiore, *Rabbinic Literature and Gospel Teachings*, pp. 103f. Quoted by Major, Manson, and Wright, *The Mission and Message of Jesus* (Dutton, 1938), p. 344.

than one neighbor who wishes for their sakes to resist evil will be unable to avoid resisting the evildoer as well. With prophetic indignation, therefore, Jesus denounced those who were evil as well as impersonal forms of evil itself. This he did from neighbor-centered preferential love, although so far as his life alone was concerned he showed no preference for his own personal welfare and did not resist evildoers when evil fell upon him.

When the two perspectives, Jesus' personal ethic of nonresistance and the beginning in him of a preferential ethic of protection, are not kept quite separate the resulting blend is some form of nonviolent or passive *resistance*. This permits more concern for the self in relation to the single neighbor than by its nature *nonresisting* Christian love allows, and at the same time limits what such love may find needs to be done when weighing the claims of more neighbors than one and the actual ways they may be served. Whether the whip Jesus used in driving the money-changers out of the Temple was plaited of straw or of leather, whether he applied it to animals or to men, whether the decisive factor that day was the force of his own powerful personality justifiably indignant on behalf of a righteous cause or the threatening multitude of people gathered in Jerusalem who forestalled the immediate use of the Temple police, in any case some form of resistance was raised that day not only against perverse practices but also against the men who engaged in them. Force does not become any less resistant because of its "spirituality," or resistance wrong to a greater degree because it takes material form. Circumstances similar to those which warranted a change from Jesus' announced ethic of nonresistance to any manner of resistance he may have used in cleansing the Temple may not only permit but even on occasion require Christian love to adopt physical methods of resistance.

A recent study of Christian attitudes toward war and peace puts the issue of a preferential ethic of protection in terms of Jesus' story of the Good Samaritan: "And now arises one of the unanswerable 'ifs' of literary history. What would Jesus have made the Samaritan do while the robbers were still at their fell work?" In answering this question, the author, apparently without any hesitation, substitutes Jesus' personal ethic in relation to a single neighbor, and all his apocalyptically derived strenuous teachings having to do with this simple situation, for what might have been his ethic in multilateral relation to two or more neighbors. He writes, "The protection of one life would have seemed to Jesus no excuse at all for taking the life of another, even a robber." Surely the most that can be said is that quite plainly the protection of *his own* life did not seem to Jesus any excuse for ceasing to express nonresisting love for another. It may be "there is no evidence for the suggestion that Jesus would have had him wield his traveler's sword."[7] Still, in the rudiments of preferential ethics to be found in Jesus' attitude toward the perpetrators of injustice there is some suggestion that he *might*, at least no decisive evidence that he would *not*, have approved such action. We perhaps should not go to the other extreme so far as to say, "When I try to imagine what would have happened had Jesus come upon the scene a little earlier than the Good Samaritan, I find it more natural to suppose that he would have helped the traveler in his struggle with the thieves than that he would have waited until the man was injured and the thieves departed before coming to his aid."[8] To say the least this would have been a different ethical situation from the one pictured in the story or from an attack by thieves upon Jesus himself. The difference is precisely that nonresisting, unself-defensive love must determine its responsibility in the one case toward more than one neighbor, in the other simply toward the neighbor or "the enemy" when injurious consequences of the decision will fall upon the agent himself alone.

> To express love at all in some situations one must seem to deny it. Jesus said: "If any man smite you on one cheek turn the other also"; here the situation is relatively simple—you and your enemy. But Jesus did not say: "If any man smite one of your friends, lead him to another friend that he may smite *him* also." Not only is it clear that Jesus could have made no such statement, but also that he would have felt that the involvement of the interests of others (that is, others besides one's self and one's enemy) transformed the whole moral situation and placed our obligations with respect to it in a radically different light.[9]

Jesus once told the parable of a servant whom a merciful king released from debt to the fantastic amount of ten million dollars who nevertheless insisted that a fellow servant pay in full a debt of twenty dollars. "Then his lord summoned him and said to him, 'You wicked servant! I forgave you all that debt because you besought me; and should not you have had mercy on your fellow servant, as I had mercy on you?' And in anger his lord delivered him to the jailers, till he

7. T. S. K. Scott-Craig, *Christian Attitudes to War and Peace* (New York: Scribner's, 1938), p. 43.

8. L. A. Garrard, *Duty and the Will of God* (Oxford: Blackwell, 1938), p. 78.

9. John Knox's essay in the symposium *The Christian Answer*, ed. H. P. Van Dusen, (New York: Scribner's, 1945), p. 173.

should pay all his debt" (Matt. 18:32,33). From this story it is evident that love which for itself claims nothing may yet for the sake of another claim everything, that any one who unhesitatingly and times without number renounces "what is due" when he himself alone bears the brunt of such a decision may nevertheless turn full circle and insist with utter severity upon full payment of what is due to others; and what is due to others is never simply just payment but full forgiveness "as I had mercy on you," never exact justice alone but Christian love. This may be called neighbor-centered rather than self-centered severity, forgiving love which pronounces judgment on all that is not love, an attitude which gives up judging men in terms of their conformity to some legal or moral code and yet insists that men are judged in terms of the demands of unconditional self-giving. "So also my heavenly Father will do to every one of you, if you do not forgive your brother from your heart" (Matt. 18:35).

A CHRISTIAN ETHIC OF RESISTANCE

Whether or not so much preferential ethics of protection may be seen in Jesus himself, beyond question Christian ethics soon developed such a view, the primitive pacifism generally practiced by early Christians so long as they were in a minority giving way to what were judged more effective means for assuming responsibility for the whole of organized society. Although decades before their time individual Christians had begun to accept service in the Roman legions, often with the explicit approval of church authorities, St. Ambrose (A.D. 340–396) and his great convert St. Augustine (A.D. 354–430) were the first to give fully elaborated theoretical defense of Christian participation in armed conflict. Since Christian ethics is not a legalism concerned with external deeds only or even mainly, it would be a great mistake to regard Christianity's accommodation to Constantine's empire as necessarily a compromise of its genius or a "fall" from the pristine purity of its ethic. As a matter of fact, careful examination of the first literary defense of Christian participation in war gives striking evidence that underneath the obvious reversal of tactic, the general strategy of Christian love continued without abatement and without any alteration in its fundamental nature.

While first formulating for Christian thought a theory of *justum bellum*, both St. Ambrose and St. Augustine continued to teach that when a man himself alone is concerned he ought never to resist "one who is evil." Both combine their justification of war because of a

Christian's responsibility for public protection with an utter denial that under any circumstances he ever has any right of private self-defense. No Christian, they said, should save his own life at the expense of another; yet when other persons than himself are involved in the decision, no Christian ought to fail to resist evil by effective means which the state alone makes available to him. This combination of ideas, which seems strange to men today, is clear proof that nonresisting love was still the groundwork of all reasoning about Christian participation in conflict of arms; and indeed this continued to be true down to the "holy war" enthusiasm of the crusades, as can be seen in the requirement that a private soldier do penance for the evil he may have done or thought while participating even in just wars he *should* have joined.

Commenting on a passage from Cicero, St. Ambrose asked the question, Should a wise man in case of shipwreck take away a plank from an ignorant sailor? Leaving aside the consideration that an emaciated philosopher probably would not prove victor in struggle with an ignorant sailor, *ought* he try to save his own life at the expense of another? Ambrose answered this question in the negative, and likewise for all one-one neighbor situations.

> Some ask whether a wise man ought in case of a shipwreck to take away a plank from an ignorant sailor? Although it seems better for the common good that a wise man rather than a fool should escape from shipwreck, yet I do not think that a Christian, a just and wise man, ought to save his own life by the death of another; just as when he meets with an armed robber he cannot return his blows, *lest in defending his life he should stain his love toward his neighbor.* The verdict on this is plain and clear in the books of the Gospel. . . . What robber is more hateful than the persecutor who came to kill Christ? But Christ would not be defended by the wounds of the persecutor, for He willed to heal all by His wounds.[10]

A Christian ought never to value his own possessions so highly as to be willing, for his own sake, to take the life of another person, though from identically the same sort of neighbor-love he will value the possessions of another enough to resist, for his sake, a criminal attempt against them. This he will do not only occasionally but in the vocation of police or judge as well. When he alone is imperiled he will not presume to estimate the comparative worth of his own wisdom or

---

10. *The Duties of the Clergy*, III, iv, 27, vol. 10 of *Nicene and Post-Nicene Fathers*, 2d ser. (New York: Scribner's, 1908) (italics mine).

righteousness and another man's lack of these qualities, though in the vocation of prince or soldier such judgments about relative justice must be made by a comparison of the righteousness of one conflicting side or party with another.

In the views of St. Augustine we can penetrate more deeply the reason for this strange combination of doctrines, why for Christian ethics generally *self-defense is the worst of all possible excuses for war or for any other form of resistance or any sort of preference among other people.* Augustine makes this distinction between public and private protection when considering the more general question "whether *Libido* dominates also in those things which we see too often done."

> For me the point to be considered first is whether an on-rushing enemy, or an assassin lying in wait may be killed with no wrong-headed desire (for the saving) of one's life, or for liberty or for purity. . . . How can I think that they act with no inordinate desire who fight for that (*i.e.,* some creaturely good), which they can lose without desiring to lose it? . . . Therefore the law is not just which grants the power to a wayfarer to kill a highway robber, so that he may not be killed (by the robber); or which grants to any one, man or woman, to slay an assailant attacking, if he can, before he or she is harmed. The soldier also is commanded by law to slay the enemy, for which slaying, if he objects, he will pay the penalty by imperial order. Shall we then dare to say that these laws are unjust, or more, that they are not laws? For to me a law that is not just appears to be no law. . . . For that he be slain who lays plans to take the life of another is less hard (to bear) than the death of him who is defending his own life (against the plotter). And acting against the chaste life of a man in opposition to his own will is much more evidently wrong than the taking of the life of him who so does violence by that one against whom the violence is done. Then again the soldier in slaying the enemy is the agent of the law (in war), wherefore he does his duty easily with no wrong aim or purpose. . . . That law therefore, which for the protection of citizens orders foreign force to be repulsed by the same force, can be obeyed without a wrong desire: and this same can be said of all officials who by right and by order are subject to any powers. But I see not how these men (who defend themselves privately), while not held guilty by law, can be without fault: for the law does not force them to kill, but leaves it in their power. It is free therefore for them to kill no one for those things (life or possessions) which they can lose against their own will, which things therefore they ought not to love. . . . Wherefore again I do not blame the law which permits such aggressors to be slain: but by what reason I can defend those who slay them I do not find. . . . How indeed are they free to sin before Providence, who for those things

which ought to be held of less worth are defiled by the killing of a man?[11]

When a judge on the bench renders decision between two parties other than himself, it is universally agreed, he will likely be more impartial and clear-headed about justice than when he judges in his own case. Now, Augustine believed that the decision of a prince or a man acting in some public capacity might well be of this same sort. In multilateral relationships a man can weigh what is just and unjust without undue influence on account of his selfish partiality. In this way he may express decided preference, but from neighbor-regarding considerations, not simply on account of what pleases him best from the point of view of his own personal welfare. The contrary is true, he believed, in all cases of private self-defense, even instances which a third party would call entirely just. Every man is so centrally interested in his own preservation that, Augustine believed, private self-defense could only arouse or proceed from some degree of inordinate self-love or "wrong-headed desire." In defending himself a man's egoism either manifests or gains control over his action, and the passion of selfishness, *concupiscence,* or libido warps his moral judgment so far as to render him totally incapable of deciding rightly between himself and his neighbor. If he should happen to defend the right person in defending himself, if he should actually save the life of the person a third party would assist or protect, this would be only by chance; it would be because of egotism, not because of justice or love.

Now, Ambrose and Augustine doubtless need to be criticized for their rather unqualified acceptance of public protection and also for their complete rejection of private self-defense. They tend to understate the danger that in conflict between nations collective egotism will be so aroused that the judgment of any individual member of the group will come rather fully under the sway of self-interest. Even in his vocation, where multilateral neighbor-relationships intersect, an individual finds himself drawn not by neighbor-love alone or by considerations of justice alone but by selfish preference or personal affinity, for *these* persons rather than *those*. In actual conflict situations he is already inextricably bound to one side or the other by geography or language or existing mutual interest. In short, he *always* judges his own case; and, though he is sinfully incompetent ever to judge in such a situation, he cannot, like a judge of some court, disqualify himself

11. *De libero arbitrio,* bk. I, chap. v, trans. F. E. Tourscher (Peter Reilly, 1937), pp. 25–29. Cf. Ep. XLVII,6.

and let some one else decide the issue. Love for neighbor must necessarily be exercised from points of view which are never quite those of an impartial observer. Beyond question there takes place grave exaggeration of the claims to righteousness made on behalf of the relatively innocent individual or nation even by those who more or less "unselfishly" champion them.

On the other hand, Ambrose and Augustine were perhaps too extreme in excluding private self-defense as in every case unjustified for the Christian. Luther disagreed with them on this point, but he did so only after surrounding the exercise of any right of personal self-defense with extreme conditions:

> You ask, Why may I not use the sword for myself and for my own cause, with the intention by so doing not of seeking my own interest, but the punishment of evil? I answer, Such a miracle is not impossible, but quite unusual and hazardous. Where there is such affluence of the Spirit it may be done. . . . No one but a real Christian and one who is full of the Spirit will follow this example. If reason also should follow this example, it would indeed pretend not to be seeking its own, but this would be untrue. It cannot be done without grace. Therefore, first become like Samson, and then you can also do as Samson did.[12]

We must ask, What moral conditions will be effected by being full of the Spirit? The answer to this question should be given in light of the fact that Christian ethics always recognizes the Holy Spirit as the spirit of Christ. If from the motivating strategy of Christian love there can be vocational resistance and Christian vocations in society using protective coercion, may there not also be such a thing as vocational self-protection? A Christian does whatever love requires, and the possibility cannot be ruled out that on occasion defending himself may be a duty he owes to others. Whenever sacrificing himself, or in any degree failing to protect himself and his own, actually would involve greater burdens or injury to others, surely then a Christian should stick to his post whether he wants to or not. In such circumstances self-protection becomes a duty, a form of neighbor-regarding love, the protection of others performed first and most effectively upon oneself. Making use of the distinction between "self-defensive self-protection" and "neighbor-regarding self-protection," self-defense may be but an extreme instance of those "duties to the self" which are a part of Christian vocational obligation. This we can conclude without in any way ignoring the fact that Christian ethics from

12. *Secular Authority: To What Extent It Should Be Obeyed*, in *Works*, Muhlenberg ed., 3:249–50.

Ambrose to Tolstoy has always, quite correctly, looked upon self-defensiveness and any other form of selfish preferential love with profound suspicion. The Christian point of view, we should always remember, also surrounds an act of giving one's body to be burned with just as grave doubt.

During the height of the submarine warfare in the North Atlantic [during World War II], four chaplains gave over their lifebelts to four "ignorant sailors" and went down with the ship. This was, so far as men may judge, a Christian act of self-sacrifice. Suppose the captain of the vessel, himself not involved in the case, had presumed to choose among these men, by his command saying whose life should be saved, whose lost. In order to make such a decision, the captain would have to take many factors into account; on the side of the sailors, their greater service to immediate military ends; against one of them, the fact that he had broken ship's rule by going to sleep without his lifebelt on, that he was unmarried and had few fixed responsibilities to others, that he was not so wise or well-trained or likely to serve humanity in more than ordinary ways; on the side of one of the chaplains, that he was married and the father of several children, moreover a "wise man" and a man of rare character and capacity for unusual service. Now arises the crucial question: In the absence of a third, impartial party responsible for the decision, should a wise man ever refuse to give up his lifebelt to an ignorant sailor? Ought ever an individual act in favor of himself, making the same choice between two lives, his own and his neighbor's, which every one would regard as entirely just, even obligatory, when such a decision is rendered by some third person not himself involved in the issue?

Men, being evil, may nevertheless know how to give good gifts to their children (Matt. 7:11). Just as selfish partiality is never completely absent from decisions about public protection, so also partiality for the interests of one's neighbors need not be completely excluded from decisions and actions which actually undertake to protect the self. Enlightened weighing of a person's responsibilities to others may not only permit saving one's life "for better accounting even if it means only a more promising opportunity for sacrifice" by the merely *negative* act of keeping possession of a lifebelt or failing to pause and help countless other refugees trekking out of Burma. Care for others for whom a person is vocationally responsible, closely and obviously bound in with protecting himself, may also require more *positive* action, actually taking away the lives of others, as can be seen in the following modern version of "taking away a plank from an ignorant sailor":

> Today Tom, one of our ambulance drivers of whom I have spoken, went to China. He wanted to go, and yet he did not want to go. The reason he did not want to go was that he found India pleasant, and besides this, he was attached to us as we were to him.
>
> The reason he wanted to go was this: When we were coming out of Burma, before we had to abandon our trucks and start walking, we came across a company of wounded Chinese soldiers near Katha. There must have been two hundred of them. My guess is that they had been evacuated from the battlefield to the south and had progressed to Katha. Here the railroad was hopelessly blocked with the tangle of fleeing traffic and the soldiers were thrown on their own to get away from the Japanese who were closing in on all of us. In the staggering heat of that day they saw our convoy of trucks rolling toward them on the dusty road. They must have said to themselves, "Here is perhaps a way of escape. We are desperate men." When our trucks, which had to proceed haltingly for all the traffic, dust, and crowds of evacuees thronging the road, drew opposite them, they hobbled out and swarmed all over the trucks, stopping us.
>
> I cannot find it in me to say a word of blame for what Tom did. I was spared this fearful problem by losing my truck in the muddy bottom of the last river we tried to cross by fording. We were under strict orders not to take on anybody else. To take anybody else would prejudice the hopes we held of getting our already large, weary, half-sick crowd through safely. We had been without enough to eat, without much sleep for forty-eight hours, and the dust was a distressing coat on our eyelids.
>
> With all these things, elemental, physiological, and spiritual in the setting, *Tom got out and pushed the wounded Chinese soldiers off his truck* as the only means of being able to carry on.—More than one night on the walk out and later in Assam he told me, "I owe the Chinese a debt." When he left today he went to pay it.[13]

The foregoing analysis, it should at once be granted, comes dangerously close to one of Raskolnikov's justifications for his "right to crime" in Dostoyevsky's *Crime and Punishment.*

> I simply hinted that an "extraordinary" man has the . . . inner right to decide in his own conscience to overstep . . . certain obstacles, and only in case it is essential for the practical fulfillment of his idea (something, perhaps, of benefit to the whole of humanity). . . . I maintain that if the discoveries of Kepler and Newton could not have been made known except by sacrificing the lives of one, a dozen, a hundred or more men, Newton would have had the right, would indeed have

13. Paul Geren, *Burma Diary* (New York: Harper and Row, 1943), pp. 55–56 (italics mine).

been duty bound . . . to *eliminate* the dozen or the hundred for the sake of making his discoveries known to the whole of humanity. . . . But if such a one is forced for the sake of his idea to step over a corpse or wade through blood, he can, I maintain, find within himself, in his conscience, a sanction for wading through blood—that depends on the idea and its dimensions, of course.[14]

What, if anything, is the difference between this line of reasoning and a justifiably Christian ethic of protection? For one thing, the Christian does not suppose that *he* is "extraordinary," but that *his duty* is extraordinary, or in another sense ordinary, all too ordinary, human, all too human. For another, the Christian acts not for the sake of "the idea and its dimensions" or primarily for the sake of some abstract truth. He acts on behalf of his neighbors and their concrete needs which may have to be served on occasion by the employment of unpleasant means. Christian morality does not permit him even to disguise his private self-assertion under the rubric of abstract concern for "benefit to the whole of humanity." This Raskolnikov finally confesses was the true analysis of the nature of his crime. As for wanting to be an extraordinary man who really has the right to step over corpses, he says later:

> Of course that's all nonsense, its almost all talk! . . . I wanted *to have the daring* . . . I wanted to murder without casuistry, to murder for my own sake, for myself alone . . . I didn't do the murder to gain wealth and power and to become a benefactor of mankind. Nonsense! I simply did it; I did the murder for myself, for myself alone . . . I wanted to find then and quickly . . . whether I can step over barriers or not.[15]

Purified of such perverse self-concern, the Christian nevertheless must adjudicate and decide one way or another among the claims and needs of neighbors he is to serve. In doing so, he at least omits to serve some, and in this sense he wades through blood and suffering. If such a one is forced for the sake of his neighbors visibly to step over a corpse, he can, I maintain, find within himself, in his Christian conscience, a sanction which depends on a proper reading of his actual situation, and the needs of neighbors determining his vocation. The only way of avoiding this conclusion is by recourse to "intuition" as the basis of obligation. This would be a form of "unenlightened unselfishness" which surely requires for justification more than the fact of man's proneness to sin in using his intelligence.

14. Part 3, Chap. 5, Modern Library ed., pp. 247, 248.
15. Ibid., part 5, chap. 4, pp. 392, 395.

No doubt a man stands always in grave peril of choosing only the manifestation of love which pleases him best. He faces this same peril of deceiving himself and others and loving no one but himself even when he sacrifices himself and others. This . . . gives special relevance and validity to Christian love as a requirement in every action. Men who are always surrounded on every side by complex relationships delineating their vocational obligations, and whose moral decisions can never escape from these bonds, for this very reason have special need of a sense that they still "owe the Chinese a debt," they need some St. Francis to walk by their side troubling them. Since *there is always more than one neighbor*, men have special need of an ethic which defines with utter clarity and rigor their full duty toward any and every one of them. Whether Jesus intentionally or from his sense of apocalypse pictured the simplest possible moral situation, the result is undeniable: men may see in his strenuous teachings how they ought conscientiously to act toward every neighbor. Walking beside this unqualified disclosure of the pure will of God, measuring their lives in this mirror, Christians find repeated stimulus for remembering all their obligation, even though they are always surrounded by a vast network of neighbor-claims which converge and create for each of them some specific vocation. The essential meaning of Christian vocation, therefore, is not simply some worldly position interpreted in general religious fashion as *God-given*. Christian vocation means the secular occupation, the "station" and its full, often obnoxious duties, to which an individual feels himself assigned by Christian love or by the love of Christ controlling him.

The fundamental meaning of Christian ethics may be thrown into bolder relief by comparing the entire expulsion of legitimate private self-defense by Ambrose and Augustine with what has happened in much modern pacifism. Modern pacifists frequently revealed their non-Christian rootage by making quite the reverse combination of ideas from that which prevailed for centuries in Christian ethics. Early Christian thought, we have seen, was concerned to deny any analogy between private and public defense in order to say that a Christian, who might participate in armed and bloody conflict for the sake of public protection, would *of course* not resist even by mild or passive means any neighbor who might assault him when his own goods and life alone were threatened. In direct contrast, much modern pacifism also attempts to break down all analogy between private and public defense, but for purpose of establishing almost the reverse conclusion, namely, that *of course* individuals ought to resist by going to law if someone wishes to take away their coat and with possibly bloodless methods in case they individually (and certainly when their grandmothers) are violently attacked. We need have no great sympathy for the "grandmother argument" often presented by draft boards to "conscientious objectors" to military service. Nevertheless, it is clear that modern pacifists, in withdrawing completely from resistance on behalf of national defense, frequently make greater accommodation to the supposed natural necessity of self-defense (or some sort of multilateral ethic of defense limited to the private area where extreme violence need not be used) than ever occurred to the great thinkers who first forged a Christian theory of justum bellum.

Searching for an explanation, we may be driven to reflect that both the pacifism of early Christians and their shift over to resistance in the light of increasing responsibility were basically grounded in Christian love, while in contrast a good deal of contemporary pacifism is grounded in horror and revulsion at the sight of violence or bloodshed and in an ethic which values life above everything else. Violence and bloodshed are no doubt horrifying, especially in destructive, total war, but the word *unlovely* has in Christian ethics a mainly spiritual, not a mainly physical, meaning. A selfish act is the most unlovely thing, and an unselfish motive may lead the Christian to perform necessary responsibilities which prove not so "nice" in terms of physical contamination. For a Christian outlook, sin came first into the world, death followed; sin, or the contrary of love, is the greatest evil from which men need to be delivered, death is only the last enemy of mankind which shall be destroyed, and the sting of death is in fact sin (I Cor. 15:26,56). For many pacifists, however, bloodshed and death are the worst evils, life a conditional or even the highest value which ought never to be violated. And as a consequence they are willing to approve resistance in those forms and under circumstances, in court or at fisticuffs or by aiming low, when a man may hope to stop short of bringing death to an opponent.

Such a view has more in common with dualistic pacifism in the ancient world or with otherworldly Indian religious ethics than with early Christian pacifism. As we have seen, Christian ethics first of all approved public protection and the defense of organized justice as the only means of loving the neighbor with all his concrete physical and social needs in *this* world, and judged that such action might be unselfish even if hopelessly bloody. Centuries later Christian ethics approved private self-defense, which doubtless is nicer but almost always more selfish.

Moreover, it is still true that emotional horror over physical evils may indicate stronger love for ourselves than love for neighbor.

> Today we had to move the evacuee patients out of one hospital building into another. It was a filthy job because so many patients had dysentery. The man whom this foul disease clutches soon becomes unable to move or do anything for himself. He fouls his clothing, the bedding, the stretcher on which we have put him. There is no fresh clothing and bedding to change him. Piles of it lie all about the place all the day unwashed.
>
> It rains every day and no one has the resolution to start the cleansing job since he could never get the things dry. Patients, soiled bedding, soiled clothing all join to send up a reeking stench like a burnt offering to some perverse devil.
>
> Three of us stood surveying the preparations for moving: an American boy who had joined the British Army before we got into the war, his British soldier comrade and I. We saw that the patients had to be moved and that the sweepers who had been assigned to the task were not getting along very quickly with it. If the others were feeling what I felt, we were all dreading to get on any more intimate terms with the stench and handle it. The American turned to his British comrade and said, "I am very glad at this moment that I am agnostic."
>
> I do not know how seriously he intended this. However that is, the conclusion which he implied certainly held: Since he did not believe in the love of Christ he could leave the handling of these dysentery victims to the sweepers. Since his friend did believe in it, he was not free to stand by and watch. Nor was I. Get down in it! Pick the patients up! Soil yourself with this disease! St. Francis kissed the beggars' sores. However this ended in him, it must have begun as the practice of the only medicine he knew. There is no need to call this filthiness sweet, or to start enjoying it through a strange inversion. Only one thing is necessary: for love's sake it must be done.[16]

Participation in regrettable conflict falls among distasteful tasks which sometimes become imperative for Christian vocation. Only one thing is necessary: for love's sake it must be done. All things now are lawful, all things are now permitted, yet everything is required which Christian love requires, everything without a single exception.

16. Geren, *Burma Diary*, pp. 51–52.

5

JUSTICE IN WAR

In *War and the Christian Conscience,* published in 1961, Ramsey deepened
his discussion of resistance on behalf of victims unjustly attacked. The Roman Catholic tradition of justified war became a welcome resource in his
contest against fellow Protestant thinkers who relied too much on a purely
pragmatic moral approach. His concern with forms of right conduct whose
justification resists mere utilitarian calculation of effective means to desired
ends led him to stress two implications of the love commandment regarding
armed resistance. The first, of course, is that the innocent should be protected; the second is that what *justifies* recourse to violence also *limits* its
employment. Agape, therefore, requires the immunity of noncombatants
from direct attack in wartime. By seeking to ground both the warrant and the
limit of organized violence in Christian love, Ramsey sought to drive a wedge
between "pacifists" who reject war *because* it has no limit and "realists" who
insist that wars must in justice be fought, *albeit* (and tragically in the modern
age) *without limit.* These implications are usefully sketched in the essay
below. (From *The Just War,* pp. 141–47)

═══

Question: How do porcupines make love?
Answer: Carefully!
This is a parable of the nations in a multinational world. They
can't get along with and they can't get along without one another.
They make love and reach settlements, or they make war when they
cannot reach or postpone settlements—all, carefully!
There is nothing more like a pacifist than a believer in massive
deterrence: *both* think it possible to banish the use of force from
human history before banishing the porcupine nation-states from off
this planet. To them may be added what Walter Lippman called the

"war *whoop*" party in this country, which thinks we won't ever need to use nuclear weapons if only we say loudly enough that we are going to. So do we as a people—whether by confidence in moral suasion and omnicompetence of negotiation or by confidence in our deterrent technology or by confidence in our superior bluffing ability— avoid facing up to the moral economy governing an actual *use* of the weapons we possess. With peace and the nation-state system as our premises, we have designed a war to end all war: God may let us have it.

Since, however, the porcupine-nations are unlikely soon to be banished, since they are armed with massive nuclear weapons, and since somewhere, sometime, a nation is likely to find itself so vitally challenged that it will believe that even in the atomic era war can be an instrument of its justice, we are today forced to reexamine an ancient set of teachings which many people thought was out of date. This is the doctrine of the "just war," or the morality governing a resort to arms which is only an elaboration of the morality governing the use of power generally.

One of the "tests" in this body of teachings about the morality of warfare is the principle of "proportionate grave reason," or the justification of one good or evil effect only by weighing the greater good or lesser evil of the other effects let loose in the world. This is a test in terms of consequences, and this criterion has been the focus of significant developments in recent years both in Christian analysis, Protestant and Roman Catholic, and in the communist theory of "just war."

In this chapter, however, I want to deal with the *origin* and the *meaning* of another criterion for the morality of war's conduct. It is a more intrinsic one, having to do with the justice or injustice of an *act* of war, considered apart from its consequences. In the course of tracing its origin, the systematic meaning of "just conduct" in war will be exhibited. This is the distinction between *legitimate* and *illegitimate* military actions. This distinction cuts across all distinctions among weapons systems and applies to them all, even though it is nuclear weapons that have decisively raised the question whether there are just and unjust acts of war by raising the question whether these particular weapons can possibly be used in a just manner. To learn the meaning of "justice in war" (and its origin out of love-informed reason) will be to learn what it means to say, in connection with military policy, that the end does not justify the means and that it can never be right to do wrong for the sake of some real or supposed good.

The Western theory of the just war originated, not primarily from considerations of abstract or "natural" justice, but from the interior of the ethics of Christian love, or what John XXIII termed "social charity." It was a work of charity for the Good Samaritan to give help to the man who fell among thieves. But one step more, it may have been a work of charity for the innkeeper to hold himself ready to receive beaten and wounded men, and for him to have conducted his business so that he was solvent enough to extend credit to the Good Samaritan. By another step it would have been a work of charity, and not of justice alone, to maintain and serve in a police patrol on the Jericho road to prevent such things from happening. By yet another step, it might well be a work of charity to resist, by force of arms, any external aggression against the social order that maintains the police patrol along the road to Jericho. This means that, where the enforcement of an ordered community is not effectively present, it may be a work of justice and a work of social charity to resort to other available and effective means of resisting injustice: what do you think Jesus would have made the Samaritan do if he had come upon the scene while the robbers were still at their fell work?

Now, I am aware that this is no proper way to interpret a parable of Jesus. Yet, these several ways of retelling the parable of the Good Samaritan quickly exhibit something that is generally true about the teachings of Jesus—namely, that by deed and word he showed the individual the meaning of being perfectly ready to have the will of God reign and God's mercy shed abroad by his life and actions. These versions quickly exhibit how a social ethic emerged from Christian conscience formed by this revelation, and what the early Christians carried with them when they went out into the world to borrow, and subsequently to elevate and refine, Stoic concepts of natural justice.

While Jesus taught that a disciple in his own case should turn the other cheek, he did not enjoin that his disciples should lift up the face of another oppressed man for *him* to be struck again on *his* other cheek. It is no part of the work of charity to allow this to continue to happen. Instead, it is the work of love and mercy to deliver as many as possible of God's children from tyranny, and to protect from oppression, if one can, as many of those for whom Christ died as it may be possible to save. When choice *must* be made between the perpetrator of injustice and the many victims of it, the latter may and should be preferred—even if effectively to do so would require the use of armed force against some evil power. This is what I mean by saying that the justice of sometimes resorting to armed conflict originated in the interior of the ethics of Christian love.

Thus Christian conscience shaped itself for effective action. It allowed even the enemy to be killed only because military personnel and targets stood objectively there at the point where intersect the needs and claims of many more of our fellow men. For their sakes the bearer of hostile force may and should be repressed. Thus, participation in war (and before that, the use of any form of force or resistance) was justified as, in this world to date, an unavoidable necessity if we are not to omit to serve the needs of men in the only concrete way possible, and to maintain a just endurable order in which they may live.

There was another side to this coin. The justification of participation in conflict at the same time severely limited war's conduct. What justified also limited! Since it was for the sake of the innocent and helpless of earth that the Christian first thought himself obliged to make war against an enemy whose objective deeds had to be stopped, since only for their sakes does a Christian justify himself in resisting by any means even an enemy-neighbor, he could never proceed to kill equally innocent people as a means of getting at the enemy's forces. Thus was twin-born the justification of war and the limitation which surrounded noncombatants with moral immunity from direct attack. Thus was twin-born the distinction between combatant and noncombatant in all Christian reflection about the morality of warfare. This is the distinction between *legitimate* and *illegitimate* military objectives. The same considerations which justify killing the bearer of hostile force by the same stroke prohibit noncombatants from ever being directly attacked with deliberate intent.

This understanding of the moral economy in the just use of political violence contains, then, two elements: (1) a specific justification for sometimes killing another human being; and (2) severe and specific restrictions upon anyone who is under the hard necessity of doing so. Both are exhibited in the use of force proper to the domestic police power. It is never just for a policeman to forget the distinction between the bearer of hostile force who must be stopped and the "innocent" bystanders (no matter how mixed up they are). He may hit some innocent party accidentally; but it would never be right for him to "enlarge the target" and deliberately and directly kill any number in the crowd on Times Square *as a means* of preventing some criminal from injurious action. Nor do we allow the police the right to get a criminal's children into their power as hostages and threaten to kill them in order to "deter" him. Yet the source of the justification of such limited use of force is evidently to be found in "social charity." This is clear from the fact that a man, who in one situation could legitimately be killed if that were the only way to save other lives, would himself in another situation be saved at grave risk to the lives of the very same policemen—i.e., if that man alone is in need of rescue because he has gone off his rocker and is threatening to jump from the ledge of a building twenty stories up.

This is the moral economy which regulates the use of force *within* political communities, where it is both *morally* and *legally* binding. This same moral economy is *morally* if *not* legally binding upon the use of force between nations. It will become *both* legally and morally binding if ever there is world law and order abolishing the nation-state system. War may *in fact* be more than an extension of politics in another form, but the *laws* or war are only an extension, where war is the only available means, of the rules governing any use of political power. We are not apt ever to "abolish war" if we keep on denying that there is a morality *of* war, which is only a concise summary of right and charitable reason in the simultaneous *justification* and the *limitation* of the use of power necessary to the political life of mankind.

To summarize the theory of just or civilized conduct in war as this was developed within Christendom: love for neighbors threatened by violence, by aggression, or tyranny, provided the grounds for admitting the legitimacy of the use of military force. Love for neighbors at the same time required that such force should be limited. The Christian is commanded to do anything a realistic love commands (and so sometimes he must fight). But this also prohibits him from doing anything for which such love can find no justification (and so he can never approve of unlimited attack upon any human life not closely cooperating in or directly engaged in the force that ought to be repelled).

This means that nuclear war against the civil centers of an enemy population, the A-bomb on Hiroshima, or obliteration bombing perpetrated by both sides in World War II were all alike immoral acts of war; and that Christians can support such actions only by dismissing the entire Western tradition of civilized warfare that was originally born in the interior of that supreme compassion which always seeks if possible to wound none whom by His wounds Christ died to save. This theory of just and severely limited conflict has guided action and served as the regulative norm for military conduct for nineteen centuries. If a man cannot irresponsibly forsake those who need to be saved from an oppressor, neither can he directly and indiscriminately attack innocent people in order to restrain that same oppressor. If to protect his own children he should resist an aggressor, that gives him no leave directly to intend and directly to do the death of the aggressor's children as a means of dissuading him from his evil deeds.

If the just war theory did not already exist, Christians would have to invent it. If in the fullness of God's time and the emptiness of ours, Christ came into our present world (instead of when he did), then would the just war theory still have to be produced. Then would Christian thought bring together the notions of justice lying around in the Renaissance and the Enlightenment (if you can imagine these periods without their Christian background), as St. Augustine and other great Christian thinkers brought together the notions of justice lying around in the Graeco-Roman world, galvanized them into action, elevated and firmed them up, illumined and sensitized the justices of men to produce severer restrictions upon the forms of human conflict which the Christian or any truly just man can ever believe justified. Had I the space I could derive the same moral restrictions upon the use of force from the ethical perspectives of the Old Testament. These would have been productive of a remarkably similar just war theory, had Judaism been the predominant influence in Western civilization.

I can only briefly indicate that this distinction between combatant and noncombatant never supposed that the latter were to be roped off like ladies at a medieval tournament. The fact of twilight, as Dr. Johnson said, does not mean you cannot tell day from night. So with noncombatant status, and the difference between discriminate and indiscriminate acts of war. Moreover, it was never supposed that noncombatants were immune from all damage but only from direct, intended attack. The range of indirect, unintended, collateral damage might be quite large. Moreover, closeness of civilian cooperation, in contrast to some degree of remoteness from the force used, was sufficient to bring the civilian under the category of "combatant." But these qualifications were never the same as "enlarging the target" to include the whole of civil society as a legitimate military objective, directly damaging whole peoples in order to get at their leaders and fighters. Translated into modern terminology, this means that just or limited warfare must be *forces*-counter-*forces* warfare, and that *people*-counter-*people* warfare is wholly unjust.

At stake in preserving this distinction is not only whether warfare can be kept barely civilized, but whether civilization can be kept from barbarism. Can civilization survive in the sense that we can continue in political and military affairs to *act civilized*, or must we accept total war on grounds that clearly indicate that we have already become *totalitarian*—by reducing everyone without discrimination and everyone to the whole extent of his being to a mere means of achieving political and military goals? Even if an enemy government says that is all its people are, a Christian or any truly just man cannot agree to this.

Now pacifism teaches people what massive deterrence is built on. It "teaches people to make no distinction between the shedding of innocent blood and the shedding of any human blood. And in this way pacifism has corrupted enormous numbers of people who will not act according to its tenets. They become convinced that a number of things are wicked which are not; hence, seeing no way of avoiding 'wickedness,' they set no limits to it."[1] That is to say, pacifism teaches people to believe that there is no *significant moral* difference, except in the *ends* sought, between murder and killing in war. It seems incredible to accept that anyone really seriously believes that soldiers are only "licensed murderers" and that murderers are only unlicensed soldiers. Yet, at the operational level where the thoughts of a multitude of human hearts shall today be revealed, this seems to be what it comes down to. The desperate attempt to maintain the current state of nonwar by indiscriminately aiming weapons at people, and a fervent attempt to abolish war by declaring it in any shape to be a wickedness to which no moral limits can or should be applied, lie down peaceably together in the declaration by both parties that there is no moral economy that should or can govern the use of armed violence.

It has certainly to be admitted that all the wars of the past have been conducted more or less justly, more or less unjustly; but attacks on civilian life have been *peripheral* even if often carried out. In former ages it simply took too much muscle to fight war unlimitedly. You will understand the point on which present-day politics squirms, and military strategy squirms, if you see that in the nuclear age the nations are trying to make *unjust war* the *central war*, and to *base* strategy on the deliberate aim of attacking cities. They will never

1. Walter Stein, ed., *Nuclear Weapons and Christian Conscience* (London: Merlin, 1961), p. 56.

succeed in basing politics or purposive military strategy on such an inherently irrational and immoral plan of war.

They will never succeed in making war "carefully" by such planned disregard for the moral economy governing the use of force as an extension of the moral economy governing any purposive use of political power. It seemed reasonable for President Kennedy to say in his speech at Frankfurt, Germany, "The United States will risk its cities to defend yours because we need your freedom to protect ours."[2] This seems reasonable because the risks are still in the state of nonwar. The *plus* in front of that policy statement is within a parenthesis preceded by a *minus* sign, as shall be revealed if we ever factor the equation. Then the pluses will all become minuses. For it cannot make sense for the President to say, "The United States is *now,* this moment, accepting the destruction of its cities in order to defend yours, which are also now being destroyed along with the Russian cities, because we need your freedom to protect ours." If one perseveres in thinking the thinkable (because it is the actual, present) state of nonwar all the way through to an actual war conducted in the fashion apparently planned, he will have thought an unthinkable and a politically undoable action. He will have factored the massive deterrence—or retaliation—equation, and found that the pluses within the parenthesis all become minuses.

The traditional teaching about the conduct of war taught us that it is never right to intend or do wrong that good may come of it. Nuclear weapons have only added to this perennial truth a morally insignificant footnote: it can never do *any good* to intend or do wrong that good may come of it.[3]

---

2. *New York Times,* June 26, 1963.

3. In Chap. 11 of *The Just Wars,* "The Limits of Nuclear War," pp. 248–58, I argue that deterrence sufficient to keep war limited and just need *not* rest on the intention to do murder. This is a significant correction of the treatment of the morality of deterrence in my book *War and the Christian Conscience* (Durham, N.C.: Duke Univ. Press, 1961) [see selection 8 below—Eds.].

6

THE CASE FOR MAKING "JUST WAR" POSSIBLE

This 1962 essay is a good example of how Ramsey sought to establish order and precision in the use of moral discourse. He defends a manner of thinking and speaking that works to "make just war possible." The alternatives to this are either to submit to gross injustice without recourse to war, or to resist it through warfare that exceeds all moral limit. In the effort to make a case for the (barely) human activity of war, Ramsey evidences his belief that a major practical task of ethical reflection is to sustain a critical stance toward moral language written and spoken in church and world; for mistakes in language and thought make way for confusion and error in our social affairs. Such a stance explains his arresting comment that "war first became total in the minds of men." (From *The Just War*, 148–60, 164–65)

A recent editorial in *worldview*[1] expresses evident dissatisfaction with political "realism" and "prudential" ethics as by no means an adequate contribution of religious ethics to politics in our times. It continues by noting that the nature of modern weapons has given religious pacifists powerful new arguments that have not been adequately answered. It is symptomatic of the ills of religious ethics today, and of political and military doctrine, that the editorial writer gets from the limit he places on "realism" and "prudential" politics to the need for reopening a discussion of pacifism by a quite uncritical rejection of the only genuine alternative there is. He states as a conclusion no one today would think of challenging, that "previous norms for the 'just' war have, for all practical purposes, been rendered

1. "The Pacifist Question," *worldview* 3/7–8 (July–August 1960): 1.

obsolete"; and demands that religious leaders find out quickly whether they have anything to say about the destructiveness of modern warfare and not "salve" their "conscience by repeating the ancient rules for a 'just' war—rules which have as much relationship to an all-out modern war as such a war would have to the bow and arrow."[2]

Now obviously, you cannot indict the concept of the just war for drawing up a moral indictment of all-out nuclear warfare as intrinsically immoral; nor should anyone simply dismiss the distinction between the just and the unjust conduct of war because men and nations have the power (and are in fact planning) to violate this distinction. Too frequently the just war theory is said to be assuredly false or irrelevant or outmoded by people who would not confront the actual policies of their nation with these criteria even if proved true. Translate the traditional terminology distinguishing between just and unjust warfare into contemporary language distinguishing between counter-*forces* and counter-*people* warfare. At once it will be seen that the position that counter-forces warfare alone can be justified for arming the political purposes of a nation may reasonably be proposed as a truth to be acknowledged in military doctrine. It is certainly not irrelevant or anachronistic to say this; and the consciences of men may be not "salved" but awakened if this is said clearly by the moralist and, in collaboration with competent weapons analysis, concretely *to the point* of the dilemma we confront in modern warfare. The present chapter undertakes an initial step in this direction; first explaining *why*, under the shaping influence of Christian ethics, criteria for just conduct were enunciated by the theory of civilized warfare in the West, and then proceeding to clarify the exact *meaning* of these criteria.

It is convenient to begin with a quotation from a Roman Catholic, who is perhaps a "just war" pacifist, concerning "thirteenth century principles . . . as a minimal statement of the Christian ethic," not exhaustive or preclusive of a "higher aim." These principles, writes Robert Hovda, "made an exception (that's what it was) to the commandment 'Thou shalt not kill' in the case of a soldier or other military personnel on the opposing (clearly unjust) side in a war. The basis for this exception has been the fact that such a one is cooperating

---

2. Cf. editorial, *worldview* 2/6 (June 1959): 2; "It is more and more agreed that the concept of a 'just war' is an anachronism."

directly in the unjust action of his government and that he is therefore materially if not formally 'guilty.' Generally, moralists extended
this exception to include other citizens who were cooperating *directly* in the war effort."[3]

However, it is only when the commandment "Thou shalt not kill"
is viewed *legalistically*, and only when the actions that are licit or
illicit under it are viewed *externally*, that the Christians who formulated the just war theory can be said to have made, in regard to killing
another human being, one, single, clearly defined and limited *exception*, and nothing more.

Those persons "formally" directing or participating in the military forces, or "materially" yet closely cooperating in the force that
should be repelled and can only be repelled by violent means, these
persons are—this theory states—legitimate objects of *direct* violent
repression. The justification of warfare and of Christian participation
in it was not actually an exception (certainly not an arbitrary one, or a
compromise from the purity of Christian ethics), but instead an *expression* of the Christian understanding of moral and political responsibility. This conclusion was not simply the result of importing
into Christian ethics certain conceptions of natural justice from
Stoic and other ancient philosophies. Nor did the theory always simply result in a bifurcation of public morality, based on justice, from
private morality, based on love—that love which required the early
Christians to withdraw altogether from the resistance of evil by political and military means. Instead, intrinsic within the new foundation
laid by Christ for the entire conduct of his disciples was the conviction that love and mercy are the fulfilling of the law, of natural justice, and of the meaning expressed in the commandment "Thou shalt
not kill." When in doubt as to the actual action required by this
command, one had simply to consult again the requirements of compassion incarnating itself in serving the concrete needs of men.
Therefore in the ancient theory of just war, Christian conscience took
the form of allowing any killing at all of men for whom Christ died
only because military personnel were judged to stand, factually and
objectively, at the point where, as combatants, resistance to them was
judged to be necessary in responsibility to many other neighbors. The
combatant stood at the point of intersection of many primary claims
upon the Christian's life with and for his fellow man.

This still included undiminished fellow humanity with the en-

3. *worldview* 3/7–8 (July–August 1960): 8.

emy soldier; yet he was not the only one to take into account. The claims of many others had also be acknowledged and realistically served in the only way possible. In this world and not some other, faithfulness to all our fellow men, and not only to the enemy, must somehow be enacted. Jesus did not teach that his disciples should lift up the face of another oppressed man to be struck again on the other cheek. Out of neighbor-regarding love for one's fellow men, preferential decision among one's neighbors may and can and should be made. For love's sake (the very principle of the prohibition of killing), and not only for the sake of an abstract justice sovereign over the political realm in separation from the private, Christian thought and action were driven to posit this single "exception" (an exception only when externally viewed): that forces should be repelled and the bearers and close cooperators in military force should be directly repressed, by violent means if necessary, lest many more of God's little ones should be irresponsibly forsaken and lest they suffer more harm than need be. This, then, was not really an "exception," certainly not an arbitrary one; but a determinate expression of justice and mercy. It was an *expression* of the Christian understanding of political responsibility in terms of neighbor-regarding love. It was, and is, a regrettably necessary but still a necessary and morally justifiable expression of our being with and for men, as Christ was *the* man *for* other men. Christian love was the influence that shaped this conclusion. Therefore, the just war theory states not only what *may* but what *should* be done. This does not preclude a "higher aim" in personal relations if here one's own goods and life alone are at stake. It does not even preclude higher aims in politics, since as Augustine wrote, "it is a higher glory still to slay war itself with the word than men with the sword, and to procure and maintain peace by peace, not by war." But there can be no higher aim in military affairs, weapons policy, or among the goals of military establishments, except of course the prevention or deterrence of war by means it would be just to fight with.

This was the origin of the judgment that war can on occasion be justifiable in Christian conscience, and military forces or personnel (and close cooperators in mounting the opposing military force) be legitimate objects of direct attack. By the same stroke definite limits were placed upon the conduct of war by surrounding *noncombatants* with moral immunity from *direct* attack. Thus, a love-inspired justice going into concrete action fashioned rules for practical conduct—at once justifying war and limiting it. The Christian is commanded to do anything a realistic love commands, and he is prohibited from doing anything for which such love can find no justification. If combatants may and should be resisted directly by violent means to secure a desired and desirable victory, this also requires that noncombatants be never directly assaulted even to that same end. When out of Christian love or from definitions of justice inspired by love it was concluded that the death of an enemy might be directly intended and directly done for the sake of all God's other children within a just or a just endurable political order by which God governs and preserves human life in a fallen world, this also meant that such love could never find sufficient reason for directly intending and directly doing the death of the enemy's children in order to dissuade him from his evil deeds.

Thus, Western political thought did not until recently stand clothed only in an "aggressor-defender" concept of warfare, nor did it justify any sort of reply believed to be technically required to stop an aggressor. Warlike action was not justified, until recently, merely by a calculation of the future consequences and choice of the lesser evil in aiming at hypothetical results. Of course, no right action aims at *greater* evil in the results. But this does not mean that every action that prudently aims at good or less evil consequences is therefore right and is to be done. There is also a morality of means, of conduct, or of actions to be put forth. Since at least everyone seeks peace and desires justice, the *ends* for which wars may legitimately be fought are not nearly so important in the theory of the just war as is the moral and political wisdom contained in its reflection upon the *conduct* or means of warfare. Unless there is a morality applicable to instruments of war and intrinsically limiting its conduct, then we must simply admit that war has no limits—since these can hardly be derived from "peace" as the "final cause" of just wars. Certainly Christian ethics did not first concern itself with estimating the consequences. Instead, out of responsibility to God *for* all men before God, Christians sought to discover the meaning of just and loving *present* action toward them. Since it was for the sake of the innocent and helpless ones that the Christian first thought himself obliged to make war against an enemy whose objective deeds were judged to be evil and in need of restraint by any just and feasible means, how could he ever conclude from this that it was permitted him to destroy some "innocents" for the sake of other "innocents" closer to him in natural or social affinity? Thus was twin-born the justification of war and its limitation by the moral immunity of noncombatants (and the immunity of *remote* material cooperators in the force which should and had to be repelled).

This states *why* the theory of justifiable warfare was developed in the Christian West.[4] Whether this theory has any longer any bearing upon the conduct of nations is, however, a question that cannot be answered without first gaining a more complete and accurate understanding of the meaning of the norms expressed in terms of the ancient theory. Nothing can be more irresponsible, and less conducive to disciplined reflection in an area today sorely in need of being subjected to rational control, than to dismiss the just war theory on a mistaken understanding of it—as often happens today, from different points of view, by political realists and by resurgent pacifism. To come to terms with these terms will be our next undertaking.

---

4. Here one must simply voice sharp disagreement with Hans J. Morgenthau ("The Demands of Prudence," *worldview* 3/6 [June 1960]: 6–7. It is not the case that "the natural aspirations proper to the political sphere—and there is no difference in kind between domestic and international politics—contravene by definition the demands of the Christian ethics," or that "it is *a priori* impossible for political man to be at the same time a good politician—complying with the rules of political conduct—and to be a good Christian—complying with the demands of Christian ethics." The just war theory bridged the "unbridgeable gulf" Morgenthau thinks he sees. Its genesis shows that, as Christian ethics goes into actual practice, it fashions and shapes itself into principles for the direction of concrete action. Of course, no proposal for the *direction* or guidance of action can be a simple factual summary of the context in which that action is to be put forth. Only for the most abstract versions of natural law, however, is it true to say:"The gap between the rational postulates of natural law and the contingencies of the concrete situation within which man must act and judge is just as wide as the gulf which separates the demands of Christian ethics from the rules of political action, In truth, . . . both gaps are identical." If that is the meaning of the natural law, then it must be insisted that the theory of just conduct in war had nothing to do with it, but arose rather from a concretely oriented Christian love in-principling itself in responsible ways to serve actual man within the fabric of political life and institutions. Not without further examination should we agree with Morgenthau that, in the political sphere, man "is precluded from acting morally" and "the best he can do is to minimize the intrinsic immorality of the political act" (by choosing "the lesser evil"), or that "the best man is capable of is to be guided by the vision of a life lived in compliance with the Christian code and to narrow the gap between his conduct and that code." All this presupposes an asserted gap—between Christian ethics and politics, or between natural law and political decision—which the criteria of just action in war asserts it has at least partly bridged—not leaving the entire leap to technical reason or to that prudence to which Morgenthau appeals. Finally, it should be pointed out that Morgenthau's view that the gap can be cut down, not by any shaping of principles of political conduct, but only by the strategy of choosing the lesser evil, under the "vision" of a life lived otherwise, places him in the position of not being able even to understand correctly John Courtney Murray's remark that nuclear weapons are "from the moral point of view . . . unshootable." That, he says, is "because of the consequences of shooting them." This chapter will demonstrate that this is only the *last* reason (while a sufficient one) for calling multimegaton weapons morally unshootable.

In order to comprehend the meaning of "noncombatancy," it is necessary to understand a number of primary notions or distinctions fundamental in the traditional moral rules for the just conduct of war. The following may be cited as most important: (1) The distinction between "formal" and only "material," and between "close" and "remote," cooperation in the force that should be repelled. (2) The distinction between the "guilty" who are legitimate targets of violent repression and the "innocent" who are not. These are very misleading terms, since their meaning is exhaustively stated under the first contrast, and is reducible to degrees of actual participation in hostile force. (3) The distinction between "direct" and "indirect" attack. It was never supposed that noncombatants were morally immune from indirect injury or death on however colossal a scale, if there is proportionate grave reason for doing this. This has sometimes been expressed by saying that death to the innocent may be "permitted" to result "accidentally" from an act of war primarily directed against military forces. But if the word "accident" is used, it is in a philosophical or technical sense, and not with its usual meaning. For the "permitted" killing of noncombatants does not just happen to take place. It is foreknown and foreknown to result as a necessary effect of the same action that causes the death of political leaders or military personnel who are its legitimate targets. This brings us to (4) the analysis of acts of war as (like many other human actions) having double or multiple effects, and to the so-called rule of double effect. The latter requires that a distinction be made between (a) killing that is directly intended (in the subjective order) and directly done (in the objective, physical order) and (b) killing that is only permitted even if it is *indirectly* done (i.e., also *caused*) by the same action that causes the death of men who are its primary targets. Acts of war which directly intend and directly effect the death of noncombatants are to be classed morally with murder, and are never excusable. If the excuse is that victory requires this, then we would be saying that the end justifies an intrinsically wrong means or that men may be murdered in order to do good. A desired and desirable victory may, however, justify conduct in warfare that causes the death, and is foreknown to cause the death, of noncombatants *indirectly*. This would *not* be directly to do evil that good may come of it. There is a significant moral difference between the destruction in obliteration warfare which is deliberately wanton and murderous, and the destruction and death that is among the tragic consequences of counter-*forces* warfare. This distinction is not determined by the amount of the devastation or the number of deaths, but by the direction of the action itself, i.e., by what is deliberately intended and directly done. This permits there to be foreseeable evil consequences acceptable among the multiple effects of military action.

Whether these latter effects are acceptable, or not, must be assessed by prudential reason balancing good and evil, or lesser evil, consequences. But first one should be able to discriminate between acts of murder and acts of war. Indiscriminate bombing or counter-people warfare stands indicted as intrinsically wrong. In this sense, multimegaton weapons are "morally unshootable." To use them indiscriminately or deliberately against *society* targets would be the direct murder of the innocent as a means of victory. This, however, does not condemn every enlargement of legitimate military targets in the course of weapons development, much less the *unavoidable* enlargement of the indirect effects of counter-forces warfare. Multimegaton weapons may also be "unshootable" in this second sense: because we are, in the last place, forced to conclude that there can be no greater evil than the *consequences* of using them. Therefore, after having permitted and prohibited actions by an analysis of the intrinsic nature of each, it has yet to be determined whether military action lawful in itself should actually be done. This requires (5) a prudential estimate of the consequences to see whether there is in the good effect sufficiently grave reason for also indirectly producing the evil effect. Thus, the traditional morality of war locates in the last place, a calculus of probability and a morality of the ends in view. In the end, proper place should be given to sitting down to count the costs of a proposed action. While an effect cannot justify any means, one effect can justify another effect because of the greater good or "lesser evil" in one than in the other.

In recent years, bellicists and pacifists have united to declare that every act of war as such is intrinsically immoral. These alike declare the just war theory no longer applicable—bellicists, to the end of engaging in war without moral limitations; pacifists, to withdraw from it altogether; and many so-called Christian realists, with moderation placed only upon the political objectives for which, they say, wars should ever be fought (and *through* the ends, upon the means). In order for either of these parties to make a beginning toward reaching one of these conclusions, it is first of all necessary for them to misunderstand the criteria for the conduct of war and the rules of civilized warfare. Terms are used imprecisely in order to discredit the quite precise notions of the moral doctrine of war that has prevailed in

Western history. Therefore, the concept of "noncombatancy" has not been proved wrong by sound moral or political or military analysis. It has been rejected before having been understood. Thus, the traditional analysis of the morality of war has been thoughtlessly rejected, and the necessary totality of modern war largely conceded.

How can the "facts" of warfare between modern industrial and metropolitan societies prove that there are now no noncombatants, when this conclusion depends in every respect upon whether we have in our heads such notions as the moral significance of the degrees of proximity or remoteness of cooperation in unjust aggression, and the distinction between direct and indirect killing? Too often in Protestants and in secular writings on the subject of morality and war it is also erroneously supposed that *direct* killing is the only kind of killing that one undertakes to justify in a doctrine of war; and so it has come to be an unquestioned maxim that for war to be justly conducted, noncombatants have to be clearly and in detail distinguishable from combatants. Moreover, we would have to be sure not only *who* these people are but also that *where* they live is not within or near any legitimate target area, and that none will be slain or injured as an unavoidable indirect consequence of direct military action. As a result of faulty analysis of the morality of war, if today the moral immunity of noncombatants from direct attack is not simply ignorantly ridiculed, the nullity of it is assumed as a premise rather than as a conclusion to be reached by disciplined moral reflection. On this understanding of the matter, any act of war is either an immorality to be done out of military necessity or an immorality never to be done out of Christian love; and there are no significant moral distinctions to be made among warring actions except between those that succeed and those that do not succeed in obtaining victory, or between means that are proportionate and those disproportionate to the end of victory.

Plainly, it is necessary for most people to come to terms again with the terms of the ancient limits of civilized warfare. It is the *concept* of noncombatancy that has first been jettisoned from our minds; and this has happened because the *concept* of degrees of cooperation, the *concept* justifying the repulsion of objectively "guilty" forces as well as those "formally" or personally responsible for their direction, the *concept* of an indirect yet unavoidable and foreknown effect alongside the legitimately intended effects of military action, or the *concept* of double effects flowing from the same neutral or good action as cause, bringing along with the good result also a tragically necessary evil consequence in the limited, not directly intended, yet foreseen destruction of civilian life (still not the same as wholesale murder, nor the same as a single murder)—all these notions have eroded from the minds of men. *This*, then, is the reason we are prey to the illusion that modern industrial society has completely changed the nature of warfare, and not simply that mass defection from sound moral reasoning has rendered wholly inapplicable or indeed senseless any attempt to conduct war in accordance with the carefully constructed concepts of traditional Christian morality.

Of course, noncombatants are not in modern society roped off like spectators at a medieval tournament. In the theory of just war they never had to be. We only have to know *that* there are babies among the civilian population of any enemy nation, we do not even have to know that there are any grown men and women deserving to be classed as noncombatants in order to know *with certainty* that warfare should be forces-counter-forces warfare, and calculated attack be limited to legitimate military targets. There are many people, other than infants, going about their little human affairs whom a loving justice should surround with immunity limiting violence; and to know this we do not need to know *who* or *where* they are. This moral limit still holds, even if it had to be admitted that responsible political and military action must now place civilians with their moral immunity from direct attack in far greater danger even in a justly conducted war than ever before in human history, because (it might be asserted) there are many more legitimate targets than ever before and because the firepower of even a just war and the indirect effects of even its right conduct have enormously increased.

The difference between justifiable and wholly unjustifiable warfare can perhaps be better grasped from an examination of some current mistakes. In modern warfare, it is said, "all human and material resources are mobilized," and only "small children and the helpless sick and the aged stand outside the war effort. . . . Total war, in this sense of the involvement of the whole nation in it, cannot be avoided if we have a major war at all."[5] Now, who ever defined a "noncombatant" in such a fashion, as one who "stands outside" of any relation to his nation's action? Who ever meant by a noncombatant a person

5. "The Christian Conscience and Weapons of Mass Destruction," Dun Report of a Special Commission appointed by the Federal Council of the Churches of Christ in America, 1950, pp. 10–11.

who, to be one, would have to be utterly helpless, and incapable of any activity at all with important results for the common weal? Evident in such an undiscriminating definition of the "involvement" of a whole nation in war is no conception of the significance of degrees of remoteness or closeness of cooperation in a nation's war effort such as was essential in any definition of the moral immunity of noncombatants in the past. The foregoing statement, therefore, constitutes no objection at all to the application of the moral rules of warfare even in the case of two modern industrial societies locked in a war of attrition. Even more can it be said to have no force at all to nullify the distinction between counter-forces and counter-people warfare with present and future weapons which insure that wars will be fought quickly and not out of inventories. That brief period of Western history when counter-*factory* warfare was supposed to justify counter-*people* warfare has now come to an abrupt end.

The traditional distinction between combatant and noncombatant, it is asserted, today is "far less clear" than in the past. Evident here is no conception of the fact that, in the moral choice between direct and indirect killing of civilians, or between counter-forces and indiscriminate counter-retaliatory warfare, this distinction *does not need to be clear.* We do not need to know *who* or *where* the noncombatants are in order to know that indiscriminate bombing exceeds the moral limits of warfare than can ever barely be justified. We have only to know *that* there are noncombatants—even "only small children and the helpless sick and aged"—in order to know the basic moral difference between limited and total war.

This same mistake, in my opinion, was made by Professor John Bennett, who ordinarily writes with discernment upon this subject. "It has become increasingly difficult," he writes, "to distinguish in detail between combatants and non-combatants and sometimes the teaching about the just war has been legalistic at this point, if we grant that the use of military force is ever justified at all."[6] That unexamined statement is not worth having; and upon examining it two remarks should be made: (a) *Careful* statements as to the just conduct of war ought not to be dismissed out of hand as "legalistic." (b) To prohibit the *direct* killing (while allowing the *indirect* killing) of non-combatants, it is not at all necessary to distinguish them "in

6. "Theological and Moral Considerations in International Affairs," issued as background paper for the Fifth World Order Study Conference of the National Council of Churches, in Cleveland, 1958.

detail." We have only to know that anyone is there—children, the aged, the sick, barbers, cobblers, and Latin school teachers among the people we intend to obliterate by "enlarging the target." We only have to know that there are any civilians, whose lives are made the *intended*, direct object of violence, who are not now closely supporting the military force it would be just and necessary to resist by force limited to this.

A second instance of the misuse of the concept of noncombatancy is to be found in Bennett's correct insistence that the "official scientists" have been morally insensitive in their disregard of the effects of continued nuclear testing upon future generations, and his assertions that, while the Communists may sacrifice people now living to a future goal, we are in danger, by these tests, of sacrificing people yet unborn to present political goals. Whereupon he writes: "I think that the traditional distinction between combatants and non-combatants in war does not fit the present realities, but, on any showing, future generations should be regarded as non-combatants."[7] The assumption of the latter part of this statement seems to be that without revising the rules for the just conduct of war no action could ever be justified which brings about the death of noncombatants, and surely this has helped to produce the disparagement of the concept of noncombatancy in the first part of the statement. However, it was never supposed that noncombatants should be morally immune from being killed, but from being *directly* killed. It cannot be shown that nuclear testing is *intrinsically* wrong simply because there are evils among its effects. Here the question is whether one effect is sufficient to justify another. The question is whether there is proportionately greater good or lesser evil intentionally sought among the effects that can only be secured by testing which also unavoidably permits some grave evil effects to fall upon future generations.

Such is the only justification for most human actions and most of the inventions that have made civilized life possible on this earth. Here there is no question of using persons as a means, or of justifying an inherently wrong means because some good may come from it. In general, it is really quite astonishing how American public opinion concentrates upon the moral problem posed by these tests, since a planned policy of nuclear retaliation is much more clearly immoral. The death and devastation contemplated in the case of all-out nuclear war would be both *directly willed* and *directly done* as a means,

---

7. Letter in *worldview* 2/11 (Nov. 1959): 7.

while the death brought about by nuclear testing *as such* is only *indirectly willed* and *indirectly done* as one among several effects of the tests. The first is murder (to be justified by no calculation of consequences); the second is tragic (probably to be prohibited, if the proportionately greater good or lesser evil expected to result from weapons tests is not important enough to warrant our accepting the bad effects of testing—and if these cannot be controlled or avoided).

We were told in the National Council of Churches' report we have been analyzing that it is now "practically impossible to distinguish between guilty and innocent. Certainly men who are drafted into uniform may be among the least guilty."[8] Who ever clothed noncombatants with moral immunity from direct attack by first investigating their innocence in the highest subjective and personal sense? Who ever declared combatants (or the "guilty") to be legitimate objects of direct attack or counterattack simply because, unlike mercenaries in the past or men drafted today into "democratic" armies, they are more personally guilty than the rest of their countrymen? The statement that conscript armies, made up of men who may not wish to kill, are *therefore* made up of men who are not *unjust* aggressors and this gives no one the right to kill them, assumes that the point was to prove the guilt of combatants in a fully personal sense. Against this stands the notion of objective or functional guilt because of status in the forces that should be repelled. Against this stands also the fact that for many centuries after participation in war was said to be justified for Christian conscience, it still was never allowed that, when one's own life or goods alone were at stake, the evil intention of a clearly guilty assailant gave the Christian any right to resist or wound or kill him whom by his wounds and death Christ came to save. No amount or kind of guilt in the fully personal sense as such gave any man the intrinsic right to kill another. Instead, the permission and the duty to do this arose because of the place where the bearer of hostile force stood in relation to God's other children, and to their need to be served by Christians in the existing order of the common life by the maintenance of a tolerable justice for them. Of course, the "formal aggressors" are clearly guilty; the political commanders are among the legitimate targets if one knows who they are and can get at them. But an ordinary soldier's "guilt" is his objective and direct participation in the military offensive that has for love's sake to be repelled; and the "innocence" of noncombatants means

8. "Christian Conscience," pp. 10–11.

their lack of crucial relation or the remoteness of their cooperation in the prosecution of the war.

This demonstrates, it seems to me, that in rejecting as invalid the quite discriminating concepts of the just-war theory, all too many people have first employed insufficiently articulated terms, or block-buster concepts, all to the end of obliterating the moral wisdom deposited in the traditional view of the morality of war. No wonder, then, that we were morally ready to use blockbusters, and now metropolisbusters, in actual fact! War first became total in the minds of men. Why this happened among religious people, who should have remembered their traditions and who should cultivate conceptual clarity in moral analysis, can perhaps be partly explained by the effort to persuade the pacifists, as World War II approached, that in no way could they avoid "contributing to the war effort." Pacifist Christians may have been wrong in the religious and political judgments they made in refusing direct participation in war; but they were certainly not wrong in discerning a significant distinction between civilian and combatant status. (Pacifists make this distinction *for themselves* and *their own* society, while refusing to make the same necessary distinction between the people and forces of the enemy, which entails acceptance of positive responsibility to resist the latter by military means.) On this distinction hangs the discrimination between war and murder, between limited and unlimited war, between barely civilized and wholly uncivilized, even if technically efficient, military action.

At stake also in this discrimination is not only the defense of civilization against total war, but against totalitarianism as well. In stating so blandly that practically no one "stands outside" the war effort and no one is "innocent" and there is no one who may not be directly killed for some good cause, have we not in principle included practically everyone, to the whole extent of his being, within the direction of the common life toward political goals? When men wage wars, if they do not maintain a relation *of nonrelation,* or remote relation, between the civilian life of a nation and its fighters, they have already in principle totally politicized human life. So much is at stake in restoring the laws of civilized warfare, of fighting, if we must, in a just manner for the preservation of just orders of life. Anything else is technically efficient barbarism, no matter what "values" may be our objectives or the names we use, like fig leaves, to cover our unseemly acts. . . .

When a loving regard for fellow men draws close to them amid the realities of politics and military affairs, it discerns significant distinctions to be made within the activity of war itself. It takes into account persons' specific function, or lack of function, in the war itself in order to save as many as possible from being absorbed into the *thrust* of war. We must recognize this as the proper conduct of war if what is justly due is illuminated by the highest loving regard for men. Christian love does not simply hover over the realities of political life, as a vision of how life might be lived otherwise. It incarnates itself in the actualities and provides itself grounds for action by fashioning discriminating judgments between acts of war proposed to be put forth. The principle forbidding indiscriminate warfare pertains to the nature of warfare itself and its own proper laws—so long as this human action remains, by the skin of its teeth, a rational activity at all, so long as war is even conceivably a purposive extension of national policy, so long as war barely remains an affair in which a human being at all above the level of the beasts of the field can ever justifiably participate, or (to go higher and yet lower for a comparison) so long as engagement in war has not been reduced merely to an exercise of technical reason and efficiency.

The just war theory cannot be repealed; it can only be violated. It states the limit beyond which war as such becomes in itself a wholly nonhuman and nonpolitical activity, and the point beyond which military force becomes senseless violence, and our weapons no longer weapons of *war*. This is not because war has an "essence" or "nature" but because man has; and because political society has a nature to which military means must be kept subordinate. The distinction between "combatants" and "noncombatants" asserts that there is both some relation between a civil society and its fighters and yet nonrelation or remote relation between them. The maintenance of this distinction, or of this distance and subordination in the relation of combatants to the society they defend, is of the very essence of war that may under any circumstances be chosen by men who have not wholly lost all political morality and their political reasons. Push-buttons may be able to launch retaliatory and counterretaliatory warfare, but political man with all his faculties in exercise cannot do purposefully any such inhuman deed.

The problem today is "just war," limited war. This is not a description of the facts, opposed to other descriptions. It is rather an imperative statement, a political imperative which points the way in which alone, through intelligent moral action in direction of national policy, warfare can be enclosed again within the political purposes of nations from which it has escaped. This is the case for making just war possible. There is more to be gained from a concerted effort to make just war possible than from attempting to "prevent" war without first (or also) altering the shape it now has in reality and, first of all, in the minds of men.

7

THE USES OF POWER

Ramsey was convinced that the framework of the just war tradition set out a general approach to political reality and action. "The Uses of Power" is devoted to a description of that approach. It focuses on an essential connection between the political act and the exercise of power in the direction of the common human good of political communities. Power *and* human purpose constitute the political. American "liberals" who would pursue the humanitarian good in foreign affairs without regard for the "field of forces favorable to [American] power in the world," and "realists" who endorse "power politics" inattentive to the national and international common good, commit the same mistake in different ways. Neither operate with a full and proper grasp of the nature of political action. Ramsey develops his analysis further with a careful articulation of the related categories of order, justice, and law. (From *The Just War*, pp. 3–13)

During the 1964 contest for the Presidency between Lyndon B. Johnson and Barry Goldwater, we did not have any good national debate about United States foreign and military policy. The apparent reason for this is that attention was narrowly focused upon particular issues believed to be clear enough. The basic factor, however, preventing profound debate over how we as a people are to discharge our political responsibilities in the present age is the hardened polarization of "liberal" and "conservative" opinion in this country—endemic indeed to the modern mind. This in turn only shows that we lack an understanding of "government"—of what I shall call "political agency."

The "conservatives" and the "liberals" each have a piece of the truth and they make the error each points out in the other. Beyond this, they also share a common error.

The liberals know that in a nuclear age war cannot be an instrument of justice and there can be no "victory" if the means of violence used are disproportionate to any political goals (as well they may be). Therefore, they conclude that there can be no positive use of force of any sort or at any level of violence for political ends, that every dispute can and should be settled, and that the only sacrifice for the nation's good that is to be commended is the sacrificial spirit of diplomats who are resolved to negotiate so that negotiation will never fail.

The conservative, on the other hand, knows that there must be a positive use of armed power in the political affairs of mankind. Therefore, he seems determined to "win" all the way up the scale of the available violence.

Both believe that peace, justice, and freedom can be preserved by "bluffing"—the liberal with at most his *show* of force at the lower levels and the conservative with his *show* of force at the upper nuclear level. This is the error they have in common. Therefore, they both avoid thinking through the actual *use* of power for positive purposes, and the political morality governing such use.

Of course, a liberal President proved we would "shoot back" in the Gulf of Tonkin. This, however, is not enough doctrine for the responsible use of the power of a great nation. It only goes beyond the western gunfighter's morality, which allows the other fellow to *draw* first, by now allowing him to *shoot* first. This is, in fact, the doctrine that permits the Vietcong successes with their "insurgency warfare," which may be defined as hitting the "haves" where they have it not.

The brilliant North Vietnamese general Giap, who never went to war college, was once asked to explain his theory of war. He replied, "The first essential is to have a working politico-military doctrine."

The empires and nations of Christendom used to have such a working politico-military doctrine. Lately, however, political purposes have been split off from military doctrine. The conservatives do this by their asserted willingness to use or threaten force that cannot have any political purpose, by their determination to defend the free world and even roll back communism by simply being resolute enough, and by their belief that if only this nation *sounds* as if it is willing to use its entire nuclear arsenal it won't have to do so. The liberals split politics and military doctrine apart by their belief that only peaceful means serve any positive purpose, and that force has at most the purpose that a show of it stimulates negotiation.

The politico-military doctrine that used to be intact among the peoples of the West is the "just war" doctrine, which is better called the theory of the *justified* war. This teaching has many aspects, some of which I have explored elsewhere. Here it is important to say that the rules or principles governing the responsible use of armed force, or rather the principles which *anatomized* the nature of a responsible use of armed force, were at the same time a way of understanding human political reality and a way of delineating the nature of *any* use of power (armed or not). The just war theory was a working politico-military doctrine, and a first essential in the government of mankind. This is the heart of the matter, which I want to discuss in this chapter.

The use of power, and possibly the use of force, is of the *esse* of politics. By this I mean it belongs to politics' very *act of being* politics. You never have politics without the use of power, possibly armed force. At the same time the use of power, and possibly the use of force, is inseparable from the *bene esse* of politics. By this I mean that it is inseparable from politics' *proper* act of being politics, inseparable from the well-being of politics, inseparable from the human pursuit of the national or the international common good by political means. You never have *good* politics without the use of power, possibly armed force.

The preposition that the use of power, and possibly the use of force, belongs to the esse of politics (its *act of being*) and is inseparable from the bene esse of politics (its *proper act of being*, or its act of being *proper* politics) is denied by two views of the state, or of political community. Both of these mistaken views have gained wide currency today—the first only among some Christians, but the second among Christian and non-Christian so-called liberals. (Myself, I would prefer, if I could, to save that great word from such abuse.)

The first is Karl Barth's Christological view of the *normal* functions of political authority. His radically Christocentric understanding of politics is symbolized and exhibited in his teaching that it is the *polis* that is destined for perfection in the Kingdom of God, while the Church shall wither away. Meantime, this side resurrection, the state derives is meaning from the fact that Jesus Christ has already assumed the human reality which magistrates govern. This means, Barth writes, that "war should not on any account be recognized as a normal, fixed, and in some sense necessary part of what on the Christian view constitutes the just state, or the political order demanded by God."[1]

On a surface reading of it, of course, that statement should never be denied. We should always affirm, with Barth, that "what Christian ethics has to emphasize is that neither inwardly nor outwardly does the normal task of the state, which is at issue even in time of war, consist in a process of annihilating rather than maintaining and fostering life. . . . It is no part of the normal task of the state to wage war; its normal task is to fashion peace in such a way that life is served and war kept at bay. . . . It is when the state does not rightly pursue its normal task that sooner or later it is compelled to take up the abnormal one of war, and therefore to inflict this abnormal task on other states."[2]

Barth, however, means something more profound than this in his apprehension of the task of political authority in the light of Christ and the supernatural polis. "It is no primary concern of Christian ethics to say that [the state should exercise power], or to maintain that the exercise of power constitutes the essence of the state, i.e., its *opus proprium*, or even a part of it. What Christian ethics must insist is that it is an *opus alienum* for the state to have to exercise power."[3]

The other, more prevalent, and, in my opinion, more naive way of denying that the use of power, and possibly the use of force, is of the esse of politics is the supposition that not the advent of Christ but the advent of the nuclear age means that politics can and may and must be conducted without ever invoking power to impose solutions. This view ultimately depends (not upon the "logic" of nuclear weapons, but) upon the myth of the primeval goodness and preternatural wisdom of man. This seems to me to underlie Adlai Stevenson's Dag Hammarskjold Memorial Lecture delivered at Princeton, March 1964, and not inappropriately entitled "The Audacious Dream of Dynamic Order."[4] As we have moved from a policy of containment to

---

1. *Church Dogmatics* (Edinburgh: T. & T. Clark, 1961), vol. 3, part 4, p. 456.

2. Ibid., p. 458. To circumscribe correctly the war-making power, the last sentence above should be revised to read: "It is when any state or all states do not rightly pursue their normal task [of maintaining and fostering life] that sooner or later a state has inflicted upon it the abnormal task of war." This makes evident how statistically normal this normatively abnormal task may be in a world of finite rulers with limited wisdom (not to mention the consequence of the Fall upon political existence, which Barth's Christological viewpoint rejects as decisively important for Christian political theory).

3. Ibid., p. 456.

4. *Princeton Alumni Weekly* 64/20 (June 9, 1964): 26–30.

a policy of cease-fire, so the world is on the verge, said Mr. Stevenson, of a breakthrough to a policy of peaceful change replacing cease-fire. Containment meant limited war; cease-fire means limited peace. Peaceful change, no longer static like those former policies, would be true (and I suppose unlimited) peace, because this will be based on "a *dynamic* system of order" which will apply a "curative resolution" to the roots of hostility. "*Perhaps* Korea was the end of the road for classical armed aggression against one's next-door neighbor; *perhaps* Suez was the end of the road for colonial-type military solutions; *perhaps* Cuba was the end of the road for nuclear confrontation."

Missing is any mention of "wars of national liberation" conducted by subversion and insurgency from abroad. Mr. Stevenson simply believes that "we may have *slipped almost imperceptibly* into an era of peaceful settlement of disputes" (italics added). So imperceptible was this passage except to the eyes of faith, that, despite the ambassador's discussion of improvements yet to be made in the United Nations' peacekeeping machinery, it seems evident that Stevenson's audacious dream of a dynamically changing order changing in an orderly fashion must be based on some myth of the primeval goodness and preternatural wisdom of man. (U.N. peacekeeping machinery provides enforcement for only one policy—the still static one of cease-fire—while the dynamic resolution of disputes, it is hoped, will proceed nonviolently.) Concerning "this consensus on recourse to non-violent solutions" only, Stevenson declared, "most of the world is in agreement right now!" He added in all earnestness, and with no sense at all of the tragic irony of his remark, simply this one qualification: "There are a few who would make a small exception of his own dispute with his neighbor."

But neither the Western liberal's primeval man nor Barth's post-evil Christ-formed man is the subject of political agency or of political rule *post lapsum* and this side resurrection. Therefore, I say, the use of power, and possibly the use of armed force, is of the esse of politics and inseparably connected with those higher human goods which are the bene esse of politics in all the historical ages of mankind. This interpretation of political authority is held in common by the Augustinian tradition and its two main branches: the natural law theory of politics and the Lutheran analysis of the state as an "order of necessity" (*Notverordnung*).[5]

5. It is, of course, possible for natural law teachings so to stress the *bene esse,* the common good, that the component of power is lost from view; and for the Lutheran view to stress restraint and lose sight of justice and the other community values that

Another way to say this is as follows: politics is defined by both its *genus* (community) and its *specific difference* (the use of power). What political community has in common with other communities (friendship, economic associations, professional and cultural groups transcending national boundaries) within the genus to which they all belong may comprise the higher human qualities. Every community pursues a common good, or a good in common. But the legitimate use of decisive physical power distinguishes political community from these other communities in the formation of the life of mankind. *Generic* social values are the matter of politics; but so also is the *specific* use of power. You can say that the former comprise the higher values to which the latter is a conditional value; but not that the latter is a merely extrinsic instrument that can be dropped. In fact, in the *definitional* sense of "primary" and "secondary," *generic* community values are the secondary (i.e., the distinctly human) purpose of politics while the use of power comprises the differentiating *species* or the primary (i.e., the distinctive) modality of politics. I mean only to repeat this in the proposition: the use of power, and possibly the use of force, is of the esse of politics, and it is inseparable from the bene esse of politics. This entails no derogation of the uniquely human ends, the generic values, the bene esse, of political community. Quite the contrary. This puts power in its place in our understanding of politics by definitely placing it within the pursuit of the political good.

The ingredients of this classical understanding of the nature of political society need to be comprehended by citizens and statesmen alike if political action is to be restored to health in the present day. Ours is an era in which "liberals" face down every fact with the myth that there is a nonviolent solution to every conflict and in which even hard-headed political "realists" who define politics in terms of power still speak as if political action is therefore intrinsically immoral. The fact is that there is no domestic political action that does not erode or strengthen the power and authority of government and at the same time erode or strengthen the more human purposes of government (the common good). The one is no more "selfish" or otherwise immoral than the other.

---

also belong to the essence of political authority and the action of rulers. The encyclical of Pope John XXIII "Pacem in terris" with its "natural law optimism," is an example of the first, and *real-political* theories that sometimes emerge on Lutheran ground are examples of the second, of these divergencies from main-line Christian political theory, of which the just war doctrine is the chief prismatic case.

Likewise, there is no political action in the realm of foreign policy that does not erode or strengthen the power position of a nation and at the same time erode or strengthen the purposes of that nation in the world community—the international common good as this is viewed and acted upon by that government's power and politics. To enhance the one is no more "selfish" than to do the other; neither can be accomplished without effect upon and causal influence from the other. A political action is always an exercise of power and an exercise of purpose. Power without purpose and purpose without power are both equally nonpolitical.

In the field of foreign affairs, the United States always needs an environment or field of forces favorable to its power in the world, and we need always an environment favorable to our purposes in the world. Broadly speaking, the overriding goal of our foreign policy is to create and sustain a system of free and independent nations. We are in the business of nation building. This understanding of the international common good is the bene esse of our political actions toward foreign powers, while in our physical, economic, and other forms of power lies the esse of such actions and the way a nation takes responsibility for its purposes. Either requires the other, and each requires an environment favorable to it. To perform the political action that rightly protects our security and power in the power environment is no more immoral than an act that rightly protects our nationhood by fostering an environment of independent nations. We cannot contribute to the upbuilding of nations and the system of free and independent states without making our power felt; nor can the free nations grow strong without affecting, one way or another, the power and prestige of the United States in the security environment. Thus, the esse and the bene esse of international political agency, our exercise of power and the actualization of our agreement concerning what is morally and politically right, belong inseparably together and they fluctuate together.

This understanding of political action is enough to show that the standards of personal morality are not to be applied without more ado to political conduct. Political responsibility does not mean simply doing all the humanitarian good one can in the world, without prior attention to that which specifically differentiates the political good from the good in general, and without prior analysis of the structural difference between personal moral agency and political agency. This mistake has led many of the best people in the world today (those rather inappropriately called "liberals") to suppose that cultural exchanges, economic aid, and the Peace Corps are the only *proper* modes of politics toward which the nations are or should be moving. That would be to try to launch out toward the bene esse of politics without taking responsibility for its esse.

This does not mean, however, that personal and political actions are subject to entirely different moral standards, or that there is a double standard for individual conduct and for the actions of states. It only (but definitely) means that they are subject in different modes to the moral requirements governing conduct.

This is further in evidence when, leaving aside the use of power as politics' *act of being* politics, we take up some of the basic ethical criteria which determine politics' *proper act of being* politics.

The state, which is the "subject" of political action, has its responsibility defined by the national common good and by the international common good. These goods are not always the same.[6] There is, to say the least, a dialectic, a tension, a polarity, if there is not an actual or irremediable conflict, between the national and the international common good. The responsibility of the statesman is defined by the area of incidence, or overlap, between them. Allowing for the fact that he should strive always to envision and if possible to establish a larger area of incidence between his nation's good and the international common good, it is still this area of incidence between these goods that defines his responsibility He is not called to office to aim at all the humanitarian good that can be aimed at in the world. Instead, he must determine what he *ought to do* from out of the total humanitarian good that *ought to be.* He is not even responsible for all of the *ought to be* that *ought to be politically done,* since there are other nations and other political actors in the world. He must locate his political obligation, and that of his nation, within an area of incidence between the national and the international common good.

The theory of political anarchism is false which teaches that those goods are somehow completely congruent, so that these are but two misleading words for the same thing. Only upon a Kantian postulate that somehow the moral universe insures it can it be supposed that the *true* good of the nation (if only one could discern this) is the same as the good of all mankind (if only one could know what that is). In

---

6. Besides Pope John's omission of sufficient consideration of the problem of power, another way to characterize the defect of his encyclical "Pacem in terris" is to say that he supposed that the national and the international common good are always coincident, or can be made to be coincident in any moment of governmental decision.

any moment of historical time, it is in any case true that there are
more ways to miss the mark than to hit it (as Aristotle said), and
missing the mark cannot *simply* be defined as doing less than the
international common good alone requires.

Of course, a statesman is in danger of serving a too narrow view of
the international good and *thereby* failing to serve the best possible
good of his own nation. And of course he may serve a too narrow
national interest and *thereby* fail to serve an international common
good that was possible. But there is also the danger that he may try to
do too much of the humanitarian good that ought to be politically
done, with the result that he does less than he ought to have done for
the national common good and renders his own nation less apt to
serve either common good in the future.

Nothing can remove from among the awesome responsibilities of
magistrates the determination of where to draw these lines. If a "conservative" has any political sense, he will not simply decry all inter-
nationalism as naive "do-goodism"; nor will the "liberal" if he has
political sense meet every proposal that the present far-flung commitments of the United States be revised, and some of them liquidated,
with the cry of "isolationism." Every responsible political decision
involves some precarious determination of how the circles of the
national and the international common good are to be drawn. This is
the mode in which the ideal humanitarian good (all of which, by
definition, ought to be) specifies itself for political choice.

There is another set of terms which are determinative (or the
realities to which they point are determinative) of the morality of
political conduct. These are "order" and "justice," with a tension or
dialectic between them similar to the one we have considered between various "common goods" in our analysis so far of the bene esse
(the *proper* being) of politics.

Order is not a higher value in politics than justice, but neither is
humanitarian justice a higher value than order. Both are in some
respects conditional to the other. Order is for the sake of justice, since
the only real political justice is an ordered justice; yet justice is no
less for the sake of order, since the only real political order in which
men may dwell together in community and peace is one that is *just*
enough to command the love and allegiances of men, or at least their
acquiescence and their compliance. Power, which is of the esse of
political agency, may be a conditional value only; but order and justice, which are ever in tension yet in interrelation, both are values

that comprise the well-being, the bene esse, of political affairs and the common good which is the goal of political action.

A decision maker contemplating, for example, some positive interventionary military action should try to relate the use of power or force rationally as means to the ends of policy; but he should reckon order and justice both—and not justice only—as ends or the effects of responsible action. In deliberations about the order to be conserved or the justice to be done, his reckoning will be in accord with those summaries of political wisdom known as the "principle of proportion" and the rule of "double effect." This may not tell him what to think, but it is how he will think. He will know that "order" and "justice" both are the effects of his action. He will count the cost of one effect upon the other. He will ask how much disorder is worth a calculable preservation or extension of justice (which in turn will make for a new or better political order), or he will ask how much of the injustice in the world (none of which *ought to be*) it is his responsibility to expunge at the cost of disordering the political order in which alone political justice obtains embodiment. Whether justice warrants a disordering action or order warrants the permission of some injustice, nobody can say in advance of statesmanship which rules by which it decrees. The failure of the United States to come to the aid of the Hungarian freedom fighters [in 1956] may have been an instance of the requirements of order warranting the tragic permission of injustice. If so, this was not only because not all of the *ought to be* (the world political good) ought to be by us done, but only that part of it that is congruent with our national good. It was also because the preservation of political order against graver disorder is a part of the good of politics no less than the defense of justice against injustice.

Upon analysis the concept of order breaks down into two types of order that are politically relevant—the legal order and the order of power (for which hereinafter the word "order," or *ordo*, shall be used). This leads to a final characterization of the good of politics, this time involving three terms: *lex, ordo,* and *justitia*—or law, the order of power, and justice.

A Christian understanding of politics will be one that makes use of the concept of ordo (the order of power) in its relation to justitia on the one hand and to lex on the other. Lex refers to the *legal order*—the current state of international law and the treaties and agreements between governments and the United Nations with the nation-state system it is built upon. Justitia refers to the regulative ideal of all political action summed up, I suppose, in the word "humanitaria-nism," and to political judgments that are made in terms of the na-tional and the world common good. Between these two stands the *order of power* (for which I use the word ordo). There is an area of coincidence or overlap, but not entire congruency, between these three circles: the legal order, justice, and the power realities. States-men must take all three into account, but never one or two of them alone or at the expense of the other.

Just as not all justitia is legal justice, so not all order is legal order. The lex of international agreements and institutions may be under-stood as an effort to impose coherence upon the order of power, but this coherence also flows from the justitia that may be preserved, beyond the legalities, in the relative power positions of nations (the order of power); and there is also a (fluctuating but still definite) coherence inherent in the powers themselves in their encounters and in the mutual limitation of one nation's power of being by that of another.[7]

In the nuclear age the nations of the world seem to have an over-riding interest in identifying every actionable justice with *legal* jus-tice, and the principle of all order with the legal order. Nevertheless, a Christian theory of politics (and this was enshrined in the just war theory as a working politico-military doctrine) will not yield to this tempting prospect. Lex and ordo and justitia stand in a dialectical relationship in all responsible political agency. Doubtless the ideal is to effect the largest possible area of incidence between these norms of politics, and to see to it that every exercise of power is both legal and just.

Still, proper political doctrine will hold open the other possi-bilities. This is a world in which injustice may have the power and/or it may be legal. The use of power should not always stick by the legal boundaries, else the erosion of the order of power and of realized justice may make worse befall than a violation of the legalities. A responsible political action is never simply a legal act or simply an exertion of power or simply just. It is possible for a statesman to serve the legal order so well that he erodes the power environment and thereby contributes to the weakness even of the legal order in the future far more than he would have weakened it by not literally limit-ing himself to lex in his present action. Likewise, it is possible for him

7. Cf. Paul Tillich's analysis of encounters of power in *Love, Power and Justice* (New York: Oxford Univ. Press, 1954).

to be so concerned about national security that he fails to see the degree to which this depends on the growth and perfection of international institutions. It is not impossible for him (or at least for the citizens of a modern democracy) to be so concerned about the single norm of justice that they misdirect and trammel political action until the order of power fails to produce from its convergencies and tensions that justice which is attainable in the earthly city.

We may regard it as a triumph of law and of justice that the International Court to which the Republic of Panama appealed used the Universal Declaration of Human Rights for the first time in international adjudication in reaching its decision concerning the strife that broke out in the Zone in January 1964, when a group of students raised the Panamanian flag. But it is not immediately evident that this lex, or the treaty which gave us the canal and brought Panama into existence, or the Panamanian contention that its sovereignty reaches back before its birth, or that considerations of abstract justice should (under some conditions of our power responsibilities in the world) require the United States to abandon its power over the canal. If the power realities are now such that it would be a politically responsible act for us *basically* to renegotiate the canal treaty, the same is precisely *not* the case for Okinawa, where for the United States to grant self-determination to the inhabitants of that island would be to play false to half the globe. No more was it evident that the last British presence in the Middle East and its legal claims should have yielded to United Nations intervention in the Suez crisis and to the supposed "injustice" of all but nonviolent means. (So said President Eisenhower!) In this last instance, it is significant to note that the new legal order that has emerged has not yet guaranteed access to the Suez Canal to all nations (viz Israel) as effectively as did the old legal order that rested in some measure upon imperial power. It is also not without significance that in 1964 it seemed that Cyprus might be the next domino to fall outside the western defense perimeter, perhaps this time into that of Russia.

It is the awesome responsibility of magistrates to decide, beyond all doctrine but through an adequate political doctrine, how decision is to be made between lex and ordo and justitia, and how responsible political action is to be made out of regard for all three of these criteria. This is the political truth, even if my illustrations do not suggest the best decision to have been made in those instances.

8

THE LIMITS OF NUCLEAR WAR

On the basis of just war concepts, Ramsey concluded that the use of nuclear weapons directly to attack noncombatants is strictly forbidden under any circumstances; thus, for example, no moral warrant existed for American attacks on Hiroshima and Nagasaki during World War II. But how should we assess a strategy of nuclear deterrence in which nuclear arsenals and accompanying threats to use them are employed to keep the peace among nations? Ramsey argued that a viable deterrent could be based on a morally legitimate war-fighting capacity, one that met the *jus in bello* conditions of discrimination and proportionality. The following excerpt shows Ramsey distinguishing his position from that of "nuclear pacifism." The subsequent letter to *Newsweek* withdraws his earlier endorsement of the "bluff," in which deterrence rests on the perceived but not actual threat to use nuclear weapons directly against a political adversary's noncombatant population. (From *The Just War*, pp. 250–58)

In approaching the moral issues involved in appearing to be willing to do something that is wrong, I shall make use of a volume of essays by British Roman Catholics[1] who follow the anatomy of the just war doctrine to a conclusion altogether different from mine, namely, nuclear pacifism.

It is never right to do wrong that good may come of it. Nuclear weapons have only added to this perennial truth the footnote: it can never do *any good* to do wrong that good may come of it. Neither is it right to *intend* to do wrong that good may come of it. If deterrence

1. Walter Stein, ed., *Nuclear Weapons and Christian Conscience* (London: Marlin, 1961).

rests upon genuinely intending massive retaliation, it is clearly wrong no matter how much peace results. If weapons systems deter city exchanges only because and so far as they are *intended* to be used against cities, then deterrence involves a "conditional willingness" to do evil, and evil on a massive scale. Granting that deterrence deters before or during the war, and that it supports peace or the control of war, that alone cannot justify it. It would be justified "if, and only if, in employing this threat, we were not involved in . . . *immoral hypothetical decisions.*" The distinction between murder and killing in war, or between directly killing combatants and directly murdering noncombatants, posits an ethico-political principle that can only be violated, never abrogated. "Nothing, not even the alleged interests of peace, can save murderousness from evil," and nothing, not even the alleged interest in deterrence during war for the control of war, can save the *intention* to commit murder from being evil. Does reliance on nuclear weapons for deterrence hypothetically commit us, here and now, to murder, there and then? If so, such deterrence is wrong, and can never be anything but wickedness. This conclusion would seem to follow from the comparatively simple moral truth that "if an action is morally wrong, it is wrong to intend to do it."[2]

This is surely a correct "finding" as to the moral law. The authors of these chapters, however, intermix with this a certain "finding of fact" which may be questioned. They assert that "deterrence *rests*, in the end, on the intention to use nuclear weapons," not that in some or many of its forms it *may* or *might* rest on either present murderous intention or on a "conditional willingness" to do murder. No wonder the conclusion follows: if this is the case, deterrence "cannot but be morally repugnant for the same ultimate reason as is the use of the weapon held in reserve."[3] The following statement of the case is a better one, and by accenting the first word the fact to be questioned can be stressed: "*If*, then, we find that 'having' nuclear weapons involves intending to explode them over predominantly civilian targets, no more need be said; this intention is criminal, just as the action is criminal."[4] This is the matter of fact that needs to be determined—whether it *is* so, and must or should remain so if it is

2. Ibid., pp. 23, 36 (italics mine), 125, 71.

3. Ibid., p. 78 (italics mine). This was the analysis of deterrence which I held in 1961 and set forth in the concluding chapters of my *War and the Christian Conscience.* The moral argument, I believe, remains irrefutable, but findings of fact are not to be deduced from this.

4. Ibid., p. 73–74 (italics mine).

now the case—before we can know how the moral prohibition of intending to do wrong is to be applied in an assessment of deterrence policy.

The authors of these essays systematically fail to show that there can be no deterrent effect where there is no actual intention to use nuclear weapons directly against cities. They underrate what is pejoratively called "the argument from bluff," while admitting that if this deterred and if this is what deters there would not be an implied "conditional commitment to total war." These essays are remarkably sophisticated, and at many points suggest their own answer. "Having an H-bomb" for example, is no simple matter. It is not only that "having an H-bomb" differs from having a gun "in respect to the nature of the object possessed." One can "have" one or both these instruments with subtly but significantly different ways of "having" them. There is then a considerable difference "in respect to the nature of the 'possession' of the object" that has to be taken into account.[5] The question is whether "possession" of massive nuclear weapons is reducible to the crime of planning to use them over civilian targets. The question is whether "having" or "possession" implies a criminal intention to use them murderously, or a conditional willingness to do so. These questions cannot be answered without first exploring a spectrum of "havings" that may be possible, and indeed desirable. This further exploration of the nature of the "possession" of nuclear weapons which may be possible will determine whether deterrence by means of them before or during any war can ever be judged legitimate.

The technical possibility of deterrence before and during war can now be indicated, as can its compatibility with the moral prohibition of both the use and the intention to use nuclear (or any other) weapons in direct attacks on centers of population.

1. The collateral civilian damage that would result from counterforces warfare in its maximum form may itself be quite sufficient to deter either side from going so high and to preserve the rules and tacit agreements limiting conflict in a nuclear age. In that case, deterrence during the war and collateral civilian damage are both "indirect effects" of a plan and action of war which would be licit or permitted by the traditional rules of civilized conduct in war. To say that counterforce strikes over an enemy's own territory are licit or permitted is to say that one can morally intend and be "conditionally willing" to

engage in such a war. Whether one positively should ever do so depends on the conditions. Collateral civilian damage is certainly an unavoidable indirect effect and, in the technical sense, an "unintended" result of something a nation may and should make itself conditionally willing and ready to do. The deterrent effect, of which we are now speaking, is then, as it were, an indirect effect of the foreseeable indirect effects of legitimate military conduct.[6]

One can certainly "intend" to deter in this fashion, and oneself be similarly deterred. Not knowing the tyrannies future history may produce, one cannot say whether the one effect of successful resistance to them will justify the direct and the indirect costs. Still, we foreknow that these costs may be very great indeed. This is to say that, at least to a very great degree, perhaps a sufficient degree, nuclear warfare is a design for war that is inherently self-limiting upon rational decision makers without their having to intend to use these weapons directly to murder cities and civilians.

This is not at all a matter of "double-think about double effect."[7] To justify "possession" for the sake of deterrence one does not have to invent possibly legitimate uses for nuclear weapons, such as their use against a ship at sea. Many a military installation in the nuclear age is fifty or more miles in diameter.

2. In respect to the nature of the weapons we possess, there are two possible uses which cannot be removed from them. The dual use the weapons themselves have—the fact that they may be used either against strategic forces or against centers of population—means that *apart from intention* their capacity to deter cannot be removed from them. This means that there may be sufficient deterrence in the subjectively unintended consequence of the mere possession of these weapons. No matter how often we declare, and quite sincerely declare, that our targets are an enemy's forces, he can never be quite

6. This was a quite inadequate, indeed, an unfortunate, formulation of this first step in defense of the justice of deterrence. I should not have described "collateral deterrence" as the "indirect effect of foreseeable indirect effects" of legitimately targeted nuclear strikes. Instead, this deterrent effect should have been described as a *direct* and a *wanted* effect of the unwanted, indirect, collateral consequences of even a just use of nuclear weapons. For me to revise the language of the text above and remove this mistake would be to attribute to myself a prescience and an aptitude for words that I did not have. This would also prevent the reader from being drawn into the argument over the justice of deterrence as it unfolds in subsequent chapters. Therefore, in what follows this misleading wording will continue to be used until I was forced to supplant it by better wording for the same thought.

7. Stein, *Nuclear Weapons*, p. 57.

certain that in the fury or in the fog of war his cities may not be destroyed.

This is so certainly the case that the problem of how to deter an enemy from striking our cities ought not for one moment to impede the shift to a counter-forces policy and to the actual intention to use nuclear weapons only against forces. We should declare again and again, and give evidence by what we do, that our targets are his forces rather than his cities. Since it is morally repugnant to wage war without renouncing morally repugnant means,[8] this should be speedily done, and communicated as effectively as possible to the enemy. Still, without any hesitation or ambiguity on our part, the weapons themselves will continue to have deterrent effect because they have ambiguous uses. They always *may* be used over cities; and no enemy can *know* that this will not be done. Was [Secretary of Defense Robert] McNamara's reserved use of massive nuclear weapons for retaliation in case Russia strikes our cities really necessary, or his declared policy of conditional willingness to do this? Was not this aspect of his [1962 commencement] speech [at the University of Michigan] mainly needed to reassure domestic public opinion which is still so far from supporting any steps toward a counter-force, strategy and away from pacifistic maximal deterrence?

Similar conclusions can be reached from an analysis of the "familiar spiral of reciprocal expectations," which is an important aspect of war in the nuclear age. This spiral not only threatens to be illimitable, but it serves as a built-in dampener, which no deliberate policy nor any intention can remove. This is the truth in T. C. Schelling's contention that in the nuclear age all forms of limited war raise the risk of general war, whether intended or not. The point here is not the "threat" of general war because of some technical or human failure or some mistaken calculation The point is rather than in a nuclear age all war raises a risk of general war by an apparent *possibility* of a *politically irreversible trend*. War creates this risk which we share with the Russians. They can never "be confident that even the lack of resolution sometimes attributed to the United States could guarantee that general war would not result." "It is our sheet inability to predict the consequences of our actions and to keep things under control, and the enemy's similar inability [or our reciprocal doubt whether the other is in control], that can intimidate the enemy," and ourselves.

8. Cf. Ibid., p. 82.

If war is no longer a matter of making no threat that does not depend on our ultimate willingness to *choose* general war, it is no longer a matter of having to put forth acts or threats that involve a conditional willingness to choose general war.[9] War being sufficiently threatening, a conclusive case can be made for the proposition that massive nuclear weapons should never be intended for use against societies. The nations of the world *should* and *can* devote all their attention and intention to making only just or counter-forces war possible. A single great power *can* and *should* do this, since the other ominous possibility will always remain in the background as a shared and unintended threat.

3. Only now do we come again to the suggestion that the distinction between the *appearance* and the *actuality* of being partially or totally committed to go to city exchanges may have to be employed in deterrence policy. In that case, only the appearance should be cultivated. If the first two points above do not seem to the military analyst sufficiently persuasive, *or able to be made so,* then an *apparent* resolution to wage war irrationally or at least an *ambiguity* about our intentions may have to be our expressed policy. This is a matter, not of the nature of the weapons themselves, but of the manner in which we possess them—the "having" of them that might be necessary to sustain deterrence during justifiably conducted war.

The moralist can certainly say to the decision maker that it can never be right for him to do such a thing as attack an enemy's society, or for him actually to intend to do so, or under any conditions to be willing to match his resolution against that of the enemy by means of populated cities. He can point out to the statesman that it can never be right for him to contrive to "make" the undoable intention irrevocable, or to have the intention of doing so. He can even point out where the military analyst will be found saying the same thing about the irrationality of total committal to an irrational act of war, or even of appearing quite unambiguously to be totally and irreversibly committed.

But the moralist must be careful how he rushes in with his ethico-political principles mixed with an assortment of findings of fact and various arguments *ad horrendum.* He must be careful how he spells out his *moral* guidance for deterrence policy. For, on a sound solution

9. See T. C. Schelling, "Nuclear Strategy in Europe," *World Politics,* 14/3 (April 1962): 421–24.

of this problem the security of free societies may well depend in a nuclear age which is also an age of "megacorpses,"[10] "deracination from humanity,"[11] and "unparalleled moral landslide."[12] The moralist must be careful how he disparages the so-called argument from bluff to a morally licit form of deterrence; and he should examine whether the reasons *he* uses to dismiss this argument are telling *moral* ones or rather technical judgments he has gathered to fulfill a prejudice.

The crucial question for the moralist is whether deterrent effects that flow from a *specified kind* of studied ambiguity concerning the intention with which a nation holds nuclear weapons in reserve are *praeter intentionem* (besides or without the actual intention to attack cities) as surely as are the first two types of deterrent effects we have analyzed. To say and to act as if we might go to city exchanges is certainly a form of deception. But, if this can be done without intending to make irrational, immoral use of nuclear weapons, or even with the intention that our weapons be not so used and with the intention of revoking what had never even the appearance of total committal, such deception cannot be said to be based on the criminal intention or conditional willingness to do murder. The first thing to be said then, is that the intention to deceive is certainly a far cry from the intention to murder society, or to commit mutual homicide.

The second thing to be said is in connection with the moral problem of *deception* in politics and in wartime. A moralist need not slur over the fact that in all sorts of ways deception may be an evil, just as he need not slur over the fact that the killing of combatants is evil (though certainly not wicked). But having said this, it must then be pointed out that there are deceptions and deceptions. Or rather, the word *deception* ought perhaps to be reserved for any denial of the truth to someone to whom the truth is due, or permitting him to gather from you a false or inadequate impression concerning the exact truth which, in some sense, "belongs" to him. If this is a fair statement of the moral rule, then an experienced finding of fact must be that there are many situations in both private and public life when withholding the "truth" or even communicating an inadequate representation of the "truth" is not a lie. Relative to this, there is a teaching of long standing in the Western tradition about the virtues of

10. One million dead bodies.
11. *Nuclear Weapons*, p. 31.
12. Ibid., pp. 125–26.

a military commander, to the effect that there is nothing wrong with his having military secrets provided he does not pretend that he has none. It would be extremely difficult to support the judgment that an effective reservation about the use of the weapons we possess, or about our intention that they not be used over cities, in any sense belongs to an enemy, or that this information is due to be given him, if thereby deterrence will fail and war break out and go *whoosh!*

Finally a moralist must raise the question of whether this truth is not owed to the people of an enemy nation, if not to their military commanders. In answer to this, it goes to the point to say that this may be necessary to save *their* lives as well as those of our own civilians. Or (worse than their death from the point of view of an ethics that does not place supreme value in mere physical existence) it may be necessary in order to save them (and ourselves) from a measure of complicity in their government's conditional or actual willingness to save them by doing mass murder, or from the *tragedy* (not the *wickedness*) of actually being saved by murderous intention (if a wrongly willed deterrent worked) and some of them from the tragedy of living on in a world in which their lives have been spared in the midst of the greatest possible wrong*doing* by a government which in remote degrees of participation was still their own (if the shared intentional risk does not work). So the question resolves itself into the question whether it is ever right to withhold the truth in order to save life, to save from moral wrongdoing, to save from sheer tragedy. Does the truth that might well be "fatal" in all these senses "belong" to them? Is it "due" to be given if it can be Do we "owe" them a true report that will unambiguously quiet their fears by effectively communicating to them (if this *can* ever be done) that we have no intention of engaging with their government in intersociety warfare under any circumstances? I am so far from believing that one ought readily to justify this deception that it seems to me that the first two types of deterrence must, if at all possible, be made to work. Still, if deterrence were based on a cultivated ambiguity about our real intentions, and if "deception" in an objectionable moral sense would thus in some measure be perpetrated, it would still be an intent to deceive and not an intent possibly to do murder.

Perhaps we should say that we ought to be conditionally willing to strive for this ingredient in deterrence, that is, on the condition that it is necessary to deter and to save life. I do not grant to a physician any right to withhold from a patient knowledge of his true condition; but then I also do not believe that learning the truth about his condition can be demonstrated to be so nearly fatal as, in our present supposition, it would be for an enemy government and population to learn that we do not intend to attack people. A better analogy might be the following one. If you were trying to save a man out on the ledge of a building, threatening to commit suicide and to take you with him, would you withhold from him, and have an obligation to withhold from him, any blandishments, including "daring" him to join you inside for a duel to the death by "Russian roulette" at three paces, with no intention of ever carrying out this dissuasive dare or threat?

The military and political analysts I have consulted do *not* reject as infeasible the sort of "possession" of nuclear weapons for deterrence which we are now discussing.[13] If it is thought to be infeasible now, then the "system" may have to be studied and perfected so that it can be done. For this may be one of those customarily "unthinkable" things which, the more you think about it, will prove to be technically and politically "doable." If needed, it should be developed in many a scenario. It is on balance, I believe, morally "doable," as city-busting is not, however much you think about it. Whether this ingredient in deterrence can be adopted and exercised by a democratic society is, of course, a serious question. It requires of a people a mature "ethic of restraint, limits and silence,"[14] not moral protest always, much less punitive fury or he-man morality; and it requires a reliance on the morality and rationality of their political leaders not to be expected or (on any policy decision not so crucial) desired in a free society. For this reason, if for no other, all our attention and intention should doubtless be directed toward adopting, declaring, and implementing a policy of counter-forces warfare, with the "collateral" deterrence that policy affords. This is the doctrine which should form the consciences of free men today; and if their consciences are thus formed, it may then be possible to add to the "graduated" deterrence of a counter-force policy this last type of nonmurderous deterrence.

Then it may be possible to put, not nuclear weapons as such, but the intercity use of nuclear weapons into a category by itself, so that, while the capability still exists, the intention to attack cities will recede into the background so far as not to have actuality. Things as

13. Morton H. Halperin, *Limited War in the Nuclear Age* (Center of International Affairs, Harvard University, 1962), for example, develops at length the distinction between "communication policy" and "action policy."

14. Cf. Kenneth Thompson in "The Nuclear Dilemma—A Discussion," *Christianity and Crisis*, Nov. 27, 1961.

strange have happened before in the history of warfare. Tribes living close to death in the desert have fought cruel wars. They even used poisoned arrows, and certainly to a limited extent they fought one another by means of direct attack upon women and children. But they knew *not to poison wells!* That would have been a policy of mutual homicide, and a form of society-*contra*-society warfare that would have removed the possibility of any more bloody cruel wars, not to mention peacetime pursuits. In refraining from massive well poisoning, or in keeping that ambiguous, did these tribes, in any valid or censorable sense of the word, still "intend" to poison wells?

═══

The following letter appeared in Newsweek, *July 5, 1982:*

I am honored to have my name linked with that of Reinhold Niebuhr, America's greatest twentieth-century political analyst. However, I would like to make one important correction in your account of my views. I did once argue—in 1965—that it is morally permissible for a statesman to go so far as to "bluff" about his intention to use modern weapons deliberately aimed at an adversary's society if, but only if, that was judged necessary to deter the maximum war possible today. The "bluff" was withdrawn from my analysis of a possibly moral deterrence within the year, for two reasons: first, one's real intentions not to go to such use will be found out, and the bluff will fail to deter; and, second, even if our top political and military leaders were pure in heart, they must count on thousands of men in missile silos, planes and submarines to be conditionally willing under some circumstances, to become murderers. One should never occasion mortal sin in others, tempt them to it or enlist them for it. It is never right to do evil, or to intend to do evil, so that good may come.

PAUL RAMSEY
Princeton, N.J.

9

THE CREATED DESTINATION OF PROPERTY RIGHT

Christian Ethics and the Sit-In was an attempt to bring agape to bear on ethical questions central to the American civil rights movement, such as the purpose and limits of property rights, and the role of nonviolent resistance in transforming race relations. The next two selections consider these issues, respectively. They also show Ramsey specifying the relation between "creation" and "redemption," or "justice" and "love." Below, he defends the justice of the requirement that owners of taverns, restaurants, and inns not discriminate among persons regarding their access to food and shelter. Ramsey's use of Karl Barth's formula that creation is the external basis of covenant, and covenant the internal basis of creation, is most significant in framing the character of the relation between justice and love. (From *Christian Ethics and the Sit-In*, pp. 17–39)

The sit-ins have raised basic questions concerning law and concerning civil rights. In common justice, the right of property in our law either is or should be the "innkeeper's law" in the tradition of the Anglo-Saxon common law. Whether this *is* our law of quasipublic property is, as we shall see, a question secondary in importance only to the question what the law *should* be if it is just. But first, why should the law governing property rights express the "innkeeper's law"?

This rule stated that whoever opened an inn or tavern serving travelers with bed and food should not then discriminate among those who apply for these services he is in business to sell, and that in the possession and use of such private property he should not turn anyone away for whom he had room. That was property right as a form of fellow humanity. It meant that certain forms of property were to be destined by their owners to the common good in the service of the concrete needs of men without arbitrary distinctions. The rule was soundly based on the abstract equality of man *with* fellow man; and since this also entailed no small measure of distributive justice that took into account the concrete nature of one's fellow man, it was therefore also based squarely upon the owner's nature as a man *for* other men, and upon property right as an expression of fellow humanity.

Here was none of that erroneous notion that a man without his fellow man, and with no duties toward him, can be the bearer of absolute rights and use property in any way he pleases. The "innkeeper's law" said in effect that all must be served by any man who sets up an inn at the crossroads that weary travelers reach by nightfall, since, having established himself there as owner, he now occupies the space that otherwise might be held by an owner whose practice would be more in accord with natural justice or with the requirements of man's life with man. Man's destiny as a creature made in the image of God—in the image of God's fellow humanity—affects any of those inalienable rights he may be said to possess. Property right, and the uses of space and position on the earth in which man is given to dwell but over which no man gains *dominion*—these are in order to man in the time of his covenant with fellow man. Whether the owner knows this or not, and even if he may never say *Thou* to all or to any of his paying guests, his own humanity in its creation, and therefore the fashion of any rights he inalienably possesses, have imprinted on them the destiny toward which he was made. The "innkeeper's law" manifests the fact that the political order with its justice and its law and a man's proper relation to the things he owns are the external basis, the promise, the possibility and capability for covenant-community.

This probes the situation more deeply than did Governor LeRoy Collins in his commendable statement that while negroes may not have a "legal" right in some states to be served at segregated lunch counters, they have a "moral" right to be served in any part of an establishment whose proprietor invites them to buy goods from him in another part. Property right as a form of fellow humanity expresses more clearly why this is true, and *that* it is unquestionably true, if our rules of law succeed in instituting that justice which is natural to man. This applies also to the ownership rights of a restaurant proprietor or hotel manager who may have no other business on the premises into which he ever invites a certain class or kind of people. Collins's statement says nothing wrong, but it says not enough. So also Martin Luther King's assertion (after affirming his belief in "basic rights that should be protected concerning private property") that "we are not dealing with property that is exclusively private. We are dealing with property that is privately owned but supported by, sustained by the public and which depends on the public for its very existence."[1] If it is only hospitality that is violated when an owner trades with some people he declines to serve at a lunch counter as long as they are willing to trade on this basis, and if only the public's support of his business warrants the owner's returning their favor, then presumably he might be justified in selecting a part of the public he is in business to serve, or to serve in some part but not in all parts of his establishment. Justice in practice rests not simply on elementary fairness, but on the created destination of property as a whole to the good of fellow humanity. Even in our more populous and complex society, it may be said that, if a person who bears the human countenance arrives weary from shopping for her family and beset by two tired and thirsty children at a place on the earth where drink and food are offered for purchase, the owner of this place cannot turn her away without doing violence to the just cause among men. It is due to all who come now to this place to know that they have not gone out of the world in which God and man have time for them. Having established himself there as owner, he now occupies the space that otherwise might be held by an owner whose practice would, at the very *time* it is needed *there*, be more in accord with man's life with man. This still holds in principle, to define the right of property in union with its destination, even if there are no other persons in the vicinity as potential proprietors of whom our courts can take judicial notice who would in fact come into the possession of this property and, so far, of their own humanity in the form of fellow humanity.

NATURAL JUSTICE AND CHARITY

We can also see in this why the same may not apply to all the property to which men have title. It is certainly the case that I may invite some people into some parts of my home while not opening other parts or

1. "Are Sit-In Strikes Justifiable?" *The Nation's Future*, NBC-TV, Nov. 2, 1960. King's statement that "individuals who are in the common market with their stores should not deny individuals access to the common market" comes closest to the point. Nor should the law allow this.

the whole of it to them; and, so far as the law and justice alone are concerned, in doing this I may discriminate among kinds or races of people. My momentary obligation clearly does not allow this when Christ appears at my door disguised as the hungry, the thirsty, the homeless, or the naked. That, however, is a matter of charity, and of love-transformed justice pressing home the full meaning of man's life for man as Christ was for us. Yet even if I see my neighbors as Christs to me, still I do not generalize this to mean every man's natural right at any time to be provisioned with whatever my home supplies to any, as should be the rule in regard to the use of things and places on the earth for many business—if these are public—purposes. In the one case the distance between I and Thou is given external support; in the other, a relation is externally guaranteed to me and in me to every Thou. In the one case a measure of privacy that enables one to do what he will with his own has meaning and gives important support to man's being a fellow man at all; in the case of the "innkeeper's law" there is externally grounded the necessity that he shall be this at least in some minimal fashion, and the fact is expressed that in common justice a man has no natural right to attempt to be a man wholly in isolation from his fellow man in the use of the things he owns. Both uses of property, or both definitions of the rights of property, are necessary to fellow humanity in that both sustain externally the capacity for covenant and give real promise of this. In the one, the stress is upon the fact that I need not be absorbed into my relationships; in the other, the stress is upon the fact that I am not myself, i.e., not an I, unless, if only in some minimal way, I say Thou, and own things in order to be with and for fellow man.

As we seek to promote justice among men, Christian thought and practice should be deeply concerned over what may happen to the Thou who is every man if this is understood in terms of absolute rights of property and laws of property whose justice presupposes a man may be without fellow man. We should also be equally concerned over what may happen to the I who is every man if this comes under an only abstract justice or equality and ways of forcing men by law to be with and for others. This latter points calls for treatment later on. But first the basis in creation (or in natural justice) for the destination of property in unbreakable covenant with fellow man should be fully explored.

Karl Barth has written that, in the Christian view, creation is the external basis of covenant, creation is the promise and makes possible the history of God's covenant dealings with mankind; while His covenant is the internal basis, the meaning or purpose of creation.[2] An illustration of this can immediately be given: human sexuality, in its created nature, is to be understood properly as no individual matter, and certainly not as a mere biological fact, but as the external basis, the promise and possibility of the marriage covenant and the capability of nature for fellow humanity between man and woman, and as such this is an effective token and *image*, in fact *the* image, of God's covenant and fellow humanity with man; viewed in the other direction, the ordinance, law, or covenant of marriage is the internal basis and meaning or purpose of created human sexuality.[3]

It is worth noting, parenthetically, that sexual differentiation or the duality of man and woman is the primary form of fellow humanity and the only indestructible image of covenant in which man was created. By contrast,

> the so-called races of mankind are only variations of one and the same structure, allowing at any time the practical intermingling of the one with the other and consisting only in fleeting transitions from the one to the other. . . . In the distinction of man and woman, however, we have a structural differentiation of human existence. . . . His creatureliness is to be male or female, male and female, and human in this distinction and connection. He certainly exists in other essential and non-essential differentiations. He is necessarily a child, and this individual as opposed to others. But these distinctions as such are not structural in character. . . . He does not need to be father or mother, brother or sister, young or old, gifted or not gifted, endowed in this way or that, a man of this or that particular time or sphere or race. . . . In and with his existence as a man, and as this particular man, he is male or female, male and female. And in and with all the other essential and non-essential distinctions and connections, this is decisive and in a sense exemplary because this alone is structural and runs through all the others, maintaining, expressing and revealing itself in them. In

2. *Church Dogmatics* (Edinburgh: T. & T. Clark, 1958), vol. 3, part 1, sec. 41, 2, 3.

3. Cf. ibid., pp. 288–329, and vol. 3, part 2, sec. 45, 3, pp. 285–324. In the language and in the substance of what follows in this section I am, of course, greatly indebted to Karl Barth. His theological reflection goes before and after mine, as mine goes before (since I, too, have the Bible) and gratefully after his.

The development of a philosophy of law and an analysis of "natural" justice on the basis of covenant-creation is imperative even for a Barthian theological ethics. It is not enough simply to speak of "church law," or the human law developed within the community of believers, as "exemplary law" that may provide indirect guidance for the political order where "some form of law is sought and found, in an attempted movement from the worse to better" (ibid., vol. 4, part 2, sec. 267, 4, p. 722). Before and while this may be true, creation-covenant may provide criteria for this movement of secular law from worse to better. To show how this is so is a task for theological ethics—if, as Barth everywhere insists, Christology is not creation or anthropology, and anthropology or the doctrine of creation is not Christology.

all the common and opposing features of human existence, there is no man in isolation, but only man or woman, man and woman. In the whole reach of human life there is no abstractly human but only concretely masculine or feminine being, feeling, willing, thinking, speaking, conduct and action, and only concretely masculine and feminine co-existence and co-operation in all these things.[4]

From the primacy of the man-woman form of fellow humanity, or of the marks in sexuality of our creation for covenant, two conclusions may be drawn relevant to race relations:

1. No human law should attempt to put asunder what God has joined together, as is sought to be done by the antimiscegenation laws of many states prohibiting interracial marriages. As the Supreme Court of California said in declaring that state's antimiscegenation law unconstitutional, while a state has the power and the duty to regulate marriage, if its marriage law is "discriminatory and irrational, it unconstitutionally restricts not only religious liberty but the liberty to marry as well."[5] This 1948 decision involved petitioners of different races who were also Roman Catholics and who contended that the laws in question were unconstitutional, on the grounds, among others, that they prohibited the free exercise of their religion and denied to them the right to participate fully in the sacraments of that religion.

2. On the other hand, we are not bidden by our Creator to ignore the greater ultimacy of the creation of male and female in attempting to refashion race relations to accord more with fellow humanity. To point to the fact that the danger of intermarriage has been used by misguided white people as only a subterfuge for denying elementary justice in race relations, to recall the exploitive sexual coercion of negro women in the past by white men, and to demonstrate, quite correctly, that social intimacy and the freedom of marriage are not what is mainly wanting or at all wanted in greater justice in the relations between the races, will not be sufficient to create an abstract manhood in place of the man-womanhood God has made. Sexuality is in us His summons to fellow humanity, and where two or three are gathered together with equality and justice in other respects this summons may be expected to be heard. On all sides, this has to be acknowledged and taken realistically into account, lest, because of the sins of their fathers, our children's covenants be set on edge in the years to come.

4. Ibid. vol. 3, part 2, sec. 45, p. 286.
5. *Perez v. Sharp*, 32 Cal. 2d 711, 198 P. 2d 17.

In the very nature of human sexuality, then, are marks of the indestructible force of our creation in and for fellow humanity, and of the destination of sex to our existence in covenant. This can also be expressed at once in broader social ethical terms. The state and its law as an ordinance of creation, natural justice, human and legal rights, and social institutions generally, so far as these have a positive purpose under the creative, governing, and preserving purposes of God—all are the external basis making possible the actualization of the promise of covenant; while covenant or fellow humanity is the internal basis and meaning of every right, true justice, or law. This enables us to see why the requirements of charity, or of steadfast covenant-love, and the requirements of justice, or of natural right, are ultimately inseverable. Each conditions the other, and we are told that what is required of us is only to do justice [the justice that provides an in-principled expression of divine charity or gives external basis for or promise of, or prepares in the desert a highway for God's mercy] and to love mercy [the mercy that determinately fashions our human justice] and to walk humbly in covenant with our God (Mic. 6:8).

This can be understood even more closely in the following way. In the order of charity the Christian is able and free to be, and therefore he should be, *for* other men, as Jesus Christ was *the* man *for* his fellow man and, as such, "the image of the invisible God" (Col. 1:15) or the image of that fellow humanity in which God elected Himself from the foundations of the world to be for man and resolved not without man to be God. In *this* God's very image Adam and in him all men were originally made in and for their own fellow humanity. Natural juice however, is far less than this. Justice bears only the external marks of man's destiny for steadfast covenant-love. It provides only the external possibility of covenant, or a minimum sign and promise of this. Perhaps, therefore, the fellow humanity of man that shows forth in the order of justice can best be described as the life of man *with* fellow man (not *for* him). Yet, to be *for* fellow man (charity) and to be *with* fellow man (justice) indicates the permeability of justice to charity. Charity (*for* fellow man) is the internal basis and meaning of natural justice (*with* fellow man), as justice in turn is the promise and possibility of closer meeting and steadfast covenant. This has to be said of every human right, e.g., property, of which we speak in Christian social ethics. Human rights all bear the marks of the primal justice of man's creation for fellow humanity; and property should manifest the fact that a man alone is not God's creature. Rights such as those of ownership should reflect the just cause among men (man *with* man), and man's destination for fellow humanity.

Man *with* man entails, at the minimum, a rather external system of relationships according to which each is given his exact due and regarded as abstractly equal to any other man before the law. The life of man *with* man requires at least that Aristotle's corrective or arithmetical justice be socially enforced. This we usually call "equality before the law." So "it makes no difference whether a robbery, for instance, is committed by a good man on a bad or by a bad man on a good," or by a rich man on a poor man or a negro on a white man, or vice versa:

> The law looks only to the difference created by the injury and treats the men as previously equal, where the one does and the other suffers injury, or the one has done and the other suffered harm. . . . So it is the office of a judge to make things equal, and the line, as it were, having been unequally divided, he takes from the greater part that by which it exceeds the half, and adds this on to the less. And when the whole is divided into two exactly equal portions then men say they have their own.[6]

Yet natural justice can be stretched, converted, or elevated when it is permeated by the spirit of charity. Natural justice itself shows evidence of this. For man *with* man entails also a closer and more perceptive relation with him that takes account of inequalities and the concrete details of his actual being and situation. This is man *with* man in the form of Aristotle's proportionate or distributive justice, and finally as equity. In concrete human relationships abstract equality is not enough. Justice requires also that individual differences be taken into account. The bonds of social union and reciprocation must be "according to proportion and not exact equality" alone. For Aristotle this meant that "if the persons are not equal they must not have equal shares," and that in any "division made out of common property, the shares will bear the same proportion to one another as the original contributions did."[7] Because such justice faces the concrete persons and acknowledges their differences, it is susceptible of infusion by charity, by which the life of man *with* fellow man begins to assume more of a Christian form in proportioning justice for men by distributing to them in accordance with their

6. Aristotle, *Ethics* 1132a.
7. Ibid. 1132b, 1131a, 1131b.

need for help and rescue. This is a love-transformed justice, which decides the crucial issue remaining for natural justice, i.e., whether the just community among men shall be construed largely as honoring the greatest contributors to the common weal in their inequality with others, or more largely as bending the system of relations of man *with* and (so far as may be) his life *for* fellow man in the direction of succor for the lowliest in their inequality with others.

It is in the administration of *equity* that charity can clearly make itself felt in the order of justice. For Aristotle defines the equitable as "a correction of the law, where the law is defective by reason of its universality." It is not only just to be equitable in correcting the law by sometimes making an exception in applying it to concrete cases. Considerations of equity can also provide a growing edge in the law itself, correcting, improving, and humanizing it by first transforming the universalities of man's understanding of justice. So equity can correct justice, provided there is guidance for equity to be found in charity and if equity is not confined to making justice only more just in practice. Yet even Aristotle knew that justice had finally to be coextensive with perfect virtue. Justice, fully developed and applied, and perfect virtue are "the same really, but the point of view is not the same: in so far as it has respect to one's neighbor it is justice; in so far as it is such and such a moral state it is simply virtue."[8] In order for this to be entirely acceptable to the Christian, he has simply to say that insofar as charity has respect to his neighbor it is justice brought to final completion, or the life of man *with* man transformed, through the illumination of equity, into the covenant-life of man *for* man. Thus from the beginning, to be *with* fellow man within the structures of law and institutions provides the external basis, the promise and pledge or the possibility of covenant-love *for* him; in being *for* fellow man is revealed the internal basis of any sort of justice, or the meaning and intentionality there were present all along in that life of man *with* man which God directs in creating, preserving, and governing the world by means of the social order. His rights are a man's capability to covenant. Man was made, with all his rights, to be claimed for covenant, and to have and exercise his rights with and for fellow humanity. In covenant was every man made from his birth, and without fellow humanity was not anything made that was made—no man, no rights of his, no justice, no proper law.

8. Ibid. 1137b, 1130a.

PROPERTY AND CREATION-COVENANT

Let the reader be encouraged if the foregoing seems obscure enough to be theologically profound. For it is now time to take up again the question of property and so-called ownership rights as such. From the point of view of the Christian understanding of creation-covenant, man's propensity to sin is exhibited not only in the isolation of his often wanting to be without fellow man or in imperialism against his fellow man and wanting him to be for self. It is exhibited also in the way we put ourselves forward to be with him, and in our claims for justice or rights in relation to him and his. Christians acknowledge how flimsy is the right and how questionable the justice we claim to be the bearers of apart from or only half-heartedly in covenant-relation. Yet sinful man affirms that, as an individual item, he has his humanity, his natural and human rights and justice due him, radically without his fellow man, half without him, and on some other basis than a man's own true manhood *with* other men. He claims to possess absolute rights, say, to life, or happiness, or property—adding perhaps that he will doubtless share some corner of these just possessions of his with, and in some degree make sovereign use of them for, his fellow man. Thus, a man in isolation with his rights and his just dues comes *first;* and on the basis of this, it is hoped, a surrogate for covenant may be established as a sort of bargain or contract by which an individual by his own will agrees to put himself into some measure of responsible relation with and for his fellow man, arbitrarily or according as it is in his own best interest to do so.

This is a basically mistaken view of justice and of human rights, because it is a mistaken view of God's creation in man. A man is never without his fellow man in any such fashion, nor does he reach his neighbor only by choice or contract from which he can as easily withdraw. Instead, because his creatureliness is from the beginning in the form of fellow humanity and because the creation in him is in order to covenant, and because this means he has real being only by being *with* and *for* fellow man, we have to reckon with this in everything that is said about justice and about the rights of man. His rights have their being in, with, and for covenant. The rights of man are the rights of the fellow humanity of those who bear them. If, for example, ownership and use of property is a right it is a human right (and not therefore to be sharply contrasted with "human rights"), and property as a human and not an impersonal thing means from the beginning, or, as it were, from the bottom up, that it is a right inhering in human nature because this has the form of fellow humanity. Property, like other rights, is the promise and the possibility; it is a man's capability for life *for* and *with* his fellow man, that is, it is the external basis of covenant, if we are to say in Christian social theory that it is a "natural" right based on the structure of God's creation.

This is the reason for, and a far more adequate account of, the so-called social reservation it has been necessary to introduce into more individualistic theories of the rights of man in order to give rise or effect at all to the duties of man. Thus, a man and his father before him, in the comparatively small kingdom of Denmark, may have "owned" a tree for many, many years. Yet it never becomes theirs to use as they please, an absolute property right. They may not cut it down without showing that they have specifically remembered and cared that they are men with other men now living, and with their children's children for generations yet to come who need and will continue to have need for trees to be in Denmark, no matter who says he owns them. The public authority, in this instance, stands ready to direct any exercise of individual right of ownership to, with, and for the owner's fellow man. This is a better way to express the "social reservation" and the duties of men in the midst of the rights they possess, than to say (with traditional Aristotelian-Thomistic social philosophy) that, while at its heart the *ownership* of property is a private right, its *use* must be directed (either by the owner's action or, absent that, by the state) to the common good. That is a patchwork, which says that man is man first primarily apart from fellow man in one aspect of property (ownership, or *dominion*), yet at the same time and also primarily a man with his fellow man in another aspect of it (use).

Ours is a better formulation because it is based on a unifying biblical understanding of creation-covenant, and accordingly on a man and his rights always and from the beginning having the form of fellow humanity. The right of property means the stewardship of property (of which man never has *dominion*, private or otherwise); and stewardship means that a thing may be ours in that we are persons in covenant, and that property should be held and used in fealty toward God and in recognition of His sovereign right and sole dominion and, indivisible from this, it should be held and used in fealty of life with our fellow men.

Men need property *not* because the status of their private personalities, as individual embodied persons, is precarious in them unless they have a special space or room in which to exercise the private dominion and management of their reasons over physical things. They need property and things because the status of *fellow humanity* is precarious in them. Men have a right to private property not because they mixed their reasons and wills with nature or, by individual labor, carved their own out of the state of nature where all things were once common. Nor certainly do they have a right to private property only as a grant from the state.[9] They have a right to private property and the direction of things because this is a necessary and desirable part of their created life in fellow humanity with and for fellow man. By contrast, the angels need no property—not because they are unembodied spirits needing no physical place in which to live, nor because the status, development, and exercise of their spiritual natures are not made precarious by or suffer threat from dependence on physical things. They need no property because God created each angel a separate complete species with no fellows, entirely complete in himself, a specific individual unlike any others and a being of which there are no other instances, whose thought goes swiftly to the point without need for circuitous reasoning or for any community of searching discourse with other angels, and who live always directly in the praise of God. (The angels only sing, as it happens together, but each in his own

9. An interpretation of property right based on creation-covenant escapes the extremes of individualism or collectivism, or the extremes of the absolute right of private ownership or the absolute right of society to direct these owners. On the one hand, John Locke's individualistic justification of property as a natural right "without any express compact of all the commoners" has to be rejected, along with his account of the origin of private property: "Whatsoever, then, he removes out of the state that nature hath provided and left it in, *he hath mixed his labor with*, and joined to it something that is his own, and thereby makes it is property. It being by him removed from the common state nature placed it in, it hath by this labor something annexed to it *that excludes the common right of other men.* For this labor being the unquestionable property of the laborer, no man but he can have a right to what that is once joined to"— to which some provision for the common good can only be externally appended, as when Locke continues: "at least where there is enough and as good left in common for others" to appropriate by their own isolated labors (*Second Treatise on Civil Government*, chap. 5, paras. 25, 27, italics added). On the other hand, J. J. Rousseau's exclusively social derivation of property right has equally to be rejected. "The first man," Rousseau wrote ironically, "who, having enclosed a piece of ground, bethought himself of saying *This is mine*, and found people simple enough to believe him, was the real founder of civil society. . . . It was in vain to repeat, 'I built this well; I gained this spot by my industry.' Who gave you your standing, it might be answered, and what right have you to demand payment of us for doing what we never asked you to do?" (*A Discourse on the Origin of Inequality*, part 2, Everyman ed., pp. 207, 220). Thus, an understanding of human nature as nature created in and for covenant is the foundation of any sound political or social theory, and of the natural rights of men indivisible from the duties of fellow humanity.

kind. Their harmony is predetermined, like the music of the spheres they were formerly supposed to inhabit, and their praise is not a mater of covenant-response. They do not sing *with* fellow angels, or have any other life with them. They are not creatures of the Covenant.[10] Man, however, has been placed a little higher than the angels[11] in that God created him over against himself as His own special covenant partner and created him in the very image of this same covenant partnership (of God with and for man) by giving him a humanity whose nature consists of partnership with fellow man. Everything that is said about rights, e.g., property, and about law and justice must take this fundamentally into account.

Man has rights because fellow humanity is precarious in him. How shall this be understood? The covenant is not a relationship with disappearing terms. It is not a pure internal relation with no irreducibly different beings to be related to each other. There is distance in the relation, and relatedness in the distance. Thus, the idea of *covenant*-bond stands between or beyond the idea of *contract* (in which only the surfaces of selves are engaged in action with one another), on one hand, and, on the other, the idea of *union* or merger of beings. This is clear enough in the case of God and man. God does not unite or blend his nature with man's; He covenants with him, holding him in a life-in-community in which God remains irreducibly other than man and man a creature not himself in any sense divine. I can say Thou to God only if I am maintained in difference from him as an independent creature; yet I could never say Thou to God unless this expressed the fact that in my being, however independent, I am always with and for Him, based on no will or deed of my own but on the fact that He is *my* God, i.e., because, as Christians affirm, from all eternity He is Christ for us and has bound himself not ever to be God without us.

But this is not nearly so clear in regard to man's fellow humanity *with man*. How can I avoid the defect of meeting him only in incidental, contractual ways, with only a part of my being engaged in this, without falling into either the submissive excess of identifying myself with him or the imperialistic excess of identifying him with me?

10. The writer agrees with the statement that whoever has not meditated much on God, the angels, and the *summum bonum* may possibly make a thriving earthworm, but not very much of a man.

11. The familiar verse in Ps. 8:5 in praise of the gifts with which God has shown he is mindful of man, "Thou hast made him a little lower than the angels," reads instead in the Hebrew, "Thou hast made him a little lower than God [or, to lack something from God, or the gods], and crowned him with glory and honor."

How can I have the strength to be irreducibly other than he is, and to allow him to be other than I am, and yet live with and for him from my heart? How can I be I who am I only in saying Thou to him? How can he be himself a self who has his very being only in fellow humanity with me? How can there be distance maintained without rupturing our fellow humanity? How can there be real relations between us without loss of the distinctiveness of each? In Tillich's terms, how can I have the courage to accomplish the movement in my existence of being apart, and simultaneously have the courage to accomplish the movement of being a part?[12]

We speak not of the courage and the faith to do this, but of the importance and the function of human rights in the social order based on creation and legally defined as the promise and the substantial possibility of our doing this, or as the external basis for covenant. If human rights are the rights of fellow humanity, "inalienably" connected with this human nature in us and with our life with fellow man and with our duties to other men, then rights must be whatever it is necessary for me to have in order to be with and for fellow man. If I have an inalienable, natural right to life simply by my being a man, this is because life is the single most basic precondition to human existence in covenant. It says the same thing to say that the source of the right to life is to be found in the fact that God summons us into being, for the existence into which we are called from nothingness is being in covenant. If I should have freedom, this is because there can be no fellow humanity without my being free to it, or rather free to, with, and for another. This brings us to bodily freedoms, and freedom of action, which belong also intrinsically and indefeasibly to the exercise and to the very existence of fellow humanity. My body is not alien to me or to my being with fellow man. God who created me an embodied soul or an in-souled body at the same time gave me a nature in the form of fellow humanity in the historical time and space of my existence in covenant. In existing in my body, I have life, I am free, I say Thou and in so doing am I, I am my being with other men. This is the meaning of freedoms of speech and of action.

The same can be said of "private" property or a space in which to live and means by which to live as a right of fellow humanity. This implies, of course, that I need some things to call my own in order to be with or for fellow man. Otherwise, I would be without a place on

12. Paul Tillich, *The Courage to Be* (New Haven: Yale Univ. Press, 1952), chaps. 4 and 5.

which to stand with him. He would then be without me, and I without him. I would sink into relations with the state or institutions above me which would absorb us both. There would be no distancing by which I would bring more and more of a self to the bond of covenant between us. There would be less I-ness and Thou-ness, and only between-ness there where we once attempted to stand with one another in mutual address. This is one of the meanings of saying that property as a human right finds its justification, and as well its responsible limits, in the precariousness of fellow humanity in every man, and not in the claims of a human nature that, without fellow man, demands to be supreme above physical things in appropriating them to the direction of its rational will in isolation.

At the same time, property as a natural right means simply that this right belongs to my fellow humanity in the sense that my duty to serve the just cause among men and to destine property to the common good is not an open question for me to decide. The direction of the space or place I occupy on the earth into the time of my covenant with fellow man ought not to be regarded in every respect as only an option to be chosen or not, according as this pleases me or not. This seems especially to be the case with regard to the ownership and use of property for doing business with the public. Such property is mine expressly for the sake of the life of man with man. In owning it, I belong generically to the race of mortal and needy men. The definition of such property right should itself contain an indissoluble and *unavoidable* connection between my ownership and the good of all men who in time come to that spot with needs I have so used my property as to be able to provide for. God, who creates and sustains justice among men, purposes them to live in unbreakable covenant with Him and with all who, like God in Christ, bear the human countenance. As the promise and anticipation, the precondition and the external possibility of even minimum yet unbreakable covenant between man and man, the "innkeeper's law" is clearly a rule of law found in the fashion of fellow humanity.

10

The Christian Use of Economic Pressure to Transform Race Relations

This analysis of sit-ins and economic boycotts returns to the problem of preference among neighbors in the orders of justice and love. Characteristically, Ramsey affirms the just war tradition's dual emphasis on the justifiability and limitation of resistance on behalf of neighbors in need. The account suggests a point of convergence between just war thinking and the sort of nonviolent political struggles typically associated with Mohandas Gandhi and Martin Luther King. It also makes a striking case for the resistance of victims to the oppression which besets them. It is a requirement of the "fellow humanity" in which human creatures flourish that they *not* "stand hat in hand." Resistance, indeed, is *owed* to the oppressing neighbor. With this move, reminiscent of his earlier "vocational" argument for self-defense, Ramsey was able to probe more deeply into the Christian understanding of self-love and its relation to regard for others. (From *Christian Ethics and the Sit-In*, pp. 99–123)

So far the meaning of justice and of human rights has been viewed as resting upon the foundation of the created order. This has been explained to mean the duality of one man directly with and for another man. This is the most basic form of man's fellow humanity and it fixes covenant-existence as the destiny of human life. It is now necessary, upon the basis of this primary duality of man's relation with his single neighbor, to take into account the fact that in actuality a man always stands together with many others in various groups organized for a common purpose and simultaneously in responsible multilateral relation to many neighbors. Each of these fellow men has equal claim upon him (when these are regarded one by one) to be with them through justice and for them in Christian love. This is the full context in which the question of the use of economic pressure in the transformation of race relations arises for the Christian.

Fellow humanity, or the requirements of justice upon man with other men, as well as the responsibilities of men in the order of charity are in and of themselves nonpreferential in outlook. In either case, so far as the agent alone is concerned, he should not discriminate among fellow men but would seek to live with all God's human creatures and for any man to the benefit of all for whom Christ died. Nevertheless, our first statement concerning the external possibility and internal actuality of existence in covenant with all the companions God gives us in any actual life situation must be that fellow humanity can and may and should find sufficient reason in particular actions for differentiating among men and for preferring to serve one cause rather than another. Our second statement must be that such differentiation in particular moments among our fellow men, and preference for one cause rather than another in action about to be put forth in support of greater justice in the established relationships among men, should always be with and for fellow humanity in such a way as to include also the fellow humanity of all the persons—even the "enemy"—who are now resisted or placed under pressures of one sort or another.

THE PRINCIPLE OF "JUSTIFIABLE" RESISTANCE

Always this has been the premise of Christian social ethics; and in this regard it is important to understand that the justification of resistance and the use of pressure (and, even more basic, the preference for one man over another, however ungodly) have been the problem for Christian conscience. The problem has *not* been the particular kind of resistance or pressure about to be used. This can be illustrated by the definite fashioning of principles of justice by divine charity in the concept of the *justum bellum*, or the specifications for "justifiable" warfare, in the early centuries of the church, and in the whole tradition of civilized warfare to which this gave rise and effect in the West until our present post-Christian and correspondingly barbaric times. Love and mercy, Christians believe, are the fulfilling of the law, of natural justice, and of the meaning expressed in the commandment "Thou shalt not kill." The Christians who formulated the just war theory were driven to make in this regard one, single, clearly defined and limited *exception*. That was what it was—an exception, nothing more. Those persons "formally" directing or participating in the military forces, or "materially" yet closely cooperating in the force that should be repelled and can be repelled only by violent means—these persons are, this theory states, legitimate objects of *direct* violent repression.

What was the reason for this conclusion? What was the motivation for and shaping influence upon this exception? And when these questions are answered, must we not say that the justification of limited warfare was not actually an exception but instead an expression of the Christian understanding of fellow humanity? For in that ancient theory of just war, Christian conscience took the form of allowing any killing at all of men for whom Christ died only because military personnel were judged to stand, factually or objectively, at the point where there converged many multilateral relations of a Christian to his neighbors, at the point of the intersection of many primary dualities of his life with and for fellow man. While, of course, this included undiminished fellow humanity with the enemy soldier, the claims of many others had also to be acknowledged and realistically served in the only way possible. In this world and not some other, covenant must be enacted. Out of neighbor-regarding love for all one's fellow men, preferential decision among one's neighbors may and can and should be made. For love's sake (the very principle of the prohibition of killing) Christian thought and action were driven to posit this single exception (an exception only when externally viewed): that forces should be repelled and the bearers and close cooperators in military force should be directly repressed, by violent means if necessary, lest many more of God's little ones should be irresponsibly forsaken and lest they suffer more harm than need be. This, then, was not really an "exception" but a determinate expression of justice and mercy. It was, and is, a *regrettably* necessary but still a *necessary* expression of fellow humanity.

NONVIOLENT RESISTANCE: SIT-INS AND BOYCOTTS

The same has to be said in the case of a Christian's analysis of the ethical issues in his use of economic pressures to transform race relations. Here nonresisting love can and may and must find a way to prefer at the moment to enhance the status of some rather than others of our fellow men in the fabric of the common life and a way of resisting the will and ways of these others. Such is the premise and the analysis, indeed, of action within a democracy and within its legal procedures for changing the law for the purpose of resisting and defeating the will and way of anyone or the members of any faction with whom also we share a fellow humanity. No teacher in Galilee taught us to resist them by ballots but not by bullets. The question to be resolved is how nonresisting love can take form as its apparent opposite, namely, resistance by ballots, nonviolent resistance by the pressures exerted by sit-ins or economic boycotts, or in international relations resistance by armed violence. Only in an abstract world can a significant distinction be made between resisting *discrimination* while not resisting or coercing the *people* who discriminate.[1] One cannot let go the ballot at the evil of discrimination while withholding an intention to defeat those who discriminate. He cannot let go the coercive force of sit-ins or boycotts against customs or legally protected, impersonal rights of property, while withholding the intention to oppose, with resistance and nonviolent force, the evildoers who are property owners and *men* whose convictions and practices alike may be unjust. He can do these things no more than a bombardier can let go his explosives against the impersonal power of a nation ranged, he believes, against the cause of justice, while attempting inwardly the act of withholding the intention to kill people. The question to be resolved is, therefore, how nonresisting love can take up resistance (or rather how it can remain love concretely devoted to life with and for fellow man *without* taking up resistance). In comparison with this fundamental issue, questions about the nature and type of resistance to be used are always secondary and tactical (although not, for this reason, without ethical significance).

The resistance of the evil ones by ballots is a justifiable inference drawn in Christian conscience and only in face of the fact that the multiple claims of men converge upon us and call for responsible decision among them while we strive to achieve an order of life that as far as possible includes all. As was suggested above, democracy itself

1. Cf. my *Basic Christian Ethics* (New York: Scribner's, 1950), pp. 168–69: "Although his words were, 'Do not resist *one* who is evil,' Jesus did not even draw out very explicitly the distinction between resisting *evil* and not resisting the evil-*doer*, between condemning 'the system' and denouncing people who support it, which Christians often insist was his meaning. The evil and the one who does it are in any actual situation bound so closely together that a person who, in one-one relationship to an enemy-neighbor, wishes not to resist the evil-doer can find no way of resisting evil; and a person in multilateral relationships with more than one neighbor who wishes for their sakes to resist evil will be unable to avoid resisting the evil-doer as well. With prophetic indignation, therefore, Jesus denounced those who were evil as well as impersonal forms of evil itself. This he did from neighbor-centered preferential love, although as far as his life alone was concerned he showed no preference for his own personal welfare and did not resist evil-doers when evil fell upon him."

in a very real sense is nothing more than justum bellum, both in its origin in Western history and in the principles of Christian ethics requiring participation in it as a form of regularized struggle between man and man in the midst of which alone we have in this fallen world any life with man preserved unto a higher and more open fellowship.

Such, then, would be a sound Christian understanding of the use of various forms of economic pressure, e.g., strikes, boycotts, etc., in order to bend and reshape local custom and practices in race relations. These types of direct social action should conform to the ancient principles and limitations justifying a Christian in taking up any use of force. These principles can be stated in terms of (1) the justifiability of using economic pressure and (2) the limitation upon the economic pressures employed, or, respectively, what a love-transformed and -transforming justice permits to be done and what this still requires to be not done in any area of conflict between man and man.

1. In the economic and social order there are persons who are the principle bearers or agents in unjust practices or who are close material cooperators in that injustice. These may have to be directly coerced in the struggle for justice, since pressures brought to bear upon them may be the only way to attack the impacted, customary injustice that should be resisted and changed for the sake of fellow humanity. The economic boycott of their segregated businesses; picket lines of protests in front of their stores to arouse the community, to induce people not to trade with them, and to compel them to change their policies: these things are quite in order. This need not mean that the proprietor is, in a moral and personal sense, more "guilty" of the injustice in question than other people in the community. He may only fear a greater loss of trade if he changes his practice. Still, he stands objectively at the point where some form of pressure needs to be exerted if the unjust force and pressures of social habit that should be corrected are to be overcome and changed. No more did the theory of just war imply that military personnel were more "guilty" in a personal sense than others. Still, they were combatants whose deeds had to be repressed.

2. The economic pressure employed should be limited *in its target*. This limitation is implicitly contained in the justification of any use of economic pressures to effect social change. The same fellow humanity which permits the use of direct pressure upon the agents in and through whom injustice is objectively done by segregation in hotels and restaurants, also requires that these forms of force be not intentionally directed nor objectively done directly to the economic

injury of people not directly responsible for, or closely cooperating in, the evil sought to be changed. These are "noncombatants" in the struggle for justice; and they are not legitimate targets of *direct* repression or economic injury—however much it may be admitted that some of these may be as subjectively guilty as anybody else in approving of segregation, and no matter how much many of them may have *indirectly* and *secondarily* to suffer economically from a successful boycott rightly directed against those in the forefront of the unjust practices that should be removed. Moreover, in addition to limiting the pressure in its direct objective to the principle bearers and close cooperators in the injustice sought to be corrected, responsible Christian action would seek to limit as far as possible the extent to which the indirect effects of the direct action taken fall upon anyone else who is not the primary bearer of the injustice that should be corrected.

There is contained here a moral distinction between primary and secondary boycotts, which need not be spelled out in specific detail. An illustration, however, may be given. Boycotts against stores practicing segregation at their lunch counters, and against the white citizens of Tuskegee, Alabama, who have directly supported political gerrymandering to deny negroes the right to vote in municipal elections, are certainly to be justified. But, *on the supposition* that the proprietor and the employees of a local Woolworth store in New York City have not a share in formulating the policies of the chain as a whole, nor in determining the policies of a Woolworth store located in North Carolina, a Christian use of economic pressure may and should be mounted against the proprietor in North Carolina and not against the proprietor in New York City, who is twice removed from the practices in need of correction. While admitting that, even so, economic injury will be suffered by persons not directly responsible for maintaining this policy, still economic injury may not be deliberately and directly done to other persons as a *means* of getting at the persons who are responsible for the policy sought to be corrected. Indiscriminating boycotts are the moral equivalent of obliterating people in warfare in order to get at their government, or to a direct attack upon a man's wife and children in order to restrain his own murderous intent—although it has to be admitted that there may be situations in which their lives may have to be placed in indirect but real and foreknown jeopardy in order to restrain him.

Assemblage for public protest and to manifest sympathy for and support of the sit-ins in the South should take the form, not of direct economic action against persons not directly involved in segregation, but in public parks, meeting halls, etc. Such was the action taken by the students and faculty of the Yale Divinity School in marching *en masse* down to the "village green" in New Haven for a rally, and addressing themselves to the immediate improvement of race relations in that city. The achievement of the desegregation of certain lunch counters not only by wise action by local community leaders but by voluntary action following consultation between Attorney General William P. Rogers and the heads of certain national chain stores should, of course, be applauded. But for it to be just to attain this same result by means of the force of a boycott throughout the nation would require the verification of facts contrary to those assumed in the foregoing case. The suppositions in the previous illustration might be sufficiently altered by establishing a connection between general company practice and local practice in the South, and by establishing such direct connection between the practice and the economic well-being of stores located in New York and general company policy. Then the boycott would not be secondary, but primary. It would be directed against the actual location of the unjust policy which, for love's sake and for the sake of justice, must be removed, and, indivisible from this, to the economic injury of the people directly and objectively a part of this policy. Perhaps this would be sufficient to justify an economic boycott of an entire national chain in order, by threatening potential injury to its entire economy, to effect an alteration of the policy of its local stores in the matter of segregation. Such a general boycott might still be a blunt or indiscriminating instrument, and therefore of questionable justification. Action located where the evil is concentrated will prove most decisive and is most clearly legitimate. Moreover, prudence alone would indicate that, unless the local customs are already ready to fall when pushed, the results of direct economic action everywhere upon national chain stores will likely be simply to give undue advantage to local and state stores which conform to these customs, leading to greater decentralization and local autonomy within the company, or even (as the final self-defeat of an unjust application of economic pressure to correct injustice) to its going out of business in certain sections of the country (as, for that matter, the Quakers, who once had many meetings in the pre–Civil War South, largely went out of business in that part of the country over the slavery issue, never to recover a large number of southern adherents).

In any case, anyone who fails to make significant distinction between primary and secondary applications of economic pressure would in principle already have justified that use of economic boycott as a means which broke out a few years ago or was skillfully organized by white citizens' councils in the entire state of Mississippi against every local Philco dealer in that state, in protest against a Philco-sponsored program over a national TV network on which was presented a drama showing, it seemed, a "high yellow gal" smooching with a white man. It is true, of course, that the end or objective of this action was different. But since this is a world in which people disagree about ends and goals and concerning justice and injustice, and since, in a situation where direct action and economic pressure are called for, the justice of the matter has either not been clearly defined by law or the law is not effectively present, there has to be a *morality of means* applied in every case in which people take it upon themselves to use economic pressures or other forms of force.

The need that we not give unqualified approval to any but a limited use of economic pressure directed against the actual doers of injustice is clear also in light of the fact that white citizens' councils seem resolved to maintain segregation mainly by the use of these same means and not ordinarily by physical violence. An unlimited use of economic pressures for diametrically opposite causes could devastate the preconditions of any fellow humanity as surely as this would be destroyed by the use of more obviously brutal means. The end or aim of the action, of course, is also important, especially where it is not alone a matter of changing community customs but of the use of deadly economic power to intimidate a person from stepping forward to claim his legal rights, e.g., against negroes who register to vote in Fayette County, Tennessee, at the present moment. Here the recourse is in steps to give economic sustenance to those being despoiled, and to legal remedies. This, however, is sufficient to show that more or less nonviolent resistance and economic conflict (if both sides are strong enough) can be war of all against all no less than if other means are used. It is also sufficient to show the Christian and any other champion of justice that he needs to make sure not only that his cause is just but also that his *conduct* is just, i.e., that, if economic pressure has to be resorted to, this be applied directly against those persons directly in the way of some salutary change in business or institutional practices, while, if injury fall upon others, it fall upon them indirectly and secondarily (however inevitably) and not by deliberate intent and direct action against them.

It is clear that nonviolent resistance is a mode of action in need of justification and limitation in Christian morality, like any other form of resistance. The *language* used itself often makes very clear that this is only another form of struggle for victory (perhaps to be chosen above all others). One of the sit-in leaders has said: "Nobody from the top of Heaven to the bottom of Hell can stop the march to freedom. Everybody in the world today might as well make up their minds to march with freedom or freedom is going to march over them." The present writer certainly agrees with that statement, and would also affirm this—in the order of justice. However, it is also a Christian insight to know that unless charity interpenetrates justice it is not likely to be freedom that marches forward. And when charity interpenetrates man's struggle for justice and freedom it does not simply surround this with a sentimental goodwill. It also definitely fashions conduct in the way explained above, and this means far more than in the choice of nonviolent means. R. B. Gregg has written that "non-violence and good will of the victim act like the lack of physical opposition by the user of physical jiu-jitsu, to cause the attacker to lose his moral balance. He suddenly and unexpectedly loses the moral support which the usual violent resistance of most victims would render him"; and again, that "the object of non-violent resistance is partly analogous to this object of war—namely, to demoralize the opponent, to break his will, to destroy his confidence, enthusiasm, and hope. In another respect it is dissimilar, for non-violent resistance demoralizes the opponent only to re-establish in him a new morale that is firmer because it is based on sounder values."[2]

A trial of strength, however, is made quite inevitable by virtue of the fact that anyone engaging in nonviolent resistance will be convinced that his action is based on sounder values than those of his opponent; and in warfare with any means, men commonly disagree over the justice of the cause. This makes necessary a morality of means, and principles governing the *conduct* of resistance whenever this is thought to be justified. The question, then, is whether sufficient discrimination in the use of even nonviolent means of coercion is to be found in the fact that such conduct demoralizes and overcomes the opponent while remoralizing and reestablishing him. Here it is relevant to remember that men commonly regard some causes as more important than their lives; and to them it will seem insignificant that it is proposed to defeat such causes nonviolently. A tech-

2. *The Power of Non-Violence* (New York: Fellowship Publications, 1944), pp. 43, 89.

nique by which it is proposed to enter with compulsion into the very heart of a man and determine his values may often in fact seem the more unlimited aggression.

Among Christian groups, the Mennonites have commonly been aware more than others of the fact that the nature of divine charity raises decisively the question of the Christian use of all forms of pressure. Since the will and word of God are for them concentrated in Christlike love, it seems clear to them that nonviolent resistance is quite another thing. "The primary objective of non-violence," writes the outstanding Mennonite ethicist, "is not peace, or obedience to the divine will, but rather certain desired social changes, for personal, or class, or national advantage."[3] Without agreeing with every phrase in this statement, we must certainly assert the great difference between Christian love and any form of resistance, and then go on beyond the Mennonite position and affirm that Christian love-in-action must first justify and then determine the moral principles limiting resistance. These principles we have now set forth. *Economy* in the use of power needs to be not only asserted, but clearly specified; and when this is done it will be found that the principles governing Christian resistance cut across the distinction between violent and nonviolent means, and apply to both alike, justifying either on occasion and always limiting either action. Economy in the use of power means more than inflicting a *barely intolerable* pressure upon an opponent and upon the injustice opposed. That would amount to calculating the means and justifying them wholly in terms of their effectiveness in reaching desired goals. There must also be additional and more fundamental discrimination in the use of means of resistance, violent or nonviolent. The justification in Christian conscience of the use of any mode of resistance also lays down its limitation—in the distinction between the persons against whom pressure is primarily directed, those upon whom it may be permitted also to fall, and those who may never be directly repressed for the sake even of achieving some great good. In these terms, the "economic withdrawal" of the negroes of Nashville, Tennessee, from trading in the center city, for example, was clearly justified, since these distinctions do not require that only people subjectively guilty be singled out.

We may now take up for consideration a hard case which seems to

---

3. Guy F. Hershberger, *War, Peace and Nonresistance* (Scottdale, Penn.: Herald, 1944), p. 225.

require either no action employing economic pressure or else action that would seem to violate the principles set forth above. There may be instances in which, if economic pressure is to be undertaken at all, this would have to be applied without discrimination against a whole people. An excellent article was published recently in the journal of the Church Peace Union by a South African journalist on the inhuman economic conditions of the blacks in South Africa, amounting to virtual slavery, and the economic *complicity* of both the government and the people of the United States in these conditions.[4] "Billions of American dollars, not only from capital investors but also from the pockets of U.S. taxpayers," this author states, "are being poured into South Africa to support a system dedicated to the oppression, the persecution, and the almost diabolical exploitation of 12 million people the color of whose skins happens not to be white." Both the conditions and the complicity are documented in considerable detail. This leads to the conclusion that "the fact is inescapable that America does have a say in whether or not apartheid shall continue." Our leadership in a wide economic boycott of South Africa would be not only in accord, it seems, with the moral conscience of America, not to be denied because we also as a people have widespread injustice in the relations of the races in our own country, but also in accord with our law, U.S. Code Title 19, Section 1307, which forbids the importation of goods made by forced or convict labor. Not only should this provision be enforced but other economic and political actions might be taken which, this author believes, "must surely be supported by every American who values the freedom that has been won for him and whose conscience is not so dominated by the lines in his account books that he can willingly and knowingly contribute to the enslavement of another nation."

Unfortunately, the issue of the justifiability of a widespread boycott in this instance is not entirely settled—though this is relevant—by the fact that "Africans in the Union have long discussed the question of what they would *like* the policy of other states to be in regard to South Africa. They have asked for as wide as possible a boycott of South African goods." Nor is it settled by the fact that Mr. Absalom Vilakasi, a leading African spokesman, can be quoted to this effect: "We know that a boycott will hurt us too, but we can bear it with a wry smile as we will know that, for once, the Nationalist Govern-

4. Sean Boud, "The Economics of Apartheid: The Facts Are a Challenge to the Conscience of America," *worldview* 3/7–8 (July–August 1960): 3–7.

ment are suffering, too." What people would like does not alone settle ethical issues. Can we say that counter-people economic warfare would be justified because this would at the same time be counter-forces warfare and would put pressure on the government, the white community, and the political leaders who make policy?

Politics, of course, and especially international political action, must be the science of the possible. It also is an area of deferred repentance—but not forever. If there has been no propitious moment yet in recent history for the United States to take action, or to cease daily to take the actions described in this article, that moment may soon come when, in concert with the other nations of the world, and especially in concert with the newer nations of Africa, our country can no longer defer making effective repentance for its complicity in injustice. Then we will face questions as to the use of strong and definite economic pressures with the purpose of radically assisting in the transformation of the whole structure of race relations in a country abroad. The moral issues here do not primarily revolve around whether or not one nation should interfere in the domestic affairs of another. Rank injustice is never exclusively a domestic matter; and the fact is that, by constant action originating in the United States, we are inexorably involved in supporting economically the domestic policies of the present South African government.

The chief ethical issue is whether a widespread international boycott is a limited, discriminating instrument to use, and whether it is justifiable if it is not. This is an extremely complex situation (now, also, to the fore in the relations of the United States and other American nations to Cuba[5] and the Dominican Republic), and a minimum of ethical analysis may be all that can be brought to bear upon the subject. Two comments may be in order.

   1. The first is that no Christian should be so infatuated by the

5. Our unilateral action placing a general embargo on the sale of all goods (except food and medical supplies) to Castro's Cuba may well have been an act of too non-discriminating counter-people economic warfare; and the injustice of this, as well as the fact that there is an order of justice amid the power relations of nations, may manifest itself in that the chief effects of this action are likely to be a certain solidification of the Cuban people behind the government sought to be restrained and a greater dependence of the Cuban economy and Cuba politically on the communist countries (if these countries are able and willing to avail themselves of the opportunity thus provided) sought to be prevented by this action. Effective, discriminating exertions of power are also just; and just conduct is discriminating. The violent overthrow or defeat of a government may be an unjust action not because violence is used, but if and because this has associated with it both violent and "nonviolent" forms of injuring people indiscriminately in order to bring their government to terms.

difference between nonviolent and violent resistance as to be be-
guiled into forgetting that this is not the same as the difference between total war by any means and a limited application of power
primarily against those who objectively stand at the point where
injustice reigns or closely cooperate in its maintenance. A total use of
economic blockade as a blunt instrument against a whole people is
only prudentially different from total war with metropolis-busters—
though in the same breath it should be said that expediency often
draws distinctions that are of importance for morality. Economic
pressures should therefore always be used with extreme care. We
must not engage in the use of wholesale economic pressure directly
intended and directly done against an entire people in order incidentally and indirectly to strike at the policies of their government. Instead, whatever foreseeable injury befalls the people in general should
be the indirect even if certain effect of action directly intended and
directly done against the central government itself and against its
primary bases in the economy, while limiting as far as possible, rather
than attempting to widen, the incidental consequences of economic
blockade to include people who can in no sense be termed cooperators in the injustice that should be changed. A basic South African
industry might be selected by injuring which would bring penalty and
pressure to bear primarily upon the makers of apartheid policy, while
its foreknown and quite dire but still secondary effects would fall on
the people in general only indirectly. The pressure can be selectively
begun and increased. At the same time it should be made clear, in
concert with other nations, that we stand ready to help by food and
other supplies to care for the immediate needs of people caught in the
economic line of fire; and that the conditions would be fulfilled for a
withdrawal of these pressures by a moderate enough but definite
change of governmental policy and by the adoption of deliberate steps
in the direction of greater justice. No nation or concert of states
should assume, simply because given the interrelatedness of the
world's economy we have the means to bring enormous pressure to
bear, that this gives us either the right or the power to guarantee
justice with order in South Africa.

2. Second, a sound analysis should indicate that in all such instances we have come close to the point where injustice and tyranny
have grown so great that almost any social order is better than the
existing order; but that, while this may in fact be the case, this is by
no means the same thing as saying that disorder is better than the
present unjust order. The primacy of order to justice, and, as we have

indicated, of tolerable justice to any order, can never be forgotten by the Christian who knows the basic conditions for the external possibility of any fellow humanity's being assured under God's governance of this sinful world. Man's life with man may be preserved in pretty shoddy clothing, but not with no garments at all to cover the nakedness of man against man.

So far we have spoken of the ethical issues that arise in the participation of *anyone* in the struggle for the attainment of a more just social order: by using democratic procedures to change law; by initiating litigation in the courts to invoke the law or to determine more clearly the meaning of human rights in a given concrete situation; by protest assemblage to influence public opinion; and by bringing economic pressures to bear in an effort to batter down practices of injustice that are customary. A final word, perhaps, should be said concerning the case in which the person who does these things is not just *anyone* but a victim who suffers such injustice. How shall his action be understood from a Christian point of view? Should not his external action as well as his inward heart be characterized by suffering, reconciling love? Granting that *others*, on his behalf, ought to be able to discriminate between the primary doers and the recipients of injustice, granting that others should prefer objectively the cause of some against the will and way of others of his fellow men and should enter the struggle for justice out of fellow humanity and love for all for whom Christ died, how can a victim of injustice, who also is a Christian, for his own sake enter the world of claims and counterclaims and fail to make manifest his life with and for man in the primary form of renouncing claims for himself? In answer to this question, we may say, in the words of Emil Brunner, "If, as a good Christian," anyone "is willing to endure the injustice of his position—so far as he is concerned—for the sake of others he ought not to do so."[6]

Perhaps probing more deeply and explaining this "for the sake of others" to be not only the acceptance of external relations of responsibility in the cause of justice, we may say that no one who bears the human countenance has the right to hide this from us. He has no right to stand hat in hand and not show forth the human countenance to the full measure that it is upon him. He has no right to deprive any one or all of his fellow men of the challenge to covenant which his creation constitutes. Any failure on his part to enact his fellow manhood is not only his loss; it is a deprivation of the cause between man

6. *The Divine Imperative* (New York: Macmillan, 1937), p. 431.

and man that has not been committed entirely to him alone. His inalienable right of fellow humanity is at the same time his inalienable duty to fellow man. He can never renounce this without going frontally against covenant imprinted upon him in creation and depriving another of the right not to be without him. It is not permitted him to allow another to be without him. This was God's meaning when He created him and let him loose on this planet. Our God who from eternity resolved not to be God without this man thereby resolved that no other of His creatures should be men without him. He no more has the right to hide his human countenance from us than we have to deprive him of it. Our God who lets the light of this countenance fall upon us gives us this man to face us and to complete our fellow humanity both by the benefit and by the challenge of the fact that he is, and lifts up his face.

This is the great thing that has happened in the sit-ins led by negro students. They have fulfilled the promise of covenant; they have made their humanity more fully visible; they have resolved to be there with their fellow men even if in some measure against them; they have had the courage to establish better external conditions for the possibility of man's life with man. Any failure to do this would have been a failure in them or on their side of that fellow humanity which belongs to all God's human creatures, and belongs exclusively to neither person in covenant to elect to give or withhold. The human countenance needs not to be hidden but to be shown forth, whether the question at issue is a definition of legal rights, or of natural justice, or of the meaning of love-transformed justice, or of which individual rights men have they should exercise or not exercise in the order of charity. Not only would justice falter but charity, also, without the challenge to covenant which shows in every human countenance. Even an act of charity in illuminating the meaning of justice and refashioning it more nearly to the desire at the heart of covenant, and in determining the exercise or nonexercise of the rights that men have, needs to have beheld the human countenance of this other man; and thus, also in the order of charity, natural justice is requisite.

This same thing has to be said in favor of the so-called kneel-ins. Besides this there is, in fact, not much else to be said in their behalf. Of course, on other grounds the "kneel-ins" as the self-elected creation of community can be defended as well as, or better than, the self-elected denials of community by segregation in the church of Jesus Christ, since the introduction of new symbolic or real pressures into the church no more confuses the kingdoms and instrumentalities of this world with the kingdom of God than do already established and permanently visible, if more subtle, forms of pressure. But people go to church to plead only the sacrifice of Christ and His mercy. They do not go to plead that they are white or black, just or unjust, sufferers or not from any particular wrong. Nor do they go to plead the community they have established across racial lines. They go together or separately to plead only the sacrifice and mercy of Christ, and to count only on the community that He, the Lord of Covenant, may create among men. But this means they go *with*, if only with, the human countenance lifted up toward God and facing their life with man, for which and in which they have been called out of nothing. They cannot go without the inalienable community not made by human hands, which God ordained in them as his human creatures, by creating them men who bear in their indestructible humanity (which no man made) the marks of the fact that they were destined for fellow humanity. Pleading only communion with Jesus Christ, they must acknowledge that to all eternity they cannot be men without this fellow man here and now, since Christ is God's resolve from all eternity never to be Lord and God or Man without him.

11

================

THE COVENANT OF MARRIAGE AND RIGHT MEANS

Here the idea of covenant is used in bringing a Christian ethic of marriage down to specific cases involving genetic therapy and control of our human progeny. Along the way Ramsey distinguishes his normative vision of human sexuality, permissive as it is of the use of artificial contraception, from the traditional Roman Catholic approach. A biblical view of God's creative love, and not a mere "naturalism" or "biologism," theologically grounds the prescription that the unitive and procreative aspects of human sexuality are inseparable. (From *Fabricated Man*, pp. 32–45, 47–51)

================

In relation to genetic proposals, the most important element of Christian morality—and the most important ingredient that the Christian acknowledges to be deserving of respect in the nature of man—which needs to be brought into view is the teaching concerning *the union between* the two goods of human sexuality.

An act of sexual intercourse is at the same time an act of love and a procreative act. This does not mean that sexual intercourse always in fact nourishes love between the parties or always engenders a child. It simply means that it *tends*, of its own nature, toward the strengthening of love (the unitive or the communicative good), and toward the engendering of children (the procreative good). This will be the nature of human sexual relations, provided there is no obstruction to the realization of these natural ends (for example, infertility preventing procreation, or an infirm, infertile, or incurving heart that prevents the strengthening of the bonds of love).

Now, there has been much debate between Protestants and Roman Catholics concerning whether the unitive or the procreative good is primary, and concerning the hierarchial order or value-rank to be assigned these goods. I have shown elsewhere[1] that, contrary to popular belief, there is in the present day little or no essential difference between Roman Catholic and Protestant teachings on this point. The crucial question that remains is whether sexual intercourse as an act of love should ever be separated from sexual intercourse as a procreative act. This question remains to be decided, even if the unitive and procreative goods are equal in primacy, and even if it be said that the unitive end is the higher one. It still must be asked, Ought men and women ever to put entirely asunder what God joined together in the covenant of the generating generations of mankind? Assign the supreme importance to sexual intercourse as an act of personal love, and there still remains the question whether, in what sense, and in what manner intercourse as an act of love should ever be divorced from sexual intercourse as in and of itself procreative.

Now, I will state as a premise of the following discussion that an ethics (whether proposed by nominal Christians or not) that *in principle* sunders these two goods—regarding procreation as an aspect of biological nature to be subjected merely to the requirements of *technical* control while saying that the unitive purpose is the free, human, personal end of the matter—pays disrespect to the nature of human parenthood. *Human* parenthood is not the same as that of the animals God gave Adam complete dominion over. Such a viewpoint falls out of the bounds which limit the variety of Christian positions that may be taken up by, and debated among, people who undertake to intend the world as Christians.

It is important that these outer limits be carefully defined so that we see clearly the requirements of respect for the created nature of man-womanhood, and so that we do not rule out certain actions that have traditionally been excluded. Most Protestants, and nowadays a great many Catholics, endorse contraceptive devices which separate the sex *act* as an act of love from whatever tendency there may be in the act (at the time of the act, and in the sexual powers of the parties) toward the engendering of a child. But they do *not* separate the sphere or realm of their personal love from the sphere or realm of their procreation, nor do they distinguish between *the person* with whom the bond of love is nourished and *the person* with whom procreation may be brought into exercise. One has only to distinguish what is

---

1. "A Christian Approach to the Question of Sexual Relations Outside Marriage," *Journal of Religion* 45 (April 1965): 100–118.

done in particular *acts* from what is intended, and done, in a whole series of acts of conjugal intercourse in order to see clearly that contraception need not be a radical attack upon what God joined together in the creation of man-womanhood. Where planned parenthood is not planned *un*parenthood, the husband and wife clearly do not tear their own one-flesh unity completely away from all positive response and obedience to the mystery of procreation—a power by which at a later time their own union originates the one flesh of a child.

Moreover, the fact that God joined together love and progeny (or the unitive and procreative purposes of sex and marriage) is held in honor, and not torn asunder, even when a couple for grave, or for what in their case is to them sufficient, reason adopt a lifelong policy of planned *un*parenthood. This possibility can no more be excluded by Protestant ethics than it is by Roman Catholic ethics, which teaches that under certain circumstances a couple may adopt a systematic and possibly lifelong policy of restricting their use of the unitive good to only such times as, it is believed, there is no tendency in the woman's sexual nature toward conception. The "grave reasons" permitting, or obliging this, have been extended in recent years (the original "reason" being extreme danger to a woman's life in childbirth) to include grave family financial difficulties (because the end is the procreation *and education* of the child). These "grave reasons" have been extended even to the point of allowing that the economy of the environing society and world overpopulation may be taken into account, by even the healthy and the wealthy, as sufficient reason for having fewer children or for having no more at all.[2] Once mankind's genetic dilemma is called to the attention of the church and its moral theologians, I see no intrinsic reason why these categories of analysis may not be applied to allow ample room for voluntary eugenic decisions, either to have no children or to have fewer children, for the sake of future generations.

After all, Christian teachings have always held that by procreation one must perform his duty to the future generations of men; procreation has not been a matter of the selfish gratification of would-be parents. If the fact-situation disclosed by the science of genetics can prove that a given person cannot be the progenitor of healthy individuals (or at least not unduly defective individuals) in the next generations, then such a person's "right to have children" becomes his duty

2. Gerald Kelly and John C. Ford, "Periodic Continence," *Theological Studies* 23 (December 1962): 590–624.

not to do so, or to have fewer children than he might want (since he never had any right to have children simply for his own sake). Protestant and Roman Catholic couples in practicing eugenic control over their own reproduction may (unless the latter church changes its teaching about contraception in the wake of the [Second] Vatican Council) continue to say to one another: You in your way, and I in God's! In the turmoil over the encyclical of Pope Paul VI "Humanae Vitae," one Catholic couple says, in effect, to another: You in your way, I in the church's or at least the pope's. Still, it is clear that the Roman Catholic no less than the Protestant Christian could adopt a policy of lifelong nonparenthood, or less parentage, for eugenic reasons. Such married partners would still be saying by their actions that if either has a child, or if either has more children, this will be from their own one-flesh unity and not apart from it. Their response to what God joined together, and to the claim He placed upon human life when He ordained that procreation come from sexual love, would be expressed by their resolve to hold acts of procreation (even the procreation they have not, or have no more) within the sphere of acts of conjugal love, within the covenant of marriage.

Before going on to explore the implications of Christian ethics for methods of genetic control other than voluntary, eugenically directed birth control, it may be important to correct a misinterpretation of the principle we are using (the union of conjugal love with procreation) and to show how cardinal a principle this is in theological ethics and in the way Christians understand the entire realm with which genetics deals. It might be supposed that the moral judgments defining the outer limits of responsible human conduct are based on a mere fact of biological life, on the "natural law" in this sense, on Genesis, or—as theologians would say—on the first article of the Creed which speaks of "creation" and the Creator. It is true that a Christian will refuse to place man's own sexual nature in the class of the animals over which Adam was given unlimited dominion. He will regard man as the body of his soul as well as the soul of his body, and he is not apt to locate the *humanum* of man in thought or freedom alone. He will also discern immediately that many prevalent modern views are based on other "myths of creation." Many a modern outlook would elevate personal freedom in the expression of love without in any way honoring its connection with procreation. Instead these viewpoints call upon men and women to act as if anything that technically can be done to exert dominion over procreation may, or should, be done if it is voluntary and desirable in terms of consequences. Faced with these proposals, a Christian is apt to sum them all up in a "myth of creation" that is not his, namely, by rewriting Genesis to tell of the creation of man-womanhood with two separate faculties: Sex serves the single end of manifesting and deepening the unity of life between the partners, while human offspring are born from the woman's brow and somehow impregnated through the ear by a cool, deliberate act of man's rational will.

Still, all this would be a misunderstanding of the honor and obedience the creature should render to his Creator, and of the source of a Christian's knowledge of this duty. It arises not from slavish obeisance to a fact of nature. The Prologue of John's Gospel (not Genesis) is the Christian story of creation which provides the source and standard for responsible procreation, even as Ephesians 5 contains the ultimate reference for the meaning and nature of conjugal love and the standard governing covenants of marriage. Since these two passages point to one and the same Lord—the lord who presides over procreation as well as the lord of all marital covenants—the two aspects of human sexuality belong together. The two aspects belong together not simply because they are found together in human and other animal bisexual reproduction.

It was out of His love that God created the entire world of His creatures. The selfsame love which in Ephesians 5 becomes the measure of how husbands should love their wives was, according to the Prologue, with God before all creation, and without Jesus Christ was not anything made that was made. Of course, we cannot see into the mystery of how God's love created the world. No more can we completely subdue the mystery (which is but a reflection of this) contained in the fact that human acts of love are also procreative. Nor can we know why this was made to be so (in contrast to the more "rational" myth we constructed a moment ago). Nevertheless, we procreate new beings like ourselves in the midst of our love for one another, and in this there is a trace of the original mystery by which God created the world because of His love. God created nothing apart from His love; and without the divine love was not anything made that was made. Neither should there be among men and women (whose man-womanhood—and not their minds or wills only—is in the image of God) any love set out of the context of responsibility for procreation, any begetting apart from the sphere of love. A reflection of God's love, binding Himself to the world and the world to Himself, is found in the claim He placed upon men and women in their creation when He bound the nurturing of marital love and procreation together in the nature of human sexuality. Thus, the Christian understanding of life stems from the second article of the Creed, not from the first or from facts of nature; and this is the source of the Christian knowledge that men and women should not put radically asunder what God joined together in creation. Thus a Christian, as such, intends the world as God intends the world. We men know this at the very center of the Christian faith and revelation, and here "right" and righteousness are defined in terms of aligning our wills with His.

Men and women are created in covenant, to covenant, and for covenant. Creation is *toward* the love of Christ.[3] Christians, therefore, will not readily admit that the energies of sex, for example, have any other primary *telos*, another final end, than Jesus Christ. Rather, they will find in the strength of human sexual passion (beyond the obvious needs of procreation) an evident telos of acts of sexual love toward making real the meaning of man-womanhood, nurturing covenant-love between the parties, fostering their care for one another, prefiguring Christ's love for the church—whatever other substrata of purposes sexual energy may have that can be discovered by intending the world as a biologist. And in human procreativity out of the depths of human sexual love is prefigured God's own act of creation out of the profound mystery of His love revealed in Christ. To put radically asunder what God joined together in parenthood when He made love procreative, to procreate from beyond the sphere of love (AID [Artificial Insemination by Donor], for example, or making human life in a test-tube), or to posit acts of sexual love beyond the sphere of responsible procreation (by definition, marriage), means a refusal of the image of God's creation in our own.

A science-based culture, such as the present one, of necessity erodes and makes nonsense out of all sorts of bonds and connections which a Christian sees to be the case. Thus, because of its atomistic individualism, modern thought delivers the verdict "guilty of mo-

3. In these and other statements in the explanation in the text above, I may seem no longer to be within hailing distance of normative Judaism, or of what follows from intending the world as a Jew. There is a profound, *formal* analogy, however, to be taken into account if anyone wants to understand the basic theological ethics that is, or should be, controlling in the specific teachings of Judaism. Normative Judaism, or at least the theology of the Jewish Scriptures, also understands creation from the point of view of convenant. From the center of those events in which God created a negligible tribe to be His people, they understand His will in creating anything else out of "nothing," covenanting with the sun and moon and stars. And from the point of view of God's faithfulness they interpret the fidelity or steadfastness manifest anywhere in the world, while depending on God's Messiah more than on anything else to prove this steadfastness.

nopoly" upon the definition of marriage as a mutual and exclusive exchange of right to acts which tend to the nurturing of love or unity of life, and to the engendering of children—when all that was meant by this definition is that there is a covenantal bond of life with life. And among geneticists, H. J. Muller, for one, delivers the verdict guilty of "genetic proprietorship that so many men hold dear" or "fixation on the attempted perpetuation of just his own particular genes,"[4] and "feelings of proprietary rights and prerogatives about one's own germinal material, supported by misplaced egotism"[5]— when all that is at stake in the historic ethics of the Western world, and actually in the minds of a great many people today, is the bond to be held in respect between personal love and procreation. As explained above, what is at stake is about as far from selfish proprietorship as anything can be—as far as marriage is from monopoly. There may be an irrepressible conflict between the values governing in some genetic proposals and the historic values expressed by Christians, but there is no reason for the conflict to be an irrational one, or irrationally conceived. The irrational element enters the conflict wherever there is evidently such an unparalleled breakdown of our moral tradition that men of science cannot even understand what is being said in Christian ethical judgments. The verdicts "monopoly" and "proprietorship over germinal material" become judgments upon a whole culture that produces great intelligences capable of uttering these verdicts, or incapable of understanding Christian ethics except in terms of these absurdities.[6]

4. H. J. Muller, "Means and Aims in Human Genetic Betterment," in Tracy M. Sonneborn, ed., *The Control of Human Heredity and Evolution* (New York: Macmillan, 1965), p. 117.

5. Muller, "The Guidance of Human Evolution," *Perspectives in Biology and Medicine* 3 (1959): 26.

6. "One must face the fact that there is eventually bound to be a conflict of values," said F. H. C. Crick in the discussion in *Man and His Future* (London: J. And A. Churchill, 1963), p. 380. "It is hopeful that at the moment we can get a measure of agreement, but I think that in time the facts of science are going to make us become less Christian." The subject of this discerning remark was the disagreement between Christians, with "their particular prejudice about the sanctity of the individual," and those who "simply want to try it scientifically" (whom, strangely, Crick called "humanists"!). But when it came to any of the finer points (such as those discussed in the text above) which anyone who presumes at all to take up the subject of Christian ethics makes himself responsible for knowing, Crick could only use a very blunt and unanalyzed notion of people's "right to have children" which, he asserted, is "taken for granted because it is a part of Christian ethics." Against this supposed notion, he wanted to "get across to people the idea that their children are not entirely their own business and that it is not a private matter" (p. 275). And in *Evolution and Man's*

In the preceding paragraphs I have attempted to explain the substance of that "ethics of means" which Christianity adds to scientific humanism's insistence upon the use of only voluntary means in any program of genetic control. I have tried to express what is morally at stake for the Christian religious ethics, and the rationale it lays down for determining the nature and limits of specifiably legitimate conduct in this area. We have now to resume our examination of the various methods that have been proposed for the control or improvement of man's genetic inheritance, evaluating these in the light of the requirement that there be no complete, or radical, or "in principle" separation between the personally unitive and the procreative aspects of human sexual life. By this standard there would seem to be no objection to eugenically motivated birth control, if the facts are sufficient to show that genetic defects belong among those grave reasons that may warrant the systematic, even lifelong, prevention of conception. A husband and wife who decide to practice birth control for eugenic reasons are still resolved to hold acts of procreation (even the procreation they have not, or have no more) within the sphere of conjugal love.

This understanding of the moral limits upon methods that may properly be adopted in voluntary genetic control leads, I would argue, to the permissibility of artificial conception control (no less than to the permissibility of the so-called rhythm method) and to the endorsement of voluntary sterilization for eugenic reasons. I know that many of my fellow Christians do not agree with these conclusions. Yet it seems clear that both are open for choice as means (if the ends are important enough)—provided Christian ethics is no longer restricted to the analysis of individual *acts* and is concerned instead with the coincidence of the *spheres* of personal sexual love and of procreation (the spheres to which particular actions belong). Neither the husband (or wife) who practices artificial birth control nor the husband who decides to have a vasectomy is saying by the total course of his life anything other than that *if* either marriage partner has a child, or more children, it will be within their marriage-covenant, from their own one-flesh unity and not apart from it. In

---

Progress (Hudson Hoagland and Ralph W. Burhoe, eds. [New York: Columbia Univ. Press., 1962]), Prof. D. H. Fleming, historian at Harvard, expressed some degree of reluctance about having science assume the moral leadership of mankind by the adoption of Muller's proposals, because, he said, this would "represent a passing over to science of the traditional role of religion as the fountainhead of restraints upon pleasurable conduct" (p. 65). To which the appropriate reply is: "Goshallhemlock!"

principle, they hold together, they do not put completely asunder, what God joined together—the sphere of procreation, even the procreation they have not or have no more, and the sphere in which they exchange acts that nurture their unity of life with one another. They honor the union between love and creation at the heart of God's act toward the world of His creatures, and they honor the image of this union in the union of love with procreativity in their own man-womanhood. Their morality is not oriented upon only the genetic consequences which are believed to justify any voluntary means; nor is it only an ethic of inner intention which is believed to make any sort of conduct right. They *do* something, and are constantly engaged in doing it. This gives their behavior a character that is derived neither wholly from the desired results nor from subjective intention. Through a whole course of life they actually unite their loving and their procreativity (which, incidental to this, they have not). So they do not do wrong. They do no wrong that good may come of it. They do right that good may come of it. (In this moral reasoning, the present writer can see no difference between the case for contraception and the case for voluntary contraceptive sterilization, except in not unimportant differences in the findings of fact that may warrant the one form of birth control or the other—and except for the fact that as yet sterilization is ordinarily irreversible. Even in terms of the more static formulations of the past, it should certainly be said that a vasectomy may be a far less serious invasion of nature than massive assault upon the woman's generative organism by means of contraceptive pills.)

I am aware that many Christians will not agree with these conclusions—even some who are not Roman Catholics will be in disagreement. I ask the latter simply to consider the following possible development in the basic structure of their own ethical analysis of these problems. Suppose that in the near future Roman Catholic teachings effect the shift from act-analysis (from concentrating upon features of *the act* of conjugal intercourse that ought not to be put asunder) to concentration upon these same features within the order of marriage, the sphere or realm of marriage, that ought not to be radically separated. This, I predict, will be the theological-ethical grounds for any approval of the use of contraceptive devices in acts or in a series of acts of conjugal intercourse, if Catholic teachings make this advance. Approval of contraceptive devices will not be by reference to the indirect effects of the pill in regularizing the woman's menstrual cycle: if only the pill is approved, the continued sway of act-analysis upon Catholic teachings will be evident. But if the order of marriage (with the goods that should be held together *between the parties*) comes to the fore in Catholic moral reasoning, artificial contraception will be warranted generally, where there is sufficient reason for controlling reproduction.[7]

If this is the step taken, it seems to me impossible to avoid the conclusion that voluntary male sterilization (when this is ordinarily a reversible operation) will find a place among the means of contraception. Perhaps it will even be preferable to other means that might be chosen. Then, if there are reasons for the systematic and lifelong practice of birth control (already a conclusion reached by Catholic moral theology), and if serious genetic defect finds a place among the reasons grave enough to warrant having no children at all, or no more children, then vasectomy would seem to be in principle permissible, perhaps commendable, maybe morally obligatory. Finally, where there is sufficiently grave reason for systematic, lifelong birth control, Christian moral reflection need not wait on the assured *reversibility* of vasectomy in order to accept it as a means of birth control. All this follows in the wake of taking quite seriously what I have tried to suggest by saying that a man and a women do not set creation asunder or disobey their Creator's will when they honor the union of their love with their procreativity, even the procreativity they have not, or have no more, within the covenant of marriage, which is a cause between them that is greater than they. They do not procreate from beyond their marriage, or exercise love's one-flesh unity elsewhere.

The notation to be made concerning genetic surgery, or the introduction of some antimutagent chemical intermediary, which will eliminate a genetic defect before it can be passed on through repro-

---

7. A great deal has been said about the weak reasoning—psychological, sociological, etc.—which Pope Paul VI used to support the traditional Roman Catholic prohibition of artificial conception control in his encyclical "Humanae Vitae" ("On the Regulation of Birth"), July 25, 1968. The crucial point, however, was the pontiff's mistaken conception of the viewpoint he wished to reject. "Could it not be admitted," he asked rhetorically, "that the finality of procreation pertains to the ensemble of conjugal life, rather than to its single acts?" (para. 3). That one word *ensemble* betrays the fact that for the pope the only alternative to holding the procreative and the communicative goods or "finalities" together in every single act was to hold them together in a whole series of single acts—in ensemble, first one and then the other, in a couple's conjugal life. That is still too much bound by single-act analysis. It is quite another thing to say that the nurturing of love and the transmission of life (even when the latter is limited) are to be held together *within the covenant of marriage,* with *the person* with whom one has made marriage-covenant.

duction, is simple. Should the practice of such medical genetics become feasible at some time in the future, it will raise no moral questions at all—or at least none that are not already present in the practice of medicine generally. Morally, genetic medicine enabling a man and a woman to engender a child without some defective gene they carry would seem to be as permissible as treatment to cure infertility when one of the partners bears this defect. Any significant difference arises from the vastly greater complexity of the practice of genetic surgery and the seriousness of the consequences, if because of insufficient knowledge, an error is made. The cautionary word to be applied here is simply the moral warning against culpable ignorance. The science of genetics (and medical practice based on it) would be obliged both to be fully informed of the facts and to have a reasonable and well-examined expectation of doing more good than harm by eliminating the genetic defect in question. The seriousness of this consideration arises from the serious matter with which genetic surgery will be dealing. Still, the culpability of actions performed in unjustifiable ignorance cannot be invoked as a caution without allowing, at the same time, that in the practice of genetic medicine there doubtless will be errors made in inculpable ignorance. But genetic injuries of this order would be *tragic,* like birth injuries under certain circumstances. They would not entail *wrong*doing; nor should applications of genetic science be stopped until all such eventualities are impossible. That would be an impossible demand, which no morality imposes. . . .

. . . The Christian understands the *humanum* of man to include the body of his soul no less than the soul (mind) of his body. In particular, he holds in honor the union of the realm of personal love with the realm of procreativity in man-womanhood, which is the image of God's creation in the midst of His love. Since artificial insemination by means of semen from a nonhusband donor (AID) puts completely asunder what God joined together, this proposed method of genetic control or genetic improvement must be defined as an exercise of illicit dominion over man no less than the forcing of his free will would be. Not all dominion over man's own physical nature, of course, is wrong, but *this* would be—for the reasons stated above.

In outline, H. J. Muller proposes that "germinal choice" be secured by giving eugenic direction to AID (Julian Huxley called this technique "pre-adoption"—it has already become a minority "institution" in our society). Muller also proposes that comparable techniques be developed and employed: "foster pregnancy" (artificial in-ovulation) and parthenogenesis (or stimulated asexual reproduction). The enormous difficulties in the way of perfecting punctiform genetic surgery or mutational direction by chemical intermediaries impel Muller to concentrate on presently available techniques of parental selection. Similarly, the apparently small gains for the race that can be secured by negative eugenics (because the genes will continue in great numbers as recessives in heterozygotes) impel him to advocate positive or progressive eugenics.[8] In positive genetics, one does not have to identify the genetic defects, or know that they do not add vigor in hybrids. One has only to identify the desired genotype (no small problem in itself!) and breed for it.

Muller rejects the following practices: choosing a donor who is likely to engender a child resembling the "adopting" father, using medical students (notoriously not of the highest intelligence) or barhops, using AID only when the husband is infertile or the carrier of grave genetic defect, and keeping the matter secret. Instead he proposes the selection of donors of the highest proven physical, mental, emotional, and moral traits, and he suggests that publicity be given to the practice so that more and more people may follow our genetic leaders by voluntarily deciding to bestow upon their "children" the very best genetic inheritance instead of their own precious genes.

In order for this practice to be most effective, Muller proposes that a system of deep-frozen semen banks be established and that records of phenotypes be kept and evaluated. At least twenty years should be allowed to elapse before the frozen semen is used, so that a sound judgment can be made upon the donor's capacities. The men who earn enduring esteem can thus be "manifolded" and "called upon to reappear age after age until the population in general has caught up with them."[9] It is an insufficient answer to this proposal to point out that in his 1935 book *Out of the Night*, Muller stated that no intelligent and morally sensitive woman would refuse to bear a child of Lenin, while in later versions Lenin is omitted and Einstein, Pasteur, Descartes, Leonardo, and Lincoln are nominated.[10] Muller might

---

8. "As in most defensive operations, it is dreary, frustrating business to have to run as fast as one can merely to say in the same place. Nature did better for us. Why can we not do better for ourselves?" ("Guidance," p. 17). Thus, only progressive eugenics would be the equivalent of natural selection, which was phenotypic and preserved the genes of the strongest types.

9. "Guidance," p. 35.

10. Theodosius Dobzhansky, *Mankind Evolving* (New Haven: Yale Univ. Press, 1962), p. 330; and Klein's comment in the discussion in *Man and His Future*, p. 280.

well reply either by defending Lenin or by saying that not enough time had elapsed for a sound judgment to be made on him.

To his fellow geneticists can be left the task of stating and demonstrating scientific and other socio-psychological objections, some of which follow: (1) the genes of a supposedly superior male may contain injurious recessives which by artificial insemination would become widespread throughout the population instead of remaining in small proportion, as they now do;[11] (2) the validity of this proposal is not demonstrated by the present-day children of geniuses; (3) "it might turn out that parents who looked forward eagerly to having a Horowitz in the family would discover later that it was not so fine as they expected because he might have a temperament incompatible with that of a normal family," and "it is bad enough if we take responsibility only for the environment of our children; if we take responsibility for their genetic make-up, too, the guilt may become unbearable;"[12] (4) we know nothing about the mutation rate that would continue in the frozen germ cells; (5) the IQs of criminals would be raised;[13] (6) we could not have a "healthy society" because not many men would be "emotionally satisfied by children not their own."[14] Without debating these issues, my verdict upon the eugenic use of semen banks has been negative, in terms of the morality of means which Christian ethics must use as its standard of judgment.[15]

However, a word more should be said. No disciplined analysis of the moral life should fail to say that, among wrong actions, some are wronger than others. For the Roman Catholic, for example, abortion is worse than artificial conception control. Among invasions of man's generative faculties, some are more serious than others. While Muller's proposals would constitute a very serious invasion, and an utter separation of the realm of procreation from the realm of conjugal love, it might be that, after serious reflection upon the genetic problem, a Christian moralist could reach the conclusion that the genetic motivation and probable consequences of Muller's AID would add to

11. J. Paul Scott in *Evolution and Man's Progress*, p. 48.
12. R. S. Morrison in ibid., p. 64.
13. Donald M. MacKay in *Man and His Future*, p. 298.
14. John F. Brock in ibid., p. 287. Or that, in view of the incredible diversity of opinions expressed by the scientists, it is impossible to know what we should try to educate people to do in making genetic choices (Medawar in *Man and His Future*, p. 382).
15. There is an exceedingly profound and open-minded discussion of artificial insemination, from the point of view of a Lutheran ethics, in Helmut Thielicke's *The Ethics of Sex*, trans. John W. Doberstein (New York: Harper and Row, 1964), pp. 248–68.

it a redeeming feature—but not that this feature is sufficient to place the practice in the class of *morally permitted* actions.

Moreover, the judgment that AID for genetic or any other purposes is morally wrong does not entail the conclusion that it should be prohibited by law. Not all sin should be defined as crime. Not all immoral conduct is a fit subject for prohibitive legislation, but only acts that seriously affect the common good. It can be debated whether or not one of a number of current proposals concerning AID touches the common good so deeply that it belongs in the class of those immoral practices which should also be declared illegal. It is true that AID touches the moral nature of human parenthood (and tries to define it in terms of what it is not) just as deeply as—Roman Catholics believe—legal divorce touches the nature of marriage (and attempts to define it contrary to its nature). Still, Roman Catholics do not always and everywhere teach that under no circumstances should there be legislation permitting and regulating divorce (which for them is morally impossible). When this conclusion is reached, it is by making a distinction between "sin" and "crime," or between conduct which is or is not a fit subject for prohibitive legislation— legislation which must be ever watchful to mold the common good out of the actual ethos of the people whose affairs it regulates. AID is in an area in which Anglo-American law fairly bristles with contradictions which will soon have to be cleared up by prohibitory, or permissive and regulatory legislation, or by case law. I am suggesting that it may be possible to justify the legal enactment of AID without basing this on its moral justification.[16] If so—or if, in any case, this is the cumulative judgment our society is making—then I suppose that a trial can, and will, be made to see what can be accomplished eugenically by education and action in accord with Muller's proposals.

16. The Roman Catholic legal authority Norman St. John-Stevas (*Life, Death and the Law* [Bloomington: Indiana Univ. Press, 1961], pp. 116–59), gives a good account of the theological, moral, and legal aspects of this question. He leans in the opposite direction from the position suggested in the text above.

12

REFERENCE POINTS IN DECIDING
ABOUT ABORTION

Written before *Roe v. Wade*, the U.S. Supreme Court's decision supporting a woman's right to terminate her pregnancy, the following study covers a number of themes of continuing importance in moral and legal debates over abortion. These include the role of religion in discussions about a society's common good, the relation between morality and legal prohibition, and the moral status of nascent human life. Ramsey's discussion of the third topic is particularly instructive; beyond the light it sheds on the material question of when morally protectable human life begins, it displays Ramsey's characteristic ethical method of forging a constructive position out of a process of reasoned argument and pointed rebuttal. (From John T. Noonan, ed., *The Morality of Abortion: Legal and Historical Perspectives*, pp. 60–76)

THE RELIGIOUSNESS OF ETHICAL COMMITMENTS

My first point is a plea for greater sanity in the debate over abortion laws—a plea directed against the credence currently given the contention that anyone who opposes any of the proposed legal reforms must illicitly be seeking to impose his religious opinions on the rest of us. Although persons who hold religious opinions are regarded as free to subscribe to them, it is alleged that in the matter of legislation every identifiably religious belief should be excluded from any bearing at all upon public policy.

One way to overcome any such narrow-mindedness concerning the terms of reference that are legitimately a part of public debate over abortion legislation (or any other matter in which religion, morality, and public policy are intertwined) would be to reflect for a brief

151

moment upon what counts as a conscientious "religious" opinion in our present society. Here appeal can be made to no less a theological authority than the Supreme Court of the United States. In 1961, in *Torcaso*[1] the Court pronounced as dictum that "Secular Humanism" is a religion, despite the absence of any belief in God. Dicta of the Supreme Court have a tendency to become doctrine if they are in accord with the trends of the age. So it was that in 1965, in *Seeger*,[2] the Court recognized in a conscientious objector a belief in a "lower case" supreme being which the Congress, being composed of reasonable men, must have meant by the 1948 requirement of a belief in a "higher case" Supreme Being. In the same spirit, the Court of Appeals for the Ninth Circuit recognized man's conscientious belief in "man thinking his highest, feeling his deepest and living his best" to be a religious belief.[3] In another case the same court accepted as religious a man's belief in "godness" or—if that be too traditional language— "livingness" at the heart of all the objects in the world.[4]

The test established by *Seeger* of whether or not a belief is to be regarded as religious is "whether a given belief that is sincere and meaningful occupies a place in the life of the possessor parallel to that filled by orthodox belief in God." True, the Court was interpreting the Selective Service Act and engaging in "strenuous statutory construction."[5] But in this process the Court was driven to an anatomization of "conscience" in order to find in the hearts of most men some crux, some organizing principle, some supremacy of moral claims which is the equivalent of duties arising from a relation to the Supreme Being.

This development in our law is a mirror of what we as a people really believe as a people. We believe that a deeply felt, conscientious belief in or outlook on some public question is really the same, at least in the public forum, as any belief traditionally called religious. This is the reason the Court's decision in these cases received such widespread acceptance. The conclusion that a conscientious conviction may be *functionally equivalent* to a religious belief appeared to Americans as a proper elevation of conscientious ethical beliefs. The Court judicially endowed such convictions with the sanctity that was

1. *Torcaso v. Watkins*, 397 U.S. 488 (1961) at 495, n. 11.
2. *United States v. Seeger*, 380 U.S. 193 (1965).
3. *Peter v. United States*, 324 F.2d 173 (9th Cir. 1963).
4. *Macmurray v. United States*, 330 F.2d 928 (9th Cir. 1964).
5. John H. Mansfield, "Conscientious Objection—1964 Term," *Religion and the Public Order*, ed. Donald Giannella (Chicago: University of Chicago Press, 1965), p. 6.

formerly reserved for denominationally religious beliefs. Its interpretation in these cases gained credence among us for reasons that go far beyond the particular statutes to which the Court's decision was limited.

A well-founded conclusion from this trend of American opinion is that any of the positions taken on controversial public questions having profound moral and human or value implications hold for us the functional sanctity of religious belief. The question concerning nonreligious positions is whether they any longer exist. The question is whether proponents of one or another public policy must not all be deemed religious whether they agree with this designation or not. In this ecumenical age there must be dialogue between orthodox religions and contemporary atheism and secular humanism. The latter is America's fourth religion; it is indeed our prevailing religion—even the operational religion of many churchmen and clergymen. Unless secular humanism and the religious communities wish to join forces to roll back the Court's interpretation of the religious or transcendent element in conscience, then in the debate over abortion and public policy we should hear no more charges that one party or another is trying to legislate for the whole of society a particular religious opinion. To paraphrase *Seeger*, on the question of abortion, each disputant has a religious faith in an ethical creed.

Any fundamental "outlook" productive of an "onlook" on abortion enters the public forum with the same credentials as one or another of our traditional religious teachings concerning morality and the common life. There are some who seem to *reduce* the discussion of abortion law reform to nonmoral terms, or to judgment in terms of their own moral ultimates, by shouting silence in a loud voice to members of religious communities or to anyone who holds any relic of the position once uniformly held by these communities. This simply will not do. Nor will more sophisticated attempts to reduce the terms of reference in the debate to the meanings some science might supply. "An 'outlook which rejects onlooks,'" Donald Evans writes, "is perhaps what some people have called 'the scientific attitude.'"[6] That may be a perfectly proper determination of the methods of science. But it is still an "outlook" not to be found among the contents of any science or demonstrated by any science to be the only perspective proper to take toward every question. As a proposal in the public forum for the resolution of legal and social problems, it

6. *The Logic of Self Involvement* (London: SCM, 1963), p. 254.

is on all fours with any other "onlook" concerning the individual and the common good.

SIN AND CRIME

There is, however, a certain "self-denying ordinance" that needs to be imposed on all ethical outlooks in a pluralistic society as a precondition of good public debate. A distinction must be made between what would be for us a "sin" and what would be for us a "crime." Norman St. John-Stevas, although himself adhering to generally Catholic distinctions between right and wrong, affirms that "all contraventions of natural [moral] law are not fit subjects for legislation."[7] He proposes three tests for telling when wrong practices become a fit subject for legislation: (1) the practice injuries the common good substantially, (2) the law can be enforced equitably in its incidence, and (3) its enforcement does not cause greater evils than those it represses. These criteria would exert a salutary restraint upon the propensity of at least every moralist to conclude that "there ought to be a law." They would give us pause in passing from sin or wrong to crime.

Like the lawyer's explanation that something is "contrary to public policy" or his invocation of "a reasonable man" as a norm, the assertion that something is "substantially contrary to the common good" would be the beginning and not the end of argument. This test only points us in the direction of unlimited and continuing self-government. Discussion may then lead to provisional agreement as to the meaning of the common good and of substantial injury to it. Yet a person's understanding of morality will in good measure shape his understanding of the common good; and people will disagree about action which contributes to or injures the common good as deeply as they disagree about the features of actions that are "sin."

Those among us who believe that morally abortion is, or sometimes is, a species of the sin of murder should be able to distinguish this belief from any conclusion to the question whether such abortion ought to be defined as a crime in the penal code. A weaker version of this same distinction between sin or wrong and *crime* would be

7. *Life, Death, and the Law* (Bloomington: Indiana Univ. Press, 1961), p. 94. Thomas Aquinas is frequently cited (ibid., p. 20, n. 6) in support of this distinction, widely accepted among Catholics today: "Human law does not prescribe concerning all the acts of every virtue: but only in regard to those that are ordainable to the common good," *Summa theologica* I–II, Q. XVI, arts. 2 and 3.

operative in the minds of anyone who was willing to say that not every act of abortion that he believes to be morally wrong should be prohibited by law. In the stronger version, it might be possible for a Catholic who morally would forbid all direct abortion and who himself believes this teaching to belong to the meaning of general human justice still, for purposes of jurisprudence, to treat the morality of abortion as if it were for him within the sphere of moral theology, a science based on revelation and the teaching authority of the church, rather than on natural justice.[8]

Suppose someone believes that abortion is morally a matter of taking a human life which is small and weak and wholly dependent upon others for protection. Could that person put his conscientious belief aside and refuse to allow this moral judgment decisively to shape his verdict on the effect on the common good of permitting abortion? Suppose someone who, confronting the plight of women in our urban slums or families on the very edge of collapse from the burdens of childrearing, is convinced that it is utterly shameful and a "sin" against God for the values of conscious lives to be wasted and sacrificed by antiquated laws that seek to protect mere globs of unformed tissue, or for women to be forced by our present laws to go to back-alley abortionists. Could such a person for purposes of jurisprudence suspend that conscience enough to open his mind to the greater desirability, instead, of other possible solutions that should be admitted to the public debate? *Ought* each of these persons do this? That is a question which bears equally on both.

IMPLANTATION, SEGMENTATION, AND THE GENOTYPE

If we are to ask when a new life first has a sanctity that claims protection, and if scientific findings have anything to do with the answer to that question, we must ponder four different possibilities of such a beginning: the moment of origin of the genotype, the time of implan-

---

8. This paraphrases Norman St. John-Stevas's recommendation (*Life, Death, and the Law,* p. 30) to his fellow Catholics in regard to artificial contraception—a recommendation made *before* many Catholics began to declare publicly their disagreement with the church's teaching to date on the inherent moral evil, for Catholics and non-Catholics alike, of acts of artificial intervention frustrating the natural procreative purposes of conjugal acts while performing such acts. His recommendation, therefore, accepted the intrinsic grave immorality of the very matter he placed in brackets.

tation, the time of segmentation, and the development of the fetus in the first 4–8 weeks. Compared to any one of these determinations, the difference made by capacities later discernible in the fetus, by its quickening or by birth, would seem to be lesser disjunctions in the total course of the transmission of life disclosed to us by modern knowledge. These latter, common-sense tests are as crude or gross determinations, even if not as speculative, as the Mediterranean world's old measure of forty and eighty days.

One could say that human life begins with the implantation of the fertilized egg in the uterus seven or eight days after ovulation. Such a definition is a questionable apology for the "morning after" pill now being experimentally developed. Embracing this view, Gregory Pincus, who with John Rock developed the antiovulant pill, declared that "the new pill is not an abortifacient."[9] The basis for the theoretical assertion that life begins with implantation is the merely practical consideration that the "union of sperm and ovum cannot be detected clinically unless implantation occurs." If this is the case, one might correctly draw the conclusion that a scientist's clinical knowledge that life has started begins with implantation. We could say that *pregnancy* begins with implantation, if to say this is not a redundancy. However, to declare categorically that new life begins with implantation is to make oneself by definition ignorant of the first six or seven days. This proposal can only be set down as self-serving. As a layman, I can only express surprise if it is a statement of scientific fact that fertilized ova before implantation have not been "clinically detected."[10] Such a working definition of the origin of life can only mean: our knowledge that implanted life has begun can only begin with implantation.

The segmentation of the sphere of developing cells in the case of identical twins (who have the same genotype) is entitatively distinct from implantation as a process, though this is completed at about the same time as implantation. A "primitive streak" across the hollow cluster of developing cells (the blastocyst) signals the separation of the same genotype into identical twins. This occurs by about the

9. Lawrence Lader, "Three Men Who Made a Revolution," *New York Times Magazine*, April 10, 1966, p. 8, at p. 55. On this Dr. Rock disagrees with his colleague.

10. Dr. John Rock's report of the experiments carried out at the Free Hospital for Women in Brookline, Mass., from 1938 to 1954 seems plainly to assert that fertilized ova were secured from "a two-day, two-cell egg to a 17-day ovum already implanted in the uterus" (*The Time Has Come* [New York: Alfred A. Knopf, 1963], pp. 184–85).

time of implantation, that is, on the seventh or eighth day after ovulation. It might be asserted that it is at the time of segmentation, not earlier, that life comes to be the individual human being it is ever thereafter to be. The religious word for that process would be to say that then germinating matter becomes "animate," or is informed by, or constituted, a unique human "soul."

There is a species of biological life close to us in evolution, though not in gross physical form, whose reproduction takes place in every case by, so to speak, quadruple identical "twins." Each individual of the species armadillo has the same genotype with three others arising from segmentation. Let us imagine that, similarly, every case of human reproduction resulted in identical twins. Then I suggest that, upon acquiring our modern knowledge of segmentation explaining this phenomenon, the minds of men would be strongly drawn to locate at that point, and not earlier or later, the first origins of nascent individual human life that places upon us the claims we may acknowledge to be due to any individual of our kind. If there is a moment in the development of these nascent lives of ours subsequent to fertilization and prior to birth (or graduation from college) at which it would be reasonable to believe that an individual human life begins and therefore begins to be inviolate, that moment is arguably at the stage when segmentation may or may not take place.

The argument from genotype is, to say the least, a remarkable one. The unique, never-to-be-repeated individual human being comes into existence first as a minute informational speck, and this speck has been drawn at random from still more minute informational specks his parents possessed out of the common human gene pool. Arguably, he began to be at the moment of impregnation. There was a virtually unimaginable number of combinations of the specks on his paternal and maternal chromosomes that did not come to be when these were refused and he began his life. No one else (with the single exception of an identical twin if segmentation happens seven days later) in the entire history of the human race has ever had or ever will have exactly the same genotype. Thus it might be said that in all essential respects the individual is whoever he is going to become from the moment of impregnation. He already is this while not knowing this or anything else. His subsequent development cannot be described as his becoming someone he now is not. It can only be described as a process of achieving, a process of becoming the one he already is. Genetics teaches that we were from the beginning what we essentially still are in every cell and in every generally human attribute and in every individual attribute. There are formal principles constituting us from the beginning. Thus genetics seems to have provided an approximation to the religious belief that there is a soul animating and forming a man's bodily being from the very beginning. That far, theological speculation never dared to go with theoretical certainty.

What is this but to say that we are all fellow fetuses? From impregnation to the tomb ours is a nascent and a dying life; we are bound together as congeners from our Mendelian beginnings. Any unique sanctity or dignity we may have cannot be because we are any larger than the period at the end of a sentence. Although we know only in the light of our particular span of conscious existence, this light and that darkness from which we came and toward which we go are both alike to the One who laid his hand upon us, covered us in the womb, and by whom we were fearfully and wonderfully made. We will never be anything more or anything other than the beings we always were in every cell and attribute.

In a remarkable way, modern genetics seems to teach—with greater precision and assurance than theology could ever muster— that there are "formal causes," immanent principles or constitutive elements, long before there is any shape or motion of discernible size or subjective consciousness or rationality in a human being—not merely potency for these things that later supervene, but in some sense the present, operative actuality of these powers and characteristics. These minute formal elements are already determining the organic life to be not only generally "human" but also *the* unique *individual* human being it is to be. It is now not unreasonable to assert, for the first time in the history of scientific speculation upon this question, that who one is and is ever going to be came about at the moment an ovum was impregnated.

The teachings of genetics here are about as close as science is likely to come to the doctrine of creation ex nihilo. This doctrine affirms the radical contingency of the whole created world; the world need not have been or might have been wholly otherwise. Such also, genetics seems to tell us, is the nature of that lottery by which any human creature comes to be. There were no compelling reasons, no substance simply emanating or drawn forth by necessary laws from generation to generation, no causal predetermination requiring or even making for the conception of this particular individual and not one of a myriad other possibilities. It is true, of course, that once a unique combination of informational specks comes to be, science can then give an account of him as an understandable resultant of the genes of his maternal and paternal chromosomes. Genetic clinics can unfold the preexistent factors in laws of probability; but none of these factors reaches the individual who is actualized. There can never be an account of why *he* had to be the who and what he is rather than some other individual being. In this sense, *he* was procreated "out of nothing."

So generally with the doctrine of creation ex nihilo. Any creature or the whole creation might have been quite otherwise, or might not have been and some other creation have been instead. The creation did not emanate from the divine substance, nor can we ask what necessity the recalcitrance of preexisting matter imposed on the Creator. If either of these world views were tenable, it would be theoretically possible to forecast the nature of the creation. To the contrary, creation ex nihilo means that if one wants to know who or what the creature is, one must look to see. This doctrine was a main source of the empiricism of science in the Western world; it placed upon man's way of knowing a requirement stemming from the radical contingency of the entire creation, from the fact that nothing about creation could be deduced from anything.

So with regard to the individual human being. He cannot be predictably "traduced" out from the being of his mother and father. There is no necessity, rational or nonrational, why as a particular individual he should be; nor is there any prior propensity toward his emanation from among myriad possibilities. *That* he is may be explained scientifically or romantically, but not why he is this particular one and not one of those many, many others who might have been. Once he, that is, his genotype, *is* and once his individual "determiners" *are* in the land of the living, a sort of explanation can be proffered by specifying the genes. Still, there is no explaining why he who has these characteristics and not some one else having another set of characteristics came to be. There is no explaining why he who was conceived on the particular occasion has these characteristics and not others that might just as well have been. This is the nature of our strange passage from being only a gleam in one father's eye or only an informational genetic possibility; from this nonbeing we became the actuality of the genotype each of us is for the entirety of nascent and conscious life. Some call this process the genetic "lottery." Others call it *procreation*, the transmission of life by a mechanism that serves as the occasion upon which from things that are not God calls into being the things that are.

IMPLANTATION AND THE DEVELOPMENT OF THE FETUS

Given our present knowledge of reproductive biology, there is also some evidence to support us if we take the development of the fetus, as distinct from the activity of implantation, to be the span of time in which there comes to be a human being in the womb. The signal stages in the development of the fetus take place, as we shall see, quite early. Development of the fetus is entitatively distinct from the blastocyst's activity in implanting itself in the wall of the uterus. Both lines of development, both capacities—to implant and to grow into the fetus—were contained, it can reasonably be argued, in the mere "outline" of the person or the "formal principles" contained in the genotype and in the sphere or spheres of cells. A moral "argument" based on the signal importance of the early development of the fetus, is, therefore, a kind of rebuttal of the arguments from genotype or from the time of identical twinning which we have reviewed.

This is a strong argument precisely because of the separation between the activity of implantation and the activity of development of the fetus, both of which are activities of the new life (of the blastocyst) and not of the mother-to-be. After six or seven days of cell division in the tube, if all goes well the sphere of cells enters the uterus. The blastocyst buries itself in the wall of the uterus like a parasite. More now begins to take place than the cells' single-minded self-reproduction and differentiation into the organic life to come. A "beachhead" must first be secured in this new environment. That now is crucial. The uterus alone is no place to live; and, without the preparation of a separate "system" within which the new life can live for the next nine months, the self-reproductive power of the cells and their destiny to become the differentiated organs of a human being could not proceed. If the activities of both poles of the sphere of cells proceed simultaneously, one of these—implantation—is now fundamental to the success of the other: further embryonic development. It has to be stressed that it is the sphere of cells that accomplishes both tasks, not the mother. The original "outline" contained a determination toward the execution of the task of implantation, the growth of the placental system and amniotic sac, and not solely a determination toward the human being (the fetus) in the womb and beyond.

One pole of the sphere of cells, called the trophoblast, burrows its way into the lining of the uterus.[11] This pole is later to become the placenta, which, it is important to emphasize, is a fetal and not a maternal system for sustaining the life of the fetus. The opposite pole becomes the embryo, then the fetus. In other words, the sphere of cells (the blastocyst that has grown by division of cells having the same, original genotype) now devotes some of its foreordained cellular powers to throwing out a lifeline by which it can be attached to the life of the mother. Having made the catch, the system in which the fetus is to live must then be developed in a remarkable way. This activity of implantation and development of the placenta, it can reasonably be argued, and not only the development of the fetus, was contained in the directions the original cells contained. Thus it could be argued that "the person in the womb" (I would prefer to say, the human being in the womb, who later becomes personal) comes to be with the early development of the fetus following or entitatively distinct from the blastocyst's activity in implantation. In terms of development, the fetus is more than genotype or blastocyst. Yet in a sense it is less, because implantation and placenta sprang also from the original cells.

The sphere of cells can throw out its lifeline, in rare cases, in the tubes or, in rarer cases, in the abdominal cavity. The mother's uterus is simply the appropriate place for its activity of nidation, or "nesting," where the fetal blood system can be connected with that of the mother and there is room for nine months' fetal growth. The placental system and amniotic sac are *not* to be compared with the rope that links two mountain climbers together. The rope "belongs" to both those lives. But the placental system and amniotic bag "belong" to the unborn child. This, I suppose, is the reason that the procedure of amniocentesis, that is, taking a sample from the amniotic sac, discloses to a medical investigator information about the genetic make-up or chromosomal difficulties of the unborn child, rather than those of the mother.

At the time one side of the sphere "nests" or implants, it may have become a hollow mass of several hundred cells. The decision whether

11. For the following account of fetal development, except for footnoted references and for some of the references, I draw upon a paper by Dr. André Hellegers, "Fetal Development," prepared for the Conference on Abortion sponsored by the Harvard Divinity School in cooperation with the Joseph P. Kennedy, Jr., Foundation at the Washington Hilton Hotel, Washington, D.C., Sept. 5–8, 1967. Dr. Hellegers's paper has also been published in *Theological Studies* (March 1970).

there is to be one or two or more individuals (segmentation) may still be somewhat uncertain. In any case, shelter and supply lines come first. The trophoblast burrows into the lining of the upper wall of the uterus, creating for itself a small nutritive bath of blood and broken cells for its immediately future needs. The part of the sphere of cells late to become the placenta also produces hormones. These hormones enter the mother's blood system and serve the critical function of preventing menstruation. The time interval from ovulation to menstruation is approximately fourteen days, and the developing cells have already been alive seven days in the tubes. Therefore, the implanting trophoblast has only about seven days to produce enough hormones to stop the mother from menstruating. Otherwise, the new life will be flushed out. (These hormones are also the basis for chemical tests determining pregnancy.)

The patch of cells buried in the uterine wall has work to do which it is difficult to follow. There apparently takes place a branching, fingerlike process growing larger and more numerous, to create the whole mechanism of support and sustenance (the placenta, a rather large organ) that will take care of the nutritional and chemical needs of embryo and fetus by drawing upon the mother "until birth do them part." The placenta "acts aggressively toward the tissues of the mother, takes what it needs and on the whole only what it needs, and passes out to the mother's system whatever products of its own that can be considered waste."[12] Thus the navel, which is supposed to be an external mark of the dependence of everyone since Adam and Eve, is actually a sign of an independent and entitatively distinct activity of the germinating cells. Such also is the barrier between the mother's blood and nutritional system and the fetal blood system which the original implanting patch of cells has created around the developing embryo. "These appurtenances," whose design came from the cells everyone was from conception, to be discarded later as the afterbirth, are "as truly a part of each of us as were our milk teeth."[13]

Meantime, back at the patch of cells at the opposite pole from the burrowing, hormone-producing, placenta-forming trophoblast, another line of development takes place. At the end of the second week, the patch of cells that protrudes into the uterine cavity is no longer spherical; it has stretched along one axis and has ends and sides. This aspect of the blastocyst or original sphere is now called the "embryonic plate."

12. N. J. Berrill, *The Person in the Womb* (New York: Dodd, Mead, 1968), pp. 42, 43.
13. Ibid., p. 44.

At the end of the third or fourth week following fertilization (or the second or third week after implantation), when the woman begins to wonder whether she is pregnant, the *embryo* is said to be present. This is an exceedingly crucial stage in development. While the embryo is only an elongated mass about one-third of an inch long, scientists can recognize more. "All the most important decisions and event have been made by the end of the first month."[14] There are a head, rudimentary eyes, ears and brain, a body with digestive tract, heart and bloodstream, simple kidneys and liver, two pairs of bulges where future arms and legs will grow. The differentiation is sufficient for heart pumping to occur,[15] although the human heart reaches its final four-chamber configuration later on.

Certainly by the end of six weeks all the internal organs are present in rudimentary formation. At the end of seven weeks the fetus will flex its neck if tickled on the nose. After eight weeks the embryo ceases to be called an embryo and becomes known as a fetus, to emphasize the completion of an important phase of its existence. After the end of eight weeks there is growth, not crucial development, yet to take place, although the fetus is only one inch in length. Here at eight weeks there is readable electrical activity coming from the fetal brain.[16] Fingers and toes are now recognizable. "By the end of the second month, therefore, we can say with some assurance that the person in the womb is present, with all the basic equipment and some sensitivity, although with a long, long way to go to be fully human."[17]

By the end of the ninth or tenth week the child has local reflexes such as swallowing, squinting, and movement of the tongue. By the tenth week he is capable of spontaneous movement, without any outside stimulation. By the eleventh week thumb sucking has been observed. After twelve weeks brain structure is complete, although the fetus is only 3 1/2 inches long, and growth of structure and organs (including the brain) will continue. By twelve weeks, also, a fetal heartbeat has been monitored by modern electrocardiographic (ECG) techniques, via the mother.

Between the twelfth and sixteenth weeks, "quickening" will occur. This means that fetal movements are felt by the mother—an

14. Berrill, *Person in the Womb*, p. 45.

15. J. W. C. Johnson, "Cardio-Respiratory Systems," in *Intrauterine Development*, ed. A. C. Barnes (Philadelphia: Lea and Febiger, 1968).

16. D. Goldblatt, "Nervous System and Sensory Organs, in ibid.

17. Berrill, *Person in the Womb*, pp. 45–46. "We are all there in every important way" (p. 51).

event long considered important in human sentiment and in law. "Quickening," however, "is a phenomenon of maternal perception rather than a fetal achievement."[18] The child quickens or is the source of its own motion two weeks or more earlier, at ten weeks.

Between the eighteenth and twentieth week it is possible to hear the fetal heart by simple stethoscope, not by refined ECG.

A delivery before the twentieth week is called an *abortion*; after this date it will be called a *premature delivery* in medical terminology, since a fetus one pound or more in weight and from twenty to twenty-eight weeks of gestational life has 10 percent chance of survival. The dividing line in former days was twenty-eight weeks. However, *current* possible "viability" determines for medical practice (though often not for the law) the distinction between an abortus and a premature infant. Later on, we shall return to the significance for the morality of abortion of the fact that "viability" is bound in the future to be pushed further back in the development of the fetus which we have sketched. The difference between an abortus and a premature infant is a phenomenon of medical achievement and not of medicine's perception of the fetus's actual development. The law also lags behind medicine in that a certificate of death is required for an abortus or a miscarriage only at twenty weeks and after; before that the abortus can be treated as a pathological specimen. Since 10 percent viability now begins at this point, this could mean the erasure of a class of *infants* born dead or quite nonviable. At the same time, this lag may account for a pedagogy in the law toward justifying abortion as late as twenty weeks, that is, on the border of viability, because before that the fetus is only a pathological specimen.

Albert Rosenfeld, science writer for *Life* magazine, reports that "many readers of *Life* who saw Lennart Nilsson's marvelous photographs of fetuses in their sacs, especially in the later stages of development, wrote in to say that they could never again think of their *babies* as disposable *things*. Such sentiment might well increase as fetuses become visible from the outset. And if the day of conception were to become a person's official birth date, then the act of aborting a fetus would be ending a baby of a given age."[19] Good morality, however, ought not to depend on "visual aids." Ethical judgments are not con-

18. Hellegers, "Fetal Development."
19. *The Second Genesis: The Coming Control of Life* (Englewood Cliffs, N.J.: Prentice-Hall, 1969), pp. 125–26. Nilsson's photographs were published in *Life*, April 30, 1965; and are reprinted in *The Terrible Choice: The Abortion Dilemma* (New York: Bantam, 1968).

structed out of sentiment or emotions or feelings of identification stimulated by pictures. The latter, of course, and a sympathetic imagination grasping the facts of fetal development which we have reviewed, help to sustain in us an appropriate respect for human life hitherto hidden from view. Doubtless it is our fellow-feeling and identification with children that accounts for the fact that people generally tend to *perceive* that human life begins at birth.

Ethics, however, is based on the nature of things and not on heightened imagination or feelings, however important these may be in strengthening moral behavior. Medical science knows the babies to be present in all essential respects earlier in fetal development than the women who wrote in to *Life* magazine perceived them in the pictures. It is the rational account of the nature of fetal development that matters most.

We have, then, three stages at which it is reasonable to believe that human life begins: conception, when the unique genotype originates; segmentation, or when it is irreversibly settled whether there will be one, two, or more individuals; and the early development of the fetus when the "outline" the cells contained is actualized in all essential respects, with only growth to come. By comparison, with the achievements already made by the unborn life, quickening refers to no change and birth to less significant change in the human life that is present in the womb. By "When does human life begin?" we, of course, mean to ask and possibly to answer this question in the medical-ethical context and not in the evolutionary context of the continuity of three billion years. We mean to ask and possibly to answer the question, When is there human life deserving respect and protection like any other? The fact that nascent life is minute and vulnerable and "incapable of independent existence" does not matter in determining its worth. Certainly, a religious ethics will have special regard for the near-neighbor beneath a woman's heart and the distant-neighbor in foreign lands, for the alien resident or sojourner in the womb no less than for the alien resident or sojourner in the land of Israel—for we know the heart of the stranger, the weak, and the vulnerable, and God's special redemptive care for every one of us in like circumstances. As Professor Ralph Potter of the Harvard Divinity School has written, "The fetus symbolizes you and me and our tenuous hold upon a future here at the mercy of our fellow men."[20]

20. "The Abortion Debate," *The Religious Situation 1968*, ed. Dwight Culver (Boston: Beacon, 1968), p. 157.

Anyone who seeks a clearer or better place to light upon in answering the question, When in nascent life is there a right of life in exercise? than genotype (conception), segmentation, or the early stages of fetal development will have to wait for the development of personal self-consciousness. That would be at about age one in an infant's life, when it begins to exercise the power of speech; before that, an infant is likely only potentially human by the standard of self-awareness or incipient rationality. Indeed, there is scientific confirmation of such a choice, in the fact that at about this time *full* cortical brain activity is achieved, as evidenced by the appearance of *rhythmical* markings on an electroencephalogram. Otherwise, brain and heart activity as signs of life have been evident long before birth.

These and other indices of life (except for autonomous breathing) are all present in the morphologically human, the organically complete, and interrelatedly functioning fetus in its early development. Only the growth of what the individual already is, plus breathing on its own, locomotion by crawling and by walking upright, and the final completion of cortical brain activity (at about age one) are yet to come. Every one of these achievements, indeed, may be described better as further growth, not as additional stages in development.

One may remark in passing upon the oddity of an age in which we are elevating the importance of evidences of brain activity and rejecting the singular significance of heart or lung activity when we are dealing with men in the last of life, while we seem willing to settle every question of their moral claims upon our common humanity in the continuum of life's first beginnings by reference solely to the start of spontaneous respiration which a physician evoked from every one of us (or inflicted upon us) in the birth-room, taking little or no account of the early evidence of heartbeat and brain activity in the unborn child.[21] The "breath of life" is today taken to be the sole evidence that a woman has a child or that a man and a woman have become parents, while the "breath of life" is more and more minimized among the tests for whether that same child grown up and now terminal is still alive. A proper comment upon this must be that we

21. In an article by Dr. Hannibal Hamlin of Boston, notably entitled "Life or Death by EEG" (*Journal of the American Medical Association* 190/2 [1964]), one finds the following significant description of the EEG of an unborn child: "The intra-uterine fetal brain responds to biochemical changes associated with oxygen deprivation by abnormal EEG activity similar to that produced in the adult brain. Thus at an early prenatal stage of life, the EEG reflects *a distinctly individual pattern that soon becomes truly personalized*" (italics mine).

can indulge in many a sophisticated inconsistency if we too quickly address ourselves to the solution of the serious social problem of abortion, without an adequate concept of what the life is that claims respect and protection that can cohere with our notion of what the death is that brings these claims to an end.

13

PREFACE TO *The Patient as Person*

The language of covenant stands out in this fine statement of Ramsey's method in medical ethics. The appeal to Barth is reiterated and recast. In exploring "the meaning of *faithfulness* of one human being to another" within "covenants of life with life" established by "nature, choice, or need," Ramsey is searching for "canons of loyalty" definitive of these covenants. By his own admission, these canons are to be distinguished from the "rules of practice" discussed in "The Biblical Norm of Righteousness"; where the latter, as "rules of the game," have a primarily (rule-) utilitarian justification, the former are justified by their following the pattern of God's own covenant-fidelity in Jesus Christ. Hence Ramsey develops his ethics in a fashion that grants him sharper conceptual precision and theological primacy—all the while insisting that such primacy is fully compatible with engagement in more general moral conversations not governed by Christian faith commitments. (From *The Patient as Person*, pp. xi–xviii)

This volume undertakes to examine some of the problems of medical ethics that are especially urgent in the present day. These are by no means technical problems on which only the expert (in this case, the physician) can have an opinion. They are rather the problems of human beings in situations in which medical care is needed. Birth and death, illness and injury are not simply events the doctor attends. They are moments in every human life. The doctor makes decisions as an expert but also as a man among men; and his patient is a human being coming to his birth or to his death, or being rescued from illness or injury in between.

Therefore, the doctor who attends *the case* has reason to be attentive to the patient as person. Resonating throughout his professional actions, and crucial in some of them, will be a view of man, an understanding of the meaning of the life at whose first or second exodus he is present, a care for the life he attends in its afflictions. In this respect the doctor is quite like the rest of us, who must yet depend wholly on him to diagnose the options, perhaps the narrow range of options, and to conduct us through the one that is taken.

To take up for scrutiny some of the problems of medical ethics is, therefore, to bring under examination at once a number of crucial human moral problems. These are not narrowly defined issues of medical ethics alone. Thus this volume has—if I may say so—the widest possible audience. It is addressed to patients as persons, to physicians of patients who are persons—in short, to everyone who has had or will have to do with disease or death. The question, What ought the doctor to do? is only a particular form of the question, What should be done?

This, then, is a book *about ethics*, written by a Christian ethicist. I hold that medical ethics is consonant with the ethics of a wider human community. The former is (however special) only a particular case of the latter. The moral requirements governing the relations of physician to patients and researcher to subjects are only a special case of the moral requirements governing any relations between man and man. Canons of loyalty to patients or to joint adventurers in medical research are simply particular manifestations of canons of loyalty of person to person generally. Therefore, in the following chapters I undertake to explore a number of medical covenants among men. These are the covenant between physician and patient, the covenant between researcher and "subject" in experiments with human beings, the covenant between men and a child in need of care, the covenant between the living and the dying, the covenant between the well and the ill or with those in need of some extraordinary therapy.

We are born within covenants of life with life. By nature, choice, or need we live with our fellowmen in roles or relations. Therefore we must ask, What is the meaning of the *faithfulness* of one human being to another in every one of these relations? This is the ethical question.

At crucial points in the analysis of medical ethics, I shall not be embarrassed to use as an interpretative principle the biblical norm of *fidelity to covenant*, with the meaning it gives to *righteousness* between man and man. This is not a very prominent feature in the pages that follow, since it is also necessary for an ethicist to go as far as possible into the technical and other particular aspects of the problems he ventures to take up. Also, in the midst of any of these urgent human problems, an ethicist finds that he has been joined—whether in agreement or with some disagreement—by men of various persuasions, often quite different ones. There is in actuality a community of moral discourse concerning the claims of persons. This is the main appeal in the pages that follow.

Still, we should be clear about the moral and religious premises here at the outset. I hold with Karl Barth that covenant-fidelity is the inner meaning and purpose of our creation as human beings, while the whole of creation is the external basis and condition of the possibility of covenant. This means that the conscious acceptance of covenant responsibilities is the inner meaning of even the "natural" or systemic relations into which we are born and of the institutional relations or roles we enter by choice, while this fabric provides the external framework for human fulfillment in explicit covenants among men. The practice of medicine is one such covenant. *Justice, fairness, righteousness, faithfulness, canons of loyalty,* the *sanctity* of life, *hesed, agapé,* or *charity* are some of the names given to the moral quality of attitude and of action owed to all men by any man who steps into a covenant with another man—by any man who, so far as he is a religious man, explicitly acknowledges that we are a covenant people on a common pilgrimage.

The chief man aim of the chapters to follow is, then, simply to explore the meaning of *care,* to find the actions and abstentions that come from adherence to *covenant,* to ask the meaning of the *sanctity* of life, to articulate the requirements of steadfast *faithfulness* to a fellow man. We shall ask, What are the moral claims upon us in crucial medical situations and human relations in which some decision must be made about how to show respect for, protect, preserve, and honor the life of fellow man?

Just as man is a *sacredness in the social and political order,* so he is a *sacredness in the natural, biological order.* He is a sacredness in bodily life. He is a person who within the ambience of the flesh claims our care. He is an embodied soul or ensouled body. He is therefore a sacredness in illness and in his dying. He is a sacredness in the fruits of the generative processes. (From some point he is this if he has any sanctity, since it is undeniably the case that men are never more than, from generation to generation, the products of human generation.) The sanctity of human life prevents ultimate trespass upon him even for the sake of treating his bodily life, or for the sake of others who are also only a sacredness in their bodily lives. Only a being who is a sacredness in the social order can withstand complete dominion by "society" for the sake of engineering civilizational goals—withstand, in the sense that the engineering of civilizational goals cannot be accomplished without denying the sacredness of the human being. So also in the use of medical or scientific technics.

It is of first importance that this be understood, since we live in an age in which *hesed* (steadfast love) has become *maybe* and the "sanctity" of human life has been reduced to the ever more reducible notion of the "dignity" of human life. The later is a sliver of a shield in comparison with the awesome respect required of men in all their dealings with men if man has a touch of sanctity in this, his fetal, mortal, bodily, living and dying life.

Today someone is likely to say: "Another 'semanticism' which is somewhat of an argument-stopper has to do with the sacredness or inviolability of the individual."[1] If such a principle is asserted in gatherings of physicians, it is likely to be met with another argument-stopper: It is immoral not to do research (or this experiment must be done despite its necessary deception of human beings). This is then a standoff of contrary moral judgments or intuitions or commitments.

The next step may be for someone to say that medical advancement is hampered because our "society" makes an absolute of the inviolability of the individual. This raises the spectre of a medical and scientific community freed from the shackles of that cultural norm, and proceeding upon the basis of an ethos all its own. Alternatively, the next move may be for someone to say: Our major task is to reconcile the welfare of the individual with the welfare of mankind; both must be served. This, indeed, is the principal task of medical ethics. However, there is no "unseen hand" guaranteeing that, for example, *good* experimental designs will always be morally *justifiable*. It is better not to begin with the laissez-faire assumption that the rights of men and the needs of future progress are always reconcilable. Indeed, the contrary assumption may be more salutary.

Several statements of this viewpoint may well stand as mottos over all that follows in this volume. "In the end we may have to accept the fact that some limits do exist to the search for knowledge."[2] "The end does not always justify the means, and the good things a man does

1. Wolf Wolfensberger, "Ethical Issues in Research with Human Subjects," *Science* 155 (Jan. 6, 1967): 48.
2. Paul A. Freund, "Is the Law Ready for Human Experimentation?" *Trial* 2 (October–November 1966): 49; "Ethical Problems in Human Experimentation, *New England Journal of Medicine* 273/10)Sept. 10, 1965): 692.

can be made complete only by the things he refuses to do."³ "There may be valuable scientific knowledge which it is morally impossible to obtain. There may be truths which would be of great and lasting benefit to mankind if they could be discovered, but which cannot be discovered without systematic and sustained violation of legitimate moral imperatives. It may be necessary to choose between knowledge and morality, in opposition to our long-standing prejudice that the two must go together."⁴ "To justify whatever practice we think is technically demanded by showing that we are doing it for a good end . . . is both the best defense and the last refuge of a scoundrel."⁵ "A[n experimental] study is ethical or not in its inception; it does not become ethical or not because it turned up valuable data."⁶ These are salutary warnings precisely because by them we are driven to make the most searching inquiry concerning more basic ethical principles governing medical practice.

Because physicians deal with life and death, health and maiming, they cannot avoid being conscious or deliberate in their ethics to some degree. However, it is important to call attention to the fact that medical ethics cannot remain at the level of surface intuitions or in an impasse of conversation-stoppers. At this point there can be no other resort than to ethical theory—as that elder statesman of medical ethics, Dr. Chauncey D. Leake, professor of pharmacology at the University of California Medical Center, San Francisco, so often reminds us. At this point physicians must in greater measure become moral philosophers, asking themselves some quite profound questions about the nature of proper moral reasoning, and how moral dilemmas are rightly to be resolved. If they do not, the existing medical ethics will be eroded more and more by what it is alleged *must* be done and technically *can* be done.

In the medical literature there are many articles on ethics which are greatly to be admired. Yet I know that these are not part of the daily fare of medical students, or of members of the profession when they gather together as professionals or even for purposes of conviviality. I do not believe that either the codes of medical ethics or the

3. Dunlop (1965), quoted in Douglass Hubble, "Medical Science, Society and Human Values," *British Medical Journal* 5485 (Feb. 19, 1966): 476.

4. James P. Scanlan, "The Morality of Deception in Experiments," *Bucknell Review* 13/1 (March 1965): 26.

5. John E. Smith, "Panel Discussion: Moral Issues in Clinical Research," *Yale Journal of Biology and Medicine* 36 (June 1964): 463.

6. Henry K. Beecher, *Research and the Individual: Human Studies* (Boston: Little, Brown, 1970), p. 25.

physicians who have undertaken to comment on them and to give fresh analysis of the physician's moral decisions will suffice to withstand the omnivorous appetite of scientific research or of a therapeutic technology that has a momentum and a life of its own.

The Nuremberg Code, the Declaration of Helsinki, various "guidelines" of the American Medical Association, and other "codes" governing medical practice constitute a sort of "catechism" in the ethics of the medical profession. These codes exhibit a professional ethics which ministers and theologians and members of other professions can only profoundly respect and admire. Still, a catechism never sufficed. Unless these principles are constantly pondered and enlivened in their application they become dead letters. There is also need that these principles be deepened and sensitized and opened to further humane revision in face of all the ordinary and the newly emerging situations which a doctor confronts—as do we all—in the present day. In this task none of the sources of moral insight, no understanding of the humanity of man or for answering questions of life and death, can rightfully be neglected.

There is, in any case, no way to avoid the moral pluralism of our society. There is no avoiding the fact that today no one can do medical ethics until someone first does so. Due to the uncertainties in Roman Catholic moral theology since Vatican Council II, even the traditional medical ethics courses in schools under Catholic auspices are undergoing vast changes, abandonment, or severe crisis. The medical profession now finds itself without one of the ancient landmarks—or without one opponent. Research and therapies and actionable schemes for the self-creation of our species mount exponentially, while Nuremberg recedes.

The last state of the patient (medical ethics) may be worse than the first. Still there is evidence that this can be a moment of great opportunity. An increasing number of moralists—Catholic, Protestant, Jewish, and unlabeled men—are manifesting interest, devoting their trained powers of ethical reasoning to questions of medical practice and technology. This same galloping technology gives all mankind reason to ask how much longer we can go on assuming that what can be done has to be done or should be, without uncovering the ethical principles we mean to abide by. These questions are now completely in the public forum, no longer the province of scientific experts alone.

The day is past when one could write a manual on medical ethics. Such books by Roman Catholic moralists are not to be criticized for being deductive. They were not; rather they were commendable attempts to deal with concrete cases. These manuals were written with the conviction that moral reasoning can encompass hard cases, that ethical deliberation need not remain highfalutin but can "subsume" concrete situations under the illuminating power of human moral reason. However, the manuals can be criticized for seeking finally to "resolve" innumerable cases and to give the once-and-for-all "solution" to them. This attempt left the impression that a rule book could be written for medical practice. In a sense, this impression was the consequence of a chief virtue of the authors, i.e., that they were resolved to think through a problem, if possible, *to the end* and precisely with relevance and applicability in concrete cases. Past medical moralists can still be profitably read by anyone who wishes to face the challenge of how he would go about prolonging ethical reflection into action.

Medical ethics today must, indeed, be "casuistry"; it must deal as competently and exhaustively as possible with the concrete features of actual moral decisions of life and death and medical care. But we can no longer be so confident that "resolution" or "solution" will be forthcoming.

While no one can do ethics in the medical and technological context until someone first does so, anyone can engage in the undertaking. Anyone can do this who is trained in one field of medicine and willing to specialize for a few years in ethical reasoning about these questions. Anyone can who is trained in ethics and willing to learn enough about the technical problems to locate the decisional issues. This is not a personal plea. It is rather a plea that in order to become an ethicist or a moral theologian doctors have only to quit resisting being one. An ethicist is only an ordinary man and a moral theologian is only a religious man endeavoring to push out as far as he can the frontier meaning of the practice of a rational or a charitable justice, endeavoring to draw forth all the actions and abstentions that this justice requires of him in his vocation. I am sure that by now there are a number of physicians who have felt rather frustrated as they patiently tried to explain to me some technical medical circumstance I asked about. At the same time, I can also testify to some degree of frustration as I have at times patiently tried to explain some of the things that need to be asked of the science and methods of ethics. Physicians and moralists must go beyond these positions if we are to find the proper moral warrants and learn how to think through moral dilemmas and resolve disagreements in moral judgment concerning medical care.

To this level of inquiry we are driven today. The ordinary citizen in his daily rounds is bound to have an opinion on medical ethical questions, and physicians are bound to look after the good moral reasons for the decisions they make and lead society to agree to. This, then, is a plea for fundamental dialogue about the urgent moral issues arising in medical practice.

No one can alter the fact that not since Socrates posed the question have we learned how to teach virtue. The quandaries of medical ethics are not unlike that question. Still, we can no longer rely upon the ethical assumptions in our culture to be powerful enough or clear enough to instruct the profession in virtue; therefore the medical profession should no longer believe that the personal integrity of physicians alone is enough; neither can anyone count on values being transmitted without thought.

To take up the questions of medical ethics for probing, to try to enter into the heart of these problems with reasonable and compassionate moral reflection, is to engage in the greatest of joint ventures: the moral becoming of man. This is to see in the prism of medical cases the claims of any man to be honored and respected. So might we enter thoughtfully and actively into the moral history of mankind's fidelity to covenants. In this everyone is engaged.

14

CONSENT AS A CANON OF LOYALTY, WITH SPECIAL REFERENCE TO CHILDREN IN MEDICAL INVESTIGATIONS

This portrayal of free and informed consent as a canon of loyalty in the practice of medicine is analogous to Ramsey's treatment of property rights in *Christian Ethics and the Sit-In*. Consent is a condition of "man's capacity to become joint adventurers" in the common cause of the advancement of medicine, and/or of healing the consenting patient. To use Ramsey's earlier language: since fellow humanity, or the ability really to be *"joint* adventurers,"* is precarious in us, and since there exist pressures that endanger recognition of the difference and otherness of potential partners (for example, the temptation to focus exclusively on future benefits promised by technology and medical research), protection of a patient's or experimental subject's right to consent is essential. As a central feature of current medical practice, and as an instance of "natural justice," informed consent is an external condition of covenant between human creatures. The much greater vulnerability of children, who are unable to consent, to exploitation indicates to Ramsey that no research should be performed on them that is not related to their own medical benefit. (From *The Patient as Person*, pp. 1–13, 14–17, 35–38, 38–40)

When first I had the temerity to undertake some study of ethical issues in medical practice, my resolve was to venture no comment at all—relevant or irrelevant—upon these matters until I informed myself concerning how physicians and medical investigators themselves discuss and analyze the decisions they face. One then finds himself in the midst of a remarkable professional ethics. Actual performance, of course, may often be quite different from the principles endorsed by the profession. However, whether performance falls below the stated principles cannot itself be measured except in terms of these same principles of medical ethics stated and generally agreed to. The first thing to note is, therefore, that there is no profession that comes close to medicine in its concern to inculcate, transmit, and keep in constant repair its standards governing the conduct of its members.

One need not read very far in medical ethics—and especially not in the literature concerning medical experimentation or the ethical "codes" that have been formulated since the medical cases at the Nuremberg trials—without realizing that medical ethics has not its sole basis in the overall benefits to be produced. It is not a consequence ethics alone. It is not solely a teleological ethics, to use the language of philosophy. It is not even an ethics of the "greatest possible medical benefits for the greatest possible number" of people. That calculus too easily comes to mean the "greatest possible medical benefits regardless of the number" of patients who without their proper consent may be made the subjects of promising medical investigations. Medical ethics is not solely a benefit-producing ethics even in regard to the individual patient, since he should not always be helped without his will.

As stated in the *Ethical Guidelines for Organ Transplantation* of the American Medical Association,[1] so also of medical experimentation involving human subjects: "Man participates in these procedures: he is the patient in them; or he performs them. All mankind is the ultimate beneficiary of them." Observe that the respect in which man is the patient and man the performer of medical care or medical investigation (the relation between doctor and patient/subject) places an independent moral limit upon the fashion in which the rest of mankind can be made the ultimate beneficiary of these procedures. In the language of philosophy, a deontological dimension or test holds chief place in medical ethics, beside teleological considerations. That is to say, there must be a determination of the rightness or wrongness of the action and not only of the good to be obtained in medical care or from medical investigation.

A crucial element in answer to the question, What constitutes right action in medical practice? is the requirement of a reasonably free and adequately informed consent. In current medical ethics, this is a chief *canon of loyalty* (as I shall call it) between the man who is patient/subject and the man who performs medical investigational procedures. Physicians discuss the consent requirement just as ethi-

1. Report of the Judicial Council, E. G. Shelley, M. D., Chairman, and approved by the House of Delegates of the American Medical Association, June 1968.

cists discuss fairness or justice claims: these tests must be satisfied along with the benefits (the "good") obtained.

ETHICS IN THE CONSENT SITUATION

A theologian or moralist, of course, is not the one to say anything about "ethics in the consent situation." He cannot tell us what the principle of an informed consent requires in actual application. This physicians and investigators and boards of their peers must do. That is to say, the practical applications of the requirement of an informed consent is always the work of prudence, which means not caution but practical wisdom in the appraisal of cases and specific situations. This is rightly the matter that is under discussion in the literature of medical ethics and in consultations among physicians and investigators themselves.

It is possible to parody the consent requirement by simply writing out all the details and the possible consequences that would have to be mentioned in order for a patient to be fully informed. If that is the meaning of informed consent, then major operations that are quite ordinary might get few takers, or be performed only upon patients who are frightened to death. Likewise, it is possible to analyze the motivations of normal volunteers so as to cast total doubt upon the freedom of their choice. But then one casts doubt as well upon most human decisions, such as the decision to become a physician or a minister.[2] But a choice may be free and responsible despite the fact that it began in emotional bias one way rather than another, and consent can be informed without being encyclopedic.

For this reason I referred a moment ago to "a reasonably free and adequately informed consent." It is the meaning of this that is chiefly under discussion when physicians and investigators talk about the consent requirement. They are trying to compose their prudence in aptly applying the principle or developing a common aptitude for extending the principle of consent to new sorts of cases or for making a concrete application of it in a given case. A theologian or moralist

2. "Studies have revealed that physicians are afraid of death in greater proportion than control groups of patients. This is a fascinating statistic, and, if true, it is likely to reflect the doctor's perturbation and confusion in a situation reputed to be natural" (Charles D. Aring, "Intimations of Mortality: An Appreciation of Death and Dying," *Annals of Internal Medicine* 69 [July 1968]: 139). See *Death and Dying: Attitudes of Patient and Doctor* (New York: Group for the Advancement of Psychiatry, 1965), vol. 5, Symposium 11, pp. 591–667. What similar studies, or Rorschach inkblot tests, would show about theologians or ministers, I do not know.

can as such have only some opinions about that. It is not the task of moralists to give an account of ethics in the consent situation, although they may pertinently comment upon the ethics of consent itself, as I propose to do in this chapter.

I will observe concerning applications of the consent requirement only that physicians and investigators lean on a slender reed if they suppose that "situation ethics" correctly describes how principles apply in medical practice.[3] Situation ethics proposes that our moral reasoning and practice should be based on a readiness to violate some moral requirement or to set it aside in the face of wholly unique situations that call for exceptions to be made. To the contrary, unless I have totally misunderstood the literature dealing with medical experimentation, the practical question is always about the *meaning* of the consent requirement in concrete cases of its application. About this a moralist knows nothing unless he happens also to be a physician-investigator, or has at least acquired considerable specific knowledge of all that is at stake in the case or the sort of cases in question. However, a moralist may presume to draw attention to the fact that the discussion in medical ethics is always about the meaning of the consent requirement in practical application. It is not about supposed reasons for violating or setting this principle aside, or about the justification of quantity-of-benefit "exceptions" to this requirement (which would *maxim*-ize the principle or reduce it to a mere guideline). Where the ethics of the medical profession no longer speaks of *codes*, it speaks instead of *principles*—whose meaning in

3. An example of this misconception is the excellent article by Delford L. Stickel "Ethical and Moral Aspects of Transplantation," *Monographs in the Surgical Sciences* 3/4 (1966): 267–301. Situation ethics is assumed as the framework or the approach to be taken to all medical ethical questions. This theory is set forth at some length. Yet in the substance of the ethics and the norms applied we find the following: (1) "In the care of a patient who is a prospective cadaveric donor, treatment which is solely for the purpose of obtaining a healthy graft ought not to be undertaken" (p. 289); (2) "The principle that consent by parent, guardian, or court on behalf of a minor is not valid except for procedures which benefit the minor" was left intact by the ruling in the identical-twin kidney transplant cases, which the author endorses (pp. 284–85); (3) A quotation—with evident approval—from Pope Pius XII: "I think an overwhelming majority of physician-experimenters, if not thoroughly aware of the nature of the original patient-physician relationship, are so deeply rooted in the democratic spirit that they agree and will continue to agree, that the use of force is not justified on a single person, even if millions of other lives could be saved by such an act. They realize that the act would not just save millions of lives but that, as an amoral act from the standpoint of democratic brotherhood, it might create millions of amoral sequels, and that the moral history of mankind is more important than the scientific" (Stickel, p. 274: *Acta Apostolicae Sedis* 44 [1952]: 779).

application is under constant review. The applications are for the doctor or the investigator and their peers to determine, while the principles accord with the ethics of a wider human community.

THE ETHICS OF CONSENT

Hopefully while not exceeding an ethicist's putative competence or trespassing upon the competence of medical men, I wish to undertake an analysis of the consent requirement itself. The principle of an informed consent is a statement of the fidelity between the man who performs medical procedures and the man on whom they are performed. Other aspects of medical ethics—for example, the requirement of a good experimental design and of professional skill at least as good as is customary in ordinary medical practice—treat the man as a purely passive subject or patient. These are also the requirements that hold for an ethical experiment upon animals. But any human being is more than a patient or experimental subject; he is a *personal* subject—every bit as much a man as the physician-investigator. Fidelity is between man and man in these procedures. Consent expresses or establishes this relationship, and the requirement of consent sustains it. Fidelity is the bond between consenting man and consenting man in these procedures. The principle of an informed consent is the cardinal *canon of loyalty* joining men together in medical practice and investigation. In this requirement, faithfulness among men—the faithfulness that is normative for all the covenants or moral bonds of life with life—gains specification for the primary relations peculiar to medical practice.

Consent as a canon of loyalty can best be exhibited by a paraphrase of Reinhold Niebuhr's celebrated defense of democracy on both positive and negative grounds: "Man's capacity for justice makes democracy possible; man's propensity to injustice makes democracy necessary."[4] Man's capacity to become joint adventurers in a common cause makes the consensual relation possible; man's propensity to overreach his joint adventurer even in a good cause makes consent necessary. In medical experimentation the common cause of the consensual relation is the advancement of medicine and benefit to others. In therapy and in diagnostic or therapeutic investigations, the common cause is some benefit to the patient himself; but this is still

4. *The Children of Light and the Children of Darkness* (New York: Scribner's, 1949), p. xi.

a joint venture in which patient and physician can say and ideally should both say, "I cure."

Therefore, I suggest that men's capacity to become joint adventurers in a common cause makes possible a consent to enter the relation of patient to physician or of subject to investigator. This means that *partnership* is a better term than *contract* in conceptualizing the relation between patient and physician or between subject and investigator. The fact that these pairs of people are joint adventurers is evident from the fact that consent is a continuing and a repeatable requirement. We can legitimately appeal to permissions presumably granted by or implied in the original contract only to the extent that these are not incompatible with the demands of an ongoing partnership sustained by an actual or implied *present* consent and terminable by any present or future dissent from it. For this to be at all a human enterprise—a covenantal relation between the man who performs these procedures and the man who is patient in them—the latter must make a reasonably free and an adequately informed consent. Ideally, he must be constantly engaged in doing so. This is basic to the cooperative enterprise in which he is one partner.[5]

5. Cf. "The conduct of the consent situation is decisive for the patient's or volunteer's sense of being respected as a person. . . ." "What is permanent in the consent situation is the encounter between selves when the limits of one self touch the limits of another." "The principle of *mutuality between persons,* or 'perceived effective decision making,' is the relevant ethical principle for the consent situation." In that case, there simply *are* human rights and dignity which "cut across the general social principle of least suffering" and place limits upon the ethics of medical science's mission. We must "draw the line of ethical seriousness across the activities in medical research . . . at the question of consent," even if not *only* there (John Fletcher, "Human Experimentation: Ethics in the Consent Situation," Symposium on Medical Progress and the Law, *Law and Contemporary Problems,* Autumn 1967: 632, 633, 646, 639, 632).

Thus, treating the experimental subject "as an end also" (Kant), perceived effective partnership and mutuality between the persons involved in research is the essential moral meaning of the consent requirement. This was marvelously confirmed by Renée C. Fox's *Experiment Perilous* (Glencoe, Ill.: Free Press, 1959), a sociological study of the roles and stresses of doctors and patient-subjects investigating Addison's disease, the effects of total adrenalectomy, etc. The group "dealt with patients as if they were professional equals"; they treated their patients as "personal associates and professional colleagues," correcting in part the patients' "sense of having lost the right to be active, independent and self-determining as they were in their days of health"; most of the patients felt that "the 'concern for the welfare of others' that characterized their ward made it morally superior in some ways to the 'world of wellness' from which they had been removed" (pp. 85, 105, 123, 141). This was as it should be in a joint venture among men; and then, upon this foundation, the researchers could afford to draw the line of moral seriousness elsewhere: they were most concerned about whether the good consequences for others that might come from the experimental treatments and operations they performed were worth the hazards accepted by these patients.

At the same time, just as Lincoln said concerning political covenants among men that "no man is good enough to govern another without his consent," so there is also this same negative warrant for the requirement of consent in the relation between those who perform and those who are the patients in medical procedures. No man is good enough to experiment upon another without his consent. The same can be said of the doctor-patient relation having treatment in view. No man is good enough to cure another without his consent. This holds without exception for ordinary medical practice. This is the negative premise of the contract between physician and patient, even if it serves mainly to direct us to the positive pole, to the need for a patient's partnership in his own cure.

In medical treatments, however, there is one clearly definable exception from the requirement of expressed consent, which does not weaken the general rule governing medical practice by consent alone. This is the sort or class of cases in which consent may properly be assumed or implied when men are in extreme danger and cannot themselves consent explicitly. When a physician stops on the highway to bind up the wounds of accident victims, he is not liable to suit for malpractice (where "Good Samaritan" laws are in force) on the grounds that an unconscious man "constructively" consented to procedures from which he suffered harm. The law rightly protects the doctor in such errands of mercy. Indeed we might say that if a doctor stops on the road to Jericho, instead of passing by on his way to read a research paper before a scientific gathering or to visit his regular paying customers, he is self-selected as good enough to practice medicine without the needy man's expressed consent.

In general, however, I suggest that man's propensity to overreach a joint adventurer even in a good cause makes consent necessary. This has to be said even if it is also true that this requirement is no substitute for—and indeed there can be no substitute for—the wisdom and moral integrity of the medical practitioner. That integrity still needs to be sustained in its setting in a system of medical "checks and balances" anchored in the requirement of consent.

The foregoing paragraphs describe the basis of the requirement that experimentation involving human subjects should be undertaken only when an informed consent has been secured. There are enormous problems, of course, in knowing how to subsume cases under this moral regulation expressive of respect for the man who is the subject in medical investigations no less than in applying this same moral regulation expressive of the meaning of medical care.

What is and what is not a mature and informed consent is a preciously subtle thing to determine. Then there are questions about how to apply this rule arising from those sorts of medical research in which the patient's knowing enough to give an informed consent may alter the findings sought; and there is debate about whether using prisoners or medical students in medical experimentation, or paying the participants, would not put them under too much duress for them to be said to consent freely even if fully informed. Despite these ambiguities, however, to obtain an understanding consent is a minimum obligation of a common enterprise and in a practice in which men are committed to men in definable respects. The *faithfulness* claims which every man, simply by being a man, places upon the researcher are the morally relevant considerations.[6] This is the ground of the consent rule in medical practice, though obviously medical practice has also its consequence-features.

Indeed, precisely because there are unknown future benefits and precisely because the results of the experimentation may be believed to be so important as to be overriding, this rule governing medical experimentation upon human beings is needed to ensure that for the sake of those consequences no man shall be degraded and treated as a thing or as an animal in order that good may come of it. In this age of research medicine it is not only that medical benefits are attained by research but also that a man rises to the top in medicine by the success and significance of his research. The likelihood that a researcher would make a mistake in departing from a generally valuable rule of medical practice because he is biased toward the research benefits of permitting an "exception" is exceedingly great. In such a seriously important moral matter, this should be enough to rebut a policy of being open to future possible exceptions to this canon of medical ethics. On grounds of the faithfulness claims alone, we must surely say that future experience will provide no morally significant exception to the requirement of an informed consent—although doubtless we may learn a great deal more about the meaning of this particular canon of loyalty, and how to apply it in new situations with greater sensitivity and refinement—or we may learn more and more how to practice violations of it.

6. Sir Harold Himsworth said (1953) that the spirit of the Hippocratic Oath can be given in a single sentence: Act always so as to increase trust (quoted by Ross G. Mitchell, "The Child and Experimental Medicine," *British Medical Journal* 4/1 (March 21, 1964]: 726]. This might better read: Act always so as not to abuse trust; act always so as to exhibit faithfulness, to deserve and inspire trust.

Doubtless medical men will always be learning more and more about the specific meaning which the requirement of an informed consent has in practice. Or they could learn more and more how to violate or avoid this requirement. But they are not likely to learn that it more and more does not govern the ethical practice of medicine. It is, of course, impossible to demonstrate that there could be *no* exceptions to this requirement. But with regard to unforeseeable future possibilities or apparently unique situations that medicine may face, there is this rule-assuring, principle-strengthening, and practice-upholding rule to be added to the requirement of an informed consent. *In the grave moral matters of life and death, of maiming or curing, of the violation of persons or their bodily integrity, a physician or experimenter is more liable to make an error in moral judgment if he adopts a policy of holding himself open to the possibility that there may be significant, future permissions to ignore the principle of consent than he is if he holds this requirement of an informed consent always relevant and applicable.* If so, he ought as a practical matter to regard the consent principle as closed to further morally significant alteration or exception. In this way he braces himself to respect the personal subject while he treats him as patient or tries procedures on him as an experimental subject for the good of mankind.

The researcher knows that his judgment will generally be biased by the fact that he strongly desires one of the consequences (the rapid completion of his research for the good of mankind) which he could hope to attain by breaking or avoiding the requirement of an informed consent. This, too, should strengthen adherence in practice to the principle of consent. If every doer loves his deed more than it ought to be loved, so every researcher his research—and, of course, its promise of future benefits for mankind. The investigator should strive, as Aristotle suggested, to hit the mean of moral virtue or excellence by "leaning against" the excess or the defect to which he knows himself, individually or professionally, and mankind generally in a scientific age, to be especially inclined. To assume otherwise would be to assume an equally serene rationality on the part of men in all moral matters. It would be to assume that a man is as able to sustain good moral judgment and to make a proper choice with a strong interest in results obtainable by violating the requirement of an informed consent as he would be if he had no such interest.

Thus the principle of consent is a canon of loyalty expressive of the faithfulness claims of persons in medical care and investigation. Let us grant that we cannot theoretically rule out the possibility that there can be exceptions to this requirement in the future. This, at least, is conceivable in extreme examples. It is not logically impossible. Still, this is a rule of the highest human loyalty that ought not in practice to be held open to significant future revision. To say this concerning the there and then of some future moral judgment would mean here and now to weaken the protection of coadventurers from violation and self-violation in the common cause of medical care and the advancement of medical science. The material and spiritual pressures upon investigators in this age of research medicine, the collective bias in the direction of successful research, the propensities of the scientific mind toward the consequences alone, are all good reasons—even if they are not all good moral reasons—for strengthening the requirement of an informed consent. This helps to protect coadventurers in the cause of medicine from harm and from harmfulness. This is the edification to be found in the thought that man's propensity to overreach a joint adventurer even in a good cause makes consent necessary.

This negative aspect of the ethics of medical research is essential even if only because the constraints of the consent requirement serve constantly to drive our minds back to the positive meaning or warrant for this principle in the man who is the patient and the man who performs these procedures. An informed consent alone exhibits and establishes medical practice and investigation as a voluntary association of free men in a common cause. The negative constraint of the consent requirement serves its positive meaning. It directs our attention always upon the man who is the patient in all medical procedures and a partner in all investigations, and away from that celebrated "nonpatient," the future of medical science. Thus consent lies at the heart of medical care as a joint adventure between patient and doctor. It lies at the heart of man's continuing search for cures to all man's diseases as a great human adventure that is carried forward jointly by the investigator and his subjects. Stripped of the requirement of a reasonably free and an adequately informed consent, experimentation and medicine itself would speedily become inhumane.

No one today would propose to eliminate the consent requirement directly, but this can be done more subtly, or by indirection. Even while retaining it, the consent requirement can be effectively annulled, or transformed into a disappearing, powerless guideline, simply by writing into it a "quantity-of-benefits-to-come" exception clause. Thus we could make ourselves ready to override or avoid the consent requirement in view of future good to be achieved. To do this is to make ourselves conditionally willing to use a subject in medical investigations as a mere means.

RESEARCH INVOLVING CHILDREN
OR INCOMPETENTS

From consent as a canon of loyalty in medical practice it follows that children, who cannot give a mature and informed consent, or adult incompetents, should not be made the subjects of medical experimentation unless, other remedies having failed to relieve their grave illness, it is reasonable to believe that the administration of a drug as yet untested or insufficiently tested on human beings, or the performance of an untried operation, may further *the patient's own recovery*.

Now that is not a very elaborate moral rule governing medical practice in the matter of experiments involving children or incompetents as human subjects. It is a good example of the general claims of childhood specified for application in medical care and research. It is also a qualification immediately entailed by the meaning of consent in medical investigations as a joint undertaking between men. Again, one has to be prudent (which does not mean overcautious or scrupulous) in order to know how to care for child-patients in this way. One must know the possible relation of a proposed procedure to the child's own recovery, and also its likely effectiveness compared with other methods that have been or could be tried. These considerations may provide the doctor with necessary and sufficient reason for investigations upon children, perhaps even very hazardous ones. One has to proportion the peril to the diagnostic or therapeutic needs of the child.

Practical medical judgment has undeniable and ominous room for its determinations, since a "benefit" is whatever is *believed* to be of help to the child. Still, the limits this rule imposes on practice are essentially clear: where there is no possible relation to the child's recovery, a child is not to be made a mere object in medical experimentation for the sake of good to come. The likelihood of benefits that could flow from the experiment for many other children is an equally insufficient warrant for child experimentation. The individual child is to be tended in illness or in dying, since he himself is not able to donate his illness or his dying to be studied and worked upon solely for the advancement of medicine. Again, future experience may tell us more about the meaning of this particular rule expressive of loyalty to a human child, and we may learn a great deal more about how to apply it in new situations with grater sensitivity and refinement—or we may learn more and more how to practice violations of it. But we are committed to refraining from morally significant exceptions to this rule defining impermissible medical experimentation upon children.

To experiment on children in ways that are not related to them as patient is already a sanitized form of barbarism; it already removes them from view and pays no attention to the faithfulness claims which a child, simply by being a normal or a sick or dying child, places upon us and upon medical care. We should expect no morally significant exceptions to this canon of faithfulness to the child. To expect future justifiable exceptions is, in some sense, already to have forgotten the child. . . .

To attempt to consent for a child to be made an experimental subject is to treat a child as not a child. It is to treat him as if he were an adult person who has consented to become a joint adventurer in the common cause of medical research. If the grounds for this are alleged to be the presumptive or implied consent of the child, that must simply be characterized as a violent and a false presumption.[7] Nontherapeutic, nondiagnostic experimentation involving human subjects must be based on true consent if it is to proceed as a human enterprise. No child or adult incompetent can choose to become a participating member of medical undertakings, and no one else on earth should decide to subject these people to investigations having no relation to their own treatment. That is a canon of loyalty to them. This they claim of us simply by being a human child or incompetent. When he is grown, the child may put away childish things and become a true volunteer. This is the meaning of being a volunteer: that a man enter and establish a consensual relation in some joint venture for medical progress—where before he could not, nor could anyone else, "volunteer" him for submission to unknown possible hazards for the sake of good to come.

If the requirement of parents, investigators, and state authorities

7. To base "Good Samaritan" medical care upon the implied consent of automobile accident victims is quite a different matter. A well child, or a child suffering from an unrelated disease not being investigated, is not to be compared to an unconscious patient needing specific treatment. To imply the latter's "constructive" consent is not a violent presumption, it is a life-saving presumption, though it is in some degree "false."

in regard to their wards is "Never subject children to the unknown possible hazards of medical investigations having no relation to their own treatment," we must understand that the maladies for which the individual needs treatment and protection need not already be resident within the compass of the child's own skin. He can properly be regarded as one of a population, and we can add to the foregoing words: "except in epidemic conditions." Dr. Salk tried his polio vaccine on himself and his own children first. Then it was tested on selected children within a normal population. This involved some risk for the children vaccinated, and for other children as well, that the disease *might* be contracted from the vaccine itself, or that there might be unexpected injurious results. But the normal population of children was already subjected to waves of crippling epidemic summer after summer. A parent consenting that his child be used in this trial was balancing the risks from the trial against the hazards from polio itself for that same child.

Physician-investigators are often in a quandary in which they are torn between the warrants for giving an experimental drug, and the warrants for withholding it from anyone in order to test it. Neither act seems justified, or both acts are equally warranted, when there is no available remedy and the indications are that a new drug may succeed. This situation also justifies a parent or guardian in consenting for a child, since we are supposing the hazard of the proposed treatment to be less or no greater than the hazard of the disease itself when treated by the established procedures. That would be a medical trial having clear relation to the treatment or protection of the child himself. He is not made, without his consent, the subject of medical investigations of possible benefit only to other children, other patients, or for the future advancement of medical science.

These may have been the circumstances surrounding the field trial of the vaccine for rubella (German measles) made in Taiwan, if this was in epidemic conditions, or in expectation of epidemic conditions, early in 1968 by a medical team from the University of Washington, headed by Dr. Thomas Grayston.[8] The vaccine was given to 3,269 grade-school boys in the cities of Taipei and Taichung, while roughly an equal number were left unvaccinated for comparison purposes. The latter group were given Salk polio vaccine so that they would derive some benefit from the experience to which they were subjected. This generous "payment" does not alter the moral di-

8. *New York Times*, Oct. 17, 1968.

lemma of withholding the rubella vaccine from a selected group. Yet there may have been an equipoise between the hazards of contracting rubella or other damage from the vaccine and the hazards of contracting if it not vaccinated. There could have been a likelihood favoring the vaccinated of the two comparison groups.

These considerations, we may suppose, produced the quandary in the conscience of the investigators that was partially relieved by giving the unrelated Salk vaccine to the control group. Such equipoise alone would warrant—and it would sufficiently warrant—a parent or guardian in consenting that his child or ward be used for these research purposes. In the face of actual or predictable epidemic conditions, this would be medical investigation having some measurable or immeasurable relation to a child's own treatment or protection, as surely as the catheterization of the heart of a child with congenital heart trouble may be needed in his own diagnosis and treatment; and to this type of treatment a parent may venture to consent in his child's behalf. If no gulf is to be fixed between maladies beneath the skin and diseases afflicting children as members of a population, then the consent requirement means: "Never submit children to medical investigation not related to their own treatment, except in face of epidemic conditions endangering also each individual child." This is simply the meaning of the consent requirement in application, not a "quantity-of-benefit-to-come" exception clause or a violation of this canon of loyalty to child-patients.

Indeed, a stricter construction of the necessary connection between proxy consent and the foreseeable needs of the child would permit the use of only girl children in field trials of rubella vaccine. Rubella is not the most contagious type of measles. The benefit to the subjects used in these trials (which, in addition to the consent of parents, legitimated subjecting them to experiment) was mainly to prevent their giving birth to children with congenital malformations should they later contract rubella during pregnancy. Therefore, there was stronger argument for considering only girl children as part of a population in establishing the necessary connection between experiment and "treatment."

More questionable were the earlier trials of the rubella vaccine performed upon the inmates of a retarded children's home in Conway, Arkansas. These subjects were not specially endangered by an epidemic of rubella. Few of the girls among them will ever be able to become part of the population of childbearing women, or be in danger of pregnancy while in institutions. Using them simply had the advantage that they were segregated from the rest of the population, and any degree of risk to them would not spread to other people, including women of childbearing age.

If children are incapable of truly consenting to experiments having unknown hazards for the sake of good to come, and if no one else should consent for them in cases unrelated to their own treatment, then medical research and society in general must choose a perhaps more difficult course of action to gain the benefits we seek from medical investigations. Surely it was possible to secure normal adult volunteers to consent to segregate themselves from the rest of the population for the duration of a rubella trial.[9] That method was simply more costly and inconvenient. At the same time, this illustrates the general fact that if we as a society are to proceed to the conquest of diseases, indeed, if we are to teach medical skills with fairness and justice to the poor and the ward patients, and with no violation of the basic claims of childhood, then there must be far greater encouragement generally in our society of a willingness to engage as joint adventurers for medical progress than has been achieved, or believed morally required by the principle of consent, in the past. . . .

The use of children in research by proxy consent is a prismatic case in which to see clearly the meaning of the consent requirement. In the case of the moral claims of the child upon us we can see clearly the claims of any fellow man not to be treated as a means only. The moral issue here does not actually depend on age, but on whether anyone should be made the property of another and disposition be made of him, without his will, that is not also in his behalf medically. We would not permit an older parent to consent for his son who is a grown man. This is not only because the son's consent can be consulted. It is primarily because no man is the property of another or should be made merely menial. Where the grown son cannot consent because of physical or mental disability, his parent or other relative can validly consent in his behalf if this is in his behalf medically. His welfare is then also the end in view; he is not made into an experimental means only. So also in the case of the small child.

What is at stake here is the covenantal obligations of parents to children—the protection with which a child should be surrounded,

9. The New York Times (April 5, 1969) reported that a hundred monks and nuns, from both Anglican and Roman Catholic orders, living in enclosed communities, were the voluntary subjects in testing American, British, and Belgian vaccines against German measles. This project was organized and directed by Dr. J. A. Dudgeon of London's Great Ormond Street Hospital for Sick Children.

and the meaning and duties of parenthood. In veterinary medicine, "the vet's 'patient' is an animal; but his client is the animal's owner." This means that "the operative decision lies with its owner."[10] Are we allowed to believe that an analogous situation pertains in the triadic relation of parent-child-researcher? that the parent is the physician's client? that the operative decision is the parent's consent, in effect directing the disposition of the child to ends not in his behalf? To the contrary, the doctor cannot in respect to his small patient become the agent of another person. His is a covenant with that patient, and faithfulness to him should be controlling. If perfunctory consents on hospital forms are often a kind of placebo to the experimenter's conscience, parental or guardian consent is a powerful placebo disguising the fact that these interlocking covenants among men—parent-child-physician/researcher—are on their way to being reduced to client/owner-child/object-researcher.

The issue here is the wrong of making a human being an "object" and using him in trials not in his behalf as a subject. "In some situations," it has been said, "such as with infants or with institutionalized lower-functioning retardates, there may be very little for which a researcher can ask in a request for consent because whatever a subject ordinarily has to give has never been possessed, or has already been given—or taken. . . . Unpleasant as it sounds and is, the one thing that such a person usually still has that a researcher may want is part of his bodily functioning."[11] In situations in which a part of a body's functioning is all a researcher wants, whom is he to ask? He cannot ask the small patient who has never possessed powers of consent which subjects ordinarily have to give. He cannot ask the retardate. He cannot ask those human beings who because of life's misfortunes have had taken from them that something else which normal subjects give in giving themselves along with their bodily functioning to the joint venture of research. If the researcher asks very little, still he asks too much when his exploration of a part of bodily function taken or conveyed to him by third-party consent is not medically in behalf of the patient-subject. True, the small patient or retardate cannot enter into the covenant making for medical progress as a human enterprise. However, this does not excuse parents,

10. "Decisions about Life and Death: A Problem in Modern Medicine," Church of England study pamphlet (Church Information Office, Church House, Westminister WC1, London), p. 20.

11. Wolf Wolfensberger, "Ethical Issues in Research with Human Subjects," Science 155 (Jan. 6, 1967): 48, 49.

guardians, or researchers. They can still keep covenant with the child and with the individual retardate.

Anglo-American law and the ethical substance in the law as an ordering of human reality seem very clear on this point. We should bring this briefly into view. There are two different, related aspects: harmful invasions of the body (which upon expert testimony and unless informed consent to the risk can be shown may legally be judged medical negligence) and unconsented "touching" (which are still assaults even if no harm is done).[12] In the first, the dignity or degradation of the fortress of the body is at issue; in the second merely freedom from coercion (or from a harmless offense) to the will of another person. In the second case, one wrongs another human being by doing something to him without his consent; in the first case, one wrongs him by doing something that was negligently harmful. It would seem that children could be removed from the human community and deprived of the protections of the law in both respects by medical investigations upon them. They could be placed at risk of physical harm; or, with no discernible risk, they could be offensively "touched" without risk of or actual harm—unless there is a consent that can validly enter them into medical experiments. They could be *harmfully* used, or they could simply be *used* with no harm. In fact, principles in our legal tradition generally protect children both from the degradation of the body's fortress and from being treated as a means only, and not also as an end, even when no harm is expected or can be discerned in the result. . . .

Of course, no one would have us revert to the eighteenth century, when Caroline, princess of Wales, "begged the lives" of six condemned criminals for experimental smallpox vaccination, and also procured for an additional trial "half a dozen of the charity children belonging to St. James' parish." Ours is the more subtle problem of the *use* of children in research, in which the risks are minimal or "negligible," but still not in their behalf medically. It is hard to see how this can be an expression of parental care (or of the state's care *in loco parentis*), or anything other than a violation of the nature and meaning of the responsibilities of parenthood as a covenant among the generations of men.

Dr. Henry K. Beecher stated our ethical quandary when he wrote

12. See Marcus L. Plante, "An Analysis of 'Informed Consent,'" *Fordham Law Review* 36/4 (May 1968): 639–72.

that "one can fairly raise the question as to whether those responsible for children or the mentally deficient have the right to consent to something they themselves will not experience." Dr. Beecher's own view is that research upon children may be justified when "no discernible risk" is involved.[13] One can fairly raise the question how there can be no risk or no discernible risk in an experiment. When no risk is discerned, one can still fairly raise the question whether we do not always know there to be unknown or undiscerned risks if the procedure is neither proved nor redundant. The care called for by the small patient would seem to be analogous to the ethical relation protected by our law on "offensive touching" mentioned above. "What is involved" here "is the right of each of us to determine for ourselves not alone the extent to which we will share ourselves with others, but the timing and the nature of any such sharing."[14] Since "offensive touching" or "unconsented touching" is ground for legal action for assault and battery even though there has been no damage, it seems clear that *no consent* rather than *no risk* or *no discernible risk* is the decisive point at law. Only the legal fiction of parental or other representative consent keeps experiments on children from being judged to be battery even where there is no harm. This surely is the morality of the matter: a subject can be wronged without being harmed.

The room left for ethical discretion to make situational decisions in conducting beneficial research with children comes under the determination of what is a "benefit," weighing the nearness or remoteness of possible benefits, and telling when a minor is no longer a child but is able to give an understanding consent to a particular trial for

13. "Medical Research and the Individual," in Daniel H. Labby, ed., *Life or Death: Ethics and Options* (Seattle: Univ. of Washington Press, 1968), p. 127; "Scarce Resources and Medical Advancement: Ethical Aspects of Experimentation with Human Subjects," *Daedalus*, Spring 1969: 285. In addition to the test of "no discernible risk," however, Dr. Beecher also appeals to the fact that "such work [e.g., studies of inborn errors of metabolism] is *potentially*, and sometimes unexpectedly, of direct benefit to the given subject." This, I allow, is a good reason for a seriously ill child to be subjected to experimental trial. Cf. also William J. Curran and Henry K. Beecher, "Experimentation in Children," *Journal of the American Medical Association* 210 (1969): 77–83; and Henry K. Beecher, *Research and the Individual: Human Studies* (Boston: Little, Brown, 1970), pp. 63–64.

14. Oscar M. Ruebhausen, "Experiments with Human Subjects," paper presented at the annual meeting of the American Association for the Advancement of Science in New York City, Dec. 23, 1967; *Record of the New York Bar Association* 23 (February 1968): 93.

the sake of the good of others to come. These uncertainties afford, as we have seen, such latitude that no man can relieve another of his premonitions of guilt to come whatever he decides, or lessen the stress on conscience in the situation of proxy consent to diagnostic or therapeutic investigation upon a child-life.

When one fondles or plays with an infant, he "speaks" to that child as one having individual worth; still the child may be hurt. When parents make decisions concerning a child's development or values to be imparted, and when they consent for him to undergo medical care, they have no guarantee that the benefits they seek will be forthcoming, or even that these are truly beneficial. Pediatric psychological investigations, it is often said, are always also beneficial— because the researcher gives the child more attention than the child ordinarily receives. Still, one may doubt whether more attention is always beneficial, even though a normal child has a marvelous ability to control his responses and to protect himself from "offensive observations," or he may enter freely into the game. (An anencephalitic baby discloses its impotency for further human development by the fact that it has no control of its response to environmental stimuli; such a baby has not the beginnings of the human capacity within the fortress of the body to determine the time and the nature of its sharing of himself with others). Since, however, for the foregoing argument, a benefit is whatever is *believed* to be a benefit, many eventualities are compatible with acting on the principle that we owe the individual child the highest fiduciary loyalty we know how to perform. Basically contradictory to this it would be to consent to submit a child to procedures believed not to be in the child's behalf. Parenthood was not made for this.

15

ON (ONLY) CARING FOR THE DYING

In *The Patient as Person*, Ramsey attempts to display the common ground between physicians, who are members of an ongoing tradition of medical practice, and dying patients, whose uttermost need is the comfort of a faithful human presence. Medicine's work is not exhausted when curative measures no longer offer a reasonable hope of success; nor is medicine's curative work inexhaustible, overwhelming human need by the unceasing effort to maintain life, whatever the cost. A caring response that will not abandon the patient either *through* direct killing or *to* life-prolonging technology best embodies the meaning of love of neighbor. (From *The Patient as Person*, pp. 118–36, 144–57)

ORDINARY AND EXTRAORDINARY MEANS

In any proper discussion of the physician's duty to heal and to save life, there are three interrelated distinctions that must be taken into account. These are the distinctions (1) between "ordinary" and "extraordinary" means of saving life; (2) between saving life by prolonging the living of it and only prolonging a patient's dying; and (3) between the direct killing under certain conditions of specifiable sorts of "hopeless cases" (called euthanasia) and merely allowing a patient to die by stopping or not starting life-sustaining procedures deemed not morally mandatory. By making use of all these concepts, the medical ethics developed in Western Christendom set its face resolutely against the direct killing of terminal patients, which it judged to be murder, whatever warrants may be alleged in favor of the practice. At the same time, medical ethics in the centuries before the recent achievements in scientific medicine and technology afforded reasonable grounds for refusing to "war without retreat and without quarter" against almighty God for the last shred of sentient life, worldly value, or physiological existence in the dying man.

It is necessary for us to enter this thicket if we are to gain an adequate comprehension of what is morally required in caring for the dying. This we must do if we are concerned to explore the possible bearing of religious ethics on medical practice.[1]

It is necessary for us to enter the thicket of the several meanings the moralists had in mind for yet another reason. Physicians themselves ponder this question of the care of the dying, and they repeatedly draw a distinction between "ordinary" and "heroic" measures. The generic duty to "save life" which governs medical practice is readied for application in the moral-species terms distinguishing ordinary from extraordinary means. This tells physicians the difference between a mandatory and an elective effort to save life. Therefore, the relativity in the meanings of ordinary and extraordinary procedures is precisely a chief virtue of using this distinction in the practice of medicine. It is not—as often is said—a reason for dismissing the distinction as worthless.[2] This would be the conclusion only from the premise that ethics must deal in absolutes unrelated to practice, or in principles that are inapplicable. Or else dismissal of this distinction is simply a vain effort to eliminate the role of prudence (practical

1. No one can deny the truth of Dr. Henry K. Beecher's observation: "It will be evident that Roman Catholic leaders have examined these questions with great care and have arrived at firm conclusions. It is interesting to observe that their attitudes on most such questions are remarkably similar to the Jewish. Modern Protestant theological considerations are not very helpful in the present quest" (*Research and the Individual: Human Studies* [Boston: Little, Brown, 1970], p. 187). Cf. E. Fuller Torrey's words in the preface to the volume of essays he edited, *Ethical Issues in Medicine: The Role of the Physician in Today's Society* (Boston: Little, Brown, 1968), p. viii: "If the Catholic Church seems to be unduly criticized in some chapters, let it be remembered that the Church has often taken the lead in discussing these issues."

However, to enter the thicket of these distinctions need not mean getting stuck in the brambles. It is necessary to qualify, reform, and extend the analysis of past moralists. At the same time there can be no ethics of medical practice without discourse with all those who have examined these questions of life and death with great care in the past. It is equally certain that theological moralists can make no contribution to medical ethics or shed any light upon its lasting themes by de novo starts and stops.

2. If it is said (Joseph Fletcher, "Elective Death," in Torrey, *Ethical Issues*, p. 149) that "there is no way to establish a consensus (even if desirable) as to the defining features of an extraordinary treatment," the answer is, of course not! There may be meaningful *specifications* of moral rules without *certainty* in the applications of them.

wisdom) in applying moral rules by demanding the certitude of secondary rules for the application of them.

First, we need in preliminary fashion to notice some important differences between the moralist's meaning and the physician's meaning when each uses the terms *ordinary* and *extraordinary*. It is, of course, difficult to generalize, and no doubt there are some doctors who are closer than others to the moralists on the point in question. Still as a general rule—if I have not mistaken the general tenor or emphasis in the medical literature—a doctor's understanding and a moralist's understanding of ordinary and extraordinary means are likely to be different in three important and related respects.

First, the doctor is apt to use the distinction to mean customary as opposed to unusual procedures. Physicians use these terms relative to the state of medical science and the healing art, by reference to whether or not a remedy has become a part of customary medical practice. In contrast, the moralists are somewhat more likely than doctors to use these terms relative to a patient's particular medical condition. While an unusual practice may become customary and the medical imperative change as medicine advances, it is also the case that the medical imperative ought to change according to the patient's condition and its "advances," no matter how usual the remedy may be for other patients or for this patient at other times. The first relativity is to the disease and to what is ordinarily done to remedy it. The second relativity is to the condition of the man who has the disease; these relative meanings lead to a definition of optional remedies in terms of what would be "extraordinary" for this individual.

Apart from what doctors may sometimes or often do in withholding or stopping treatments in particular cases, one observes in medical writings a tendency to define *extraordinary* in terms of "heroic" or unusual efforts. This is not only because doctors may be in danger of malpractice suits if they depart too far from customary medical practice in what they do or omit to do. In general, the doctor's conscience is formed in these terms; his imperative is likely to be to do everything medical science affords as established practice in the saving of life. He will justify refraining from trying some unusual remedy more readily than he can justify stopping or not using a customary procedure. He is likely to feel that the moralist's understanding of "extraordinary" grants him more liberty than either law or a proper medical conscience allow.

Second, for the moralist, a decision to stop "extraordinary" life-sustaining treatments requires moral warrant no greater than and in fact the same as a decision not to begin to use them. Again if I have understood the medical literature, a physician can make the decision not to institute such treatments with an easier conscience than he can make the decision to stop them once begun. "I believe that it is of primary importance," writes Dr. Jørgen Voigt, "not to get unawares into a situation in which it may be necessary to make a decision regarding the continuation of respirator treatment. Before institution of such treatment, as with every form of therapy [such as palliative interventions in inoperatable cancer patients], a decision must be taken as to whether it is *indicated.*"[3] That, of course, is true. But there should be no greater reluctance to judge that continuation of treatments is no longer indicated than to judge that they should not be begun. The moralists would support physicians in this conclusion. Since a trial treatment is often a part of diagnosis of a patient's condition, one might expect there to be greater reluctance on the part of physicians in not starting than in stopping extraordinary efforts to save life. As I understand them, physicians often have the contrary difficulty.

Putting these first two points together in summary, a doctor "is more likely to refrain from giving an antibiotic than he is to direct withholding of nourishment. He is likely to hesitate longest over switching off the machine for artificial respiration. The reasons for these variations in reactions are probably psychological rather than rational."[4]

Of course, there may be no difference between the moralist and the physician on the matter of the weight given to customary medical practice and to individual medical circumstance in defining ordinary (imperative) and elective medical care of the fatally ill, or in the matter of stopping or not starting heroic efforts to save life. If no disagreement is to be found on these two points, one is likely to arise on the third.

Third, moralists almost always understand the distinction be-

3. Jørgen Voigt, "The Criteria of Death, Particularly in Relation to Transplantation Surgery," *World Medical Journal* 14 (1967): 145.

4. "Decisions about Life and Death: A Problem in Modern Medicine," Church of England Study pamphlet (Church Information Office, Church House, Westminster SW1, London, 1965), p. 47. Yet many moralists would press the question, "To what medical lengths is there any obligation to go in order to administer nourishment?" (p. 27). "There would seem to be no valid distinction in principle between these different means, whether they be nourishment, antibiotics or the electric current which operates the apparatus for breathing" (p. 47).

tween ordinary and extraordinary procedures to refer decisively to morally relevant, nonmedical features of a particular patient's care: his "domestic economy," his familial obligations, the neighborhood that has become a part of his human existence, the person and the common good, and whether a man's fiduciary relations with God and with his fellow man have been settled. The difference between an imperative and an elective effort to save life will vary according to evaluations of these features of a human life, and a moralist's terms for expressing this final verdict are *ordinary* and *extraordinary*.

Thus, the standard definition reads as follows: "*Ordinary* means of preserving life are all medicines, treatments, and operations, which offer a reasonable hope of benefit for the patient and which can be obtained and used without excessive expense, pain, or other inconvenience. . . . *Extraordinary* means of preserving life . . . mean all medicines, treatments, and operations, which cannot be obtained without excessive expense, pain, or other inconvenience, or which, if used, would not offer a reasonable hope of benefit."[5] In explanation of the moral judgment that "one may, but need not, use extraordinary means to preserve life," another writer sums up the morally relevant factors that go into determining the meaning of this by saying, "We may define as an extraordinary means whatever here and now is very *costly* or very *unusual* or very *painful* or very *difficult* or very *dangerous*, or if the good effects that can be expected from its use are not proportionate to the difficulty and inconvenience that are entailed."[6] It is evident that theologians mean to counsel first the patient and his family and then the physician that, in deciding concerning an elective effort to save life or elective death, it is quite proper to make a balancing judgment involving decisive reference to a number of human (nonmedical) factors that constituted the worth for which that life was lived and that may discharge it from imperative continuation. Speaking as men who are doctors and in their practice, physicians may also say the same; but it is not strictly a medical judgment to say this. This is certainly not what a physician usually means when he distinguishes between ordinary and extraordinary procedures for saving life.

It may be that medical ethics will approach the position staked out by the theological moralists if its takes seriously the banner un-

5. Gerald Kelly, S. J., *Medico-Moral Problems* (St. Louis: Catholic Hospital Association, 1958), p. 129.

6. Edwin F. Healy, S. J., *Medical Ethics* (Chicago: Loyola Univ. Press, 1956), p. 67.

furled by the World Health Organization's positive definition of *health* as general human *well-being*. An erratic application of this extensive and liberal construction of a medical judgment, however, would not suffice. It would not suffice for the medical profession to invoke the psychosocial well-being of the woman as a justification for abortion while limiting professional judgment to strictly bodily considerations in caring for the hopelessly dying. That broad definition of health will either have to be withdrawn or else be consistently applied. The latter would mean that professional medical judgments assumes responsibility for the full range of human moral considerations. This would be to locate medical considerations in direct lineage with all of man's moral reflection upon the meaning of *eudaimonia* (well-being, happiness) since Aristotle!

This, I rather think, is an alarming suggestion from which the medical profession should draw back in the direction of a stricter construction of medical judgments as such. The oddity is that the medical profession seems to have adopted a comprehensive definition of health precisely in a period in which we are undertaking to conceive that inconceivable thing: a society that itself has no moral philosophy and no common assumptions as to the good or well-being of man which medicine sporadically invokes. Increasingly, the medical profession—if it moves from a strictly medical to a more extensive definition of health—would have to find the sources of its medical ethics not in the culture generally but by developing within its own community a moral ethos representative of mankind's general well-being. In this respect, medical ethics would be not unlike the ethics of church and synagogue. The ethics of no group today floats upon a sea of social ethics or upon a received moral philosophy or an understanding of man's well-being or that of society generally.

This being so, it would seem wise for the medical profession to hesitate before assuming, along with social scientific judgments, also the tasks of an entire moral philosophy under a definition of health as general human well-being. For this reason, in the equal I shall sometimes speak of *the medical imperative*, at other times of *the moral imperative* in dealing with the dying. These, of course, cannot be entirely separated, because the doctor is both a physician and a man. But this does suggest a distinction between the physician qua physician and whatever authority or role he may have as a man in relation to the well-being of the man who is his patient. It suggests a continuing distinction between the medical meaning and the theological-moral or humanistic meaning of imperative and elective procedures for saving life. This would require that the doctor lean against his understanding of the medical imperative in order to keep it optional for his patients; and that, as a man who happens also to be a doctor, he should make room for the primacy of human moral judgments on the part of the men who are his patients, the relatives of his patients, and their spiritual counselors to elect life-sustaining remedies or to elect them not. His may be the task of only caring for the dying for reasons that are not within his special competence to determine.

THE MORALITY OF (ONLY) CARING FOR THE DYING

In discussion of ordinary and extraordinary means it is commonly assumed by physicians and moralists alike that the use of all "ordinary" remedies is morally required of everyone, and that the failure to provide or use ordinary means of preserving life is the equivalent of euthanasia. The crucial question to be asked of traditional medical ethics is whether ordinary, imperative procedures can, in a proper moral judgment, become "extraordinary" and elective only. Can a patient morally refuse ordinary remedies? Can a physician morally fail to supply them or fail to continue ordinary remedies in use?

This is an unavoidable question, and one that goes to the heart of the morality of *caring*, but *only* caring, for the dying. Whoever raises this question lightly, or with a concern to disprove or dismiss past moral reflection, can only deny himself one possible source of helpful insights. Our inquiry shall concern whether and in what sense traditional medical ethical concepts and distinctions should be ethically regulative of present-day medical practice in regard to the fatally ill and the dying. During this brief journey into the meanings of the moralists, our "method" of doing medical ethics will not be to propose *replacing* definitions. Instead, our search will be for an understanding of past moral wisdom, and in this to locate places at which a *reforming* definition of one or another relevant moral concept suggests itself. In this section two such important qualifications or creative lines of development will be brought into focus which are needed to complete an ethics of caring for the dying. Then in the following section, we shall ask whether, understood in terms of these reforming definitions, the ancient distinctions between ordinary and extraordinary (as a way of telling the difference between mandatory and elective efforts to save life) do not in sum reduce to the obligations to determine when a person has begun to undergo irreversibly the process of his own particular dying; and whether with *the process of dying* (all other terms aside) there does not arise the duty only to care for the dying, simply to comfort and company with them, to be present to them. This is the positive object of our search. . . .

A good place to cut into the moralists' analysis of the question whether "ordinary" medical procedures are always imperative is with the publication of two articles by Gerald Kelly, S. J., in *Theological Studies* in 1950 and 1951.[7] Here we can plainly see how far traditional medical morality was willing to go in limiting the active use even of so-called ordinary means of sustaining life. The title of Kelly's 1950 article suggests that he answered the question just raised by distinguishing between "natural" and "artificial" among the ordinary means of preserving life. Closer examination will show that there is more to it than that; and that in fact Kelly has himself already elaborated good reasons for dispensing from ordinary natural no less than from ordinary artificial means of preserving life.

Kelly makes it quite clear that he is willing to remove "ordinary" means under certain circumstances from the class of morally or medically imperative means. Agreeing with those moralists who regard intravenous feeding as in itself an ordinary means (and who *therefore* judged it to be imperative), Kelly says instead that "even granted that it is ordinary one may not immediately conclude that it is obligatory." An ordinary means may be out of place because of the condition of a patient—as out of place as unusual or heroic procedures. In regard to the usual use of a stimulant to prolong life for only a short time, Kelly calls that also an ordinary means. In this instance he gives two reasons for dispensing with the stimulant: "Since it is artificial and since it has practically no remedial value in the circumstances, the patient is not obliged to use it."[8] It is evident, however, that in Kelly's argument the latter reason is far more important than the former. His argument is quite sufficient to make it unnecessary to distinguish between natural and artificial remedies in morally evaluating whether they should be used or not.

The argument revolves around whether the means used are really *remedies* or not. One is excused from using a proposed "remedy" if it does not offer a reasonable hope of success; it is then not a remedy. Kelly is simply intent on establishing that ordinary means may be omitted. His warrant for this is "the fine distinction between omit-

7. Gerald Kelly, S. J., "The Duty of Using Artificial Means of Preserving Life," *Theological Studies* 11 (June 1950): 203–20; "The Duty to Preserve Life," ibid. 12 (December 1951): 550–56.

8. "Using Artificial Means," p. 218.

ting an ordinary means and omitting a useless ordinary means." The uselessness of it is decisive; and it is hard to see why this does not afford us another "fine distinction," namely, that between omitting a natural means and omitting a *useless* natural means—if there is ever any need to invoke this principle in actual practice. In any case, the artificiality of the ordinary means which may be omitted Kelly puts decisively aside. Simply the fact that they are no longer *remedies* or are no longer useful in saving the life of a patient alone warrants the omission of efforts to save life. The means would have to be means-full—of use to a human life. There is no obligation to do anything that is useless.[9]

I suppose that the point in drawing attention to the fact that this argument encompasses "natural" no less than "artificial" means is simply to demonstrate how far traditionally minded moralists were in principle willing to go in ordering means to the human life they are supposed to serve. Physicians should observe this, if they are inclined in conscience to continue beyond genuine usefulness the use of means that in the course of medical progress have become "usual" or "customary," and if they are any more ready for reasons relative to the patient to omit only their spectacular or "heroic" efforts.

The present writer has removed Kelly's delaying reference to the "artificiality" of the *useless* means that may be dispensed. He, not I,

---

9. Ibid., p. 219. Fr. Kelly's argument accepts the conclusions of Joseph V. Sullivan, and seems to go further in clarifying their grounds. Sullivan had written: "A natural means of prolonging life is, per se, an ordinary means of prolonging life, yet per accidens it may be extraordinary. . . . An artificial means of prolonging life may be an ordinary means or an extraordinary means relative to the physical condition of the patient" (*Catholic Teaching on the Morality of Euthanasia* [Washington, D.C.: Catholic Univ. of America Press, 1949], p. 65, original in italics). "There is an absolute norm [sic] beyond which means are *per se* extraordinary," Sullivan writes; and it is not entirely clear whether he intends to say this of both "natural" and "artificial" means. The latter certainly are the chief practical issues, since almost all means of preserving life are "artificial." However, when Sullivan speaks of an "absolute norm" beyond which natural or artificial means become extraordinary and elective only, it is clear that the warrant for this is *relativity* to the age and physical condition of the patient. "An aged woman sick unto death with cancer would not have to use the same means toward prolonging life as a young girl, ill for the first time in her life with a hopeful future ahead. For this aged woman an operation which might prolong her life a few months or a year would be an extraordinary means" (pp. 64–65). One of this author's case illustrations justifies a physician in cutting off intravenous feeding because, however "usual" as a practice, for *a terminal patient in great pain* it is an extraordinary means and therefore need not be used (p. 72, case [R]). Here again the meaning of the medical imperative to care for the dying is relative to the physical condition of the individual patient, not alone to usual or established procedures. Then, is there any point in holding on to a distinction between "natural" and "artificial" *ordinary* means?

embraces also "natural" means—not alone in the logic of his argument but in specific cases as well. This happened in his apparent approval of the solution of two cases by Cardinal De Lugo. If a man, about to be burned to death by his enemies, has only a few buckets of water he is obliged to use the available water if he can prevent his death; but if the use of the water would only delay the inevitable he is not bound to use it. Water would seem to be a "natural" means of putting out fire, if anything is. If anyone doubts this, the second case settles the matter. Is a starving man bound to eat food brought to him by his friends? Yes, if he can get food regularly enough to ward off death. No, if by eating he only postpones his death by starvation. In sum, a prolongation of life that "may be morally considered as nothing" is *never* imperative whether the means are "natural" or "artificial," "ordinary" or "extraordinary."[10]

Several times in the foregoing paragraphs I have suggested that in an era of scientific and technical medicine, and since few people are likely to try suicide by ceasing to eat, to talk about the moral dispensability of "natural" means of saving life may be a moot question. This is not so, since so-called natural means (and also artificial means) have other uses than as *remedies* or (as "means" to any future). These are things done for no purpose except to care. To give a cup of cold water to a man who has entered upon the course of his own particular dying is to slack the thirst of a man who will soon thirst again, and thirst unto death. When a man is irreversibly in the process of dying, to feed him and to give him drink, to ease him and keep him comfortable—these are no longer given as means of preserving life. The use of glucose drip should often be understood in this way. This keeps a patient who cannot swallow from feeling dehydrated, and is often the only remaining "means" by which we can express our present faithfulness to him during his dying (since to give him water intravenously would destroy his red blood cells and directly weaken and kill him). If a glucose drip prolongs this patient's dying because of the calories that are also introduced into his system, it is not done for that purpose or as a means in a continuing useless effort to save his life.

The administration of increased dosages of pain-killing drugs in

10. Ibid., p. 208. For Kelly the test of human benefit is finally overriding in telling whether the use of any sort of means is imperative. The prime importance of humane considerations was thereafter made quite evident by the fact that, in his 1951 Note and following the suggestion of a number of other moralists, Kelly wrote the test of benefit or usefulness into the *definition* of ordinary and extraordinary means. This produced the "standard" definitions given above, which include the words "offer a reasonable hope of benefit." See Kelly, "Duty to Preserve Life," p. 550.

the care of the dying is, as it were, the "mirror image" of the glucose drip: these drugs are judged to be life-shortening (to an immeasurable degree, because to suffer extreme pain would also be debilitating), but they are properly to be given in order to keep the patient as comfortable as possible, to show that we understand his need for succor, and not as a "useful" means to push him beyond our love and care. All these procedures, some "natural," other "artificial," are appropriate means—if "means" they should be called—of only caring for the dying, of physically companying with the dying. They are the embodied and effective gestures of soul to soul. As such, these acknowledgments of solidarity in morality are due to the dying man from any of us who also bear flesh. Thus do men give answer by their presence and comfort to the faithfulness claims of persons who are passing through the acceptable death of all flesh. If death should be accepted and treatment can no longer affect it, one might even raise the question whether *glucose* water should be used to keep the dying patient comfortable. I understand that there are certain sugars which it might be possible to use to give water for hydration without metabolizing calories and prolonging the dying process.

A second place at which a liberalizing definition of our obligation to care for the dying begins to suggest itself is in Kelly's answer to the question, "Is a person who suffers from two lethal diseases obliged to take ordinary means of checking one of them when there is no hope of checking the other?" The question at issue is whether a person suffering from incurable cancer who develops diabetes is obliged to begin insulin treatment, or a diabetic who develops an incurable cancer obliged to continue on insulin, and die slowly of the cancer instead of sooner in coma. Other moralists had answered that the patient must use the insulin since that is an "ordinary" means of checking the *disease* diabetes. Kelly doubts whether a patient is bound to "prescind from the cancer in determining her obligation of using the insulin." The latter depends on two factors: that it is an ordinary means and that it offers a reasonable hope of success. The simultaneous presence of cancer throws doubt on the second stipulation. But then Kelly observes: "I think the doubt would be even stronger were there some connection between the two diseases."[11] An illus-

---

11. "Using Artificial Means," pp. 215–16. I presume that the above debate is about the dying cancer patient or a quite advanced incurable cancer. There are, of course, stages of cancer for which treatment holds out the hope of, say, ten years of relatively normal life. The diabetes of such a patient should certainly be treated. While it may be that the disease has seized him from which he one day will die, he is not yet dying of it.

tration of this would be the need for intravenous feeding *connected with* the fatal disease from which a patient is dying. Presumably Kelly would be more certain about the judgment that it is permissible to withdraw intravenous feeding in this case, although nowadays a drip is surely per se an ordinary procedure for sustaining life. Thus, in assessing mandatory and only elective remedies, Kelly moves away from judging this in terms of *single* diseases only, to connected diseases, and only hesitantly beyond that. His reasoning should be faulted only for his hesitation.

The patient is not exhaustively characterized by one disease, two separate diseases, or the interconnected diseases from which he may be suffering, both incurable, one involving prolonged dying. Ideally, Kelly wanted the description of the human act of caring for this patient to terminate in a texture of related diseases. But a proper description of the human acts of caring for mortal man terminates in that man. He is the unity of the diseases he suffers when one his quietus makes. Doctors do not treat diseases, though often they conquer them. They treat patients, and here finally all fail. If a diabetic patient need not prescind from the cancer in determining her obligation to start or to continue to use insulin, the reason is that she is the one flesh in which both diseases inhere. If to use insulin is for her quite useless, it is surely contraindicated. To move beyond the interrelation of the ills to which all flesh is heir requires that we move to *the flesh* that is heir to all its ills, indifferent to whether these ills are themselves connected or physiologically unrelated. It is this flesh, and not diseases one by one, that is the subject of medical treatment. This truth is enough to undercut the bondage of conscience to the imperativeness of "customary" or "usual" procedures for treating single diseases.

We need to ponder one further possible entailment of the reforming definition of only caring for the dying at which we have arrived. If the unity of the person in whom the diseases inhere is the important point, and not a texture of interrelated diseases, this concept has important bearing on the treatment of infants with serious congenital defects. The argument cannot always be, as Kelly seems still to contend, that "the determination of ordinary and extraordinary means begin with the mentally normal" and this be then applied without qualification to the congenitally abnormal. That requirement may hold true for the chronically defective, like infants afflicted with mongolism, who often have a satisfactory degree of human existence that is only a burden, sometimes rewarding, to others.

The theologian who recently judged that "a Downs is not a person" uttered a scandalous untruth; and the fact that our advanced societies are now launching out upon the practice of allowing to be killed in utero all who are likely to be born mentally or physically defective shows, in the prismatic case of the most vulnerable, what we are coming to think of mankind's needy and helpless life in general. Nevertheless, the "abnormal" have, at the first of life, often been seized by their particular process of dying unless medical science relentlessly intervenes. Here there are even related defects any one of which will be mortal unless we intervene to stop them in course. Since we ought not to absolutize the distinction between "usual" and "heroic" treatment of newborn babies, not to place "a monstrosity in a heating bassinet" or to stop opposing the infection to which it is prone cannot be declared morally wrong while an operation is said to be optional to provide a child who was born with congenital atresia with an artificial or implanted esophagus.[12]

"Ordinary" or imperative, and "extraordinary" or only elective treatment are, as we have seen, not fixed categories. The feeling that infants should be given the greatest protection does not alone settle what we ought to do. Life in the first of it and life in the last of it are both prismatic cases of human helplessness. The question is, What does loyalty to the newborn and to the dying require of us? Consistently, we could say that both should unqualifiedly be given every effort that might save or prolong their existence. But if a balancing judgment is permitted—even morally mandatory—concerning whether proposed remedies will be beneficial to the adult dying, the same reasoning cannot be preemptorially excluded from our care of the newborn.

If in the case of terminal patients the quality of life they can expect enters into the determination of whether even ordinary or customary measures would be beneficial and should or should not be used, cannot the same be said of infants? It is not obvious that an anencephaletic baby should be respirated while a grown man in prolonged coma should no longer be helped to breathe. In the first of life, a human being may be seized by his own unique dying. Indeed, far from taking the death of the aged and the enormous death rate of zygotes and miscarriages to be a part of the problem of evil, a religious man is likely to take this as a sign that the Lord of life has beset us behind and before in this dying life we are called to live and celebrate. There is an

12. Ibid., pp. 211–12.

acceptable death of the life of all flesh no less in the first than in the last of it. An ethical man may always gird himself to oppose this enemy, but not the religious ethical man.

THE PROCESS OF DYING

In the foregoing analysis we have drawn two pivotal conclusions: (1) that there is no duty to use useless means, however natural or ordinary or customary in practice; and (2) that the description of human acts of caring for the dying (or caring for the not yet dying) terminates in the man who is the patient of these ministrations and not in the disease or diseases he has. These are related points: in judging whether to try a given treatment one has to estimate whether there is a reasonable hope of success in saving the man's life.

A recent essay reviewing the distinction of extraordinary from ordinary means, and the different ways in which particular cases have been judged by traditional moralists, concludes that in the final analysis "the one general positive guideline from the past that will remain" may prove to be the directive that "the use of any means should be based on what is commonly termed a 'reasonable hope of success.'"[13] The residue of the distinctions we have reviewed, this author seems to suggest, is the test of usefulness. If so, the moral meaning of dispensable means would seem to reduce without remainder to a determination of an irreversible "process of dying."

This is certainly a principal component of the medical-moral imperative. It can certainly be said that our duties to the dying differ radically from our duties to the living or to the potentially still living. Just as it would be negligence to the sick to treat them as if they were about to die, so it is another sort of "negligence" to treat the dying as if they are going to get well or might get well.[14] The right medical practice will provide those who may get well with the assistance they need, and it will provide those who are dying with the care and assistance they need in their final passage. To fail to distinguish between these two sorts of medical practice would be to fail to act in accord with the facts. It would be to act in accord with some rule-book medicine. It would be to act without responsivity to those who have no longer any responsivity or recuperative powers.

13. Kieran Nolan, "The Problem of Care for the Dying," in Charles E. Curran, ed., *Absolutes in Moral Theology?* (Washington, D.C., and Cleveland: Corpus, 1968), p. 253.

14. Ibid., p. 256.

Thus would we fail to care for them as the dying men they are, just as surely as if we failed to take account of the responsivity that the living sick or the not yet dying still have. Only a physician can determine the onset of the process of dying. For all the uncertainty, he must surely make this determination. He is bound to distinguish so far as he can between that time span in which his treatment of a patient is still a part of diagnosis and treatment—diagnosis and treatment not of the disease but of a patient's particular responsivity— and a subsequent time in which the patient is irreversibly doing his own dying. The "treatment" for that is care, not struggle. The claims of the "suffering-*dying*"[15] upon the human community are quite different from the claims of those who, through suffering, still may live, or who are incurably ill but not yet dying.

In connection with all that has just been said we should not have in mind only those patients who are in deep and prolonged coma. A conscious patient as well may have begun irreversibly the process of his particular dying; and, precisely because conscious, his claims are strong upon the human community that only care and comfort and company be given him and that pretended remedies or investigative trials or palliative operations be not visited upon him as if these were hopeful therapy. Therefore, to all of the foregoing the words of David Daube, professor of law at the University of Oxford, are pertinent. "The question of at what moment it is in order to discontinue extraordinary—or even ordinary—measures to keep a person alive," Professor Daube writes, "should not be confused with the question at what moment a man is dead" or with the question whether he is conscious or unconscious. "Discontinuation of such measures is often justifiable even while the patient is conscious."[16]

This risk-filled decision concerning the onset of a man's own process of dying can be and is made by physicians. The problem is to find the courage (and perhaps legal protection) to act upon it. Dr. John R. Cavanagh defines the "dying process" as "the time in the course of an irreversible illness when treatment will no longer influence it."[17] The patient has entered a covenant with the physician for his com-

---

15. Ibid., p. 260.
16. David Daube, "Transplantation: Acceptability of Procedures and Their Required Legal Sanctions," in G. E. W. Wolstonholme and Maeve O'Connor, eds., *Ethics in Medical Progress: With Special Reference to Transplantation* (Boston: Little, Brown, 1966), pp. 190–91.
17. John R. Cavanagh, "Bene Mori: The Right of a Patient to Die with Dignity," *Linacre Quarterly*, May 1963 (unpaginated reprint).

plete *care*, not for continuing useless efforts to *cure*. Therefore, Dr. H. P. Wasserman calls for "a program of 'pre-mortem care,'" and for the training of doctors in this, and in the diverse ways in which they may fulfill their vocation to cure sometimes, to relieve often, and to comfort always.[18]

If the sting of death is sin, the sting of dying is solitude. What doctors should do in the presence of the process of dying is only a special case of what should be done to make a human presence felt to the dying. Desertion is more choking than death, and more feared. The chief problem of the dying is how not to die alone. To care, if only to care, for the dying is, therefore, a medical-moral imperative; it is a requirement of us all in exhibiting faithfulness to all who bear a human countenance. In an extraordinary article, Dr. Charles D. Aring says flatly that "it is not to be surmised that under the most adverse circumstances the patient is not aware."[19] That may be to say too much, but it strongly suggests that the sound of human voices and the clasp of the hand may be as important in keeping company with the dying as the glucose-drip "drink of cool water" or relieving their pain.

Dr. Aring tells of the case of a man who, under continuing exotic treatments, kept asking to be returned to his ward and to within the presence of his three ward companions. Instead, "he died alone, denied what he most wanted, the unspoken comfort of people—any people—around him." This physician's judgment is that this man's "want of his friends and familiar surroundings, new though they were, should have been an imperative and taken precedence over any and all technical matters." That would have been proper "pre-mortem care" of the dying. To do this, the physician needs to become aware of his own feelings about death, and to lean against his possible proneness to visit cursorily or to pass hurriedly by the room in which lies one of his "failures." And all of us in the "age of the enlightenment" need to recognize "death's growing remoteness and unfamiliarity," the masks by which it is suppressed, the fantastic rituals by which we keep the presence of death at bay and our own presence from the dying, the inferiority assigned to the dying because it would be a human accomplishment not to do so, the ubiquity of the fear of dying that is one sure product of a secular age.[20]

18. H. P. Wasserman, "Problematic Aspects of the Phenomenon of Death," *World Medical Journal* 14 (1967): 148–49.

19. Charles D. Aring, "Intimations of Mortality: An Appreciation of Death and Dying," *Annals of Internal Medicine* 69/1 (July 1968): 149.

20. Ibid., pp. 141, 137, 138, 144–45, 151.

There is a final entailment of caring for the dying that is required of priests, ministers, rabbis, and every one of us, and not only or not even mainly of the medical profession. "The process of dying" needs to be got out of the hospitals and back into the home and in the midst of family, neighborhood, and friends. This would be a "systemic change" in our present institutions for caring for the dying as difficult to bring about as some fundamental change in foreign policy or the nation-state system. Still, any doctor will tell you that by no means does everyone need to die in a hospital who today does so. They are there because families want them there, or because neighbors might think not everything was done in efforts to save them. They are there because hospitals are well equipped to "manage death," and families are ill equipped to do so.

If the "systemic change" here proposed in caring for the dying were actually brought about, ministers, priests, and rabbis would have on their hands a great many shattered families and relatives. But for once they would be shattered by confrontation with reality, by the claims of the dying not to be deserted, not to be pushed from the circle that specially owes them love and care, not to be denied human presence with them. Then God might not be as dead as lately He is supposed to be. The "sealing up of metaphysical concerns," Peter Berger recently pointed out, is one of the baneful results of a "happy" childhood—a childhood unhappily sheltered from the dying in all our advanced societies.[21] . . .

THE SAME OBJECTIONS FROM TWO OPPOSITE EXTREMES

There are physicians, of course, who entirely agree with the moralists' distinction ethically between direct killing (euthanasia) and allowing to die, and who also affirm the importance of this distinction for medical ethics. Dr. J. Russell Elkinton of the University of Pennsylvania School of Medicine, for example, calls upon his fellow physicians to attend, in addition to their obligation to save life, to their "other obligation" to allow the patient, if he is to die, to die with

21. Symposium titled "The Culture of Unbelief," held in Rome under the sponsorship of the Vatican Secretariat for Nonbelievers and the University of California at Berkeley. A second baneful effect of a happy childhood, Berger said, is "a new utopianism—a radical demand for the humanization of existing social structures," measured by "the benign character of the institutions in charge of primary socialization," family, school, playground (*New York Times*, March 26, 1969).

comfort and dignity. He acknowledges that if an extraordinary treatment (such as use of a respirator) is stopped, that is *an action*, but it is "an 'invisible act' of omission." Morally, it is decisive that "the patient dies not from that act but from the underlying disease or injury."[22] The physician simply stands aside.

For Elkinton also, in caring for the dying, it is a matter of indifference whether usual or rare and untried or new treatments are at issue. "More than 20 years ago," he writes, "I was responsible for the care of a young woman in the end state of multiple sclerosis. She was in great pain and had widespread ulcerations over the surface of her body from which she developed a septicemia (infection of her blood stream). At that time a new antibiotic, penicillin, had just become available. With the agreement of the patient's family I withheld the penicillin and the patient died quickly—her suffering was relieved. Penicillin is an ordinary treatment today but I would still make the same decision."[23] Thus, the advancement of medical science and practice is not alone sufficient to transform elective into morally imperative treatments. So also said Dr. G. B. Giertz. . . : "No step is taken with the object of killing the patient. We refrain from treatment because it does not serve any purpose. . . . I cannot regard this as killing by medical means: death has already won, despite the fight we have put up, and we must accept the fact."[24]

This is also the medical care that small children deserve. "I will fight for every day," writes Dr. Rudolf Toch of the Pediatric Tumor Clinic at Massachusetts General Hospital, "if I have even the slightest chance of doing something more than just gaining one more day. . . . On the other hand, I recall a youngster whom we recently had on the ward with osteogenic sarcoma, the lungs completely riddled with tumor, who had not responded at all to the most potent chemotherapy and for whom we really had nothing further to offer. I did not

22. J. Russell Elkinton, "The Dying Patient, the Doctor, and the Law," *Villanova Law Review* 13/4 (Summer 1968): 740, 743.

23. Ibid., p. 743, n. 4. Noteworthy also is the fact that Elkinton believes that a physician as a man should take into account the fact of age and the range of human activity in judging whether we should always oppose death. "Perhaps we have lost our perspective on death as a natural part of the life that has evolved on this planet," he writes. "Death is more natural for the old than for the young and middle-aged. A physician friend has told me of the occasion when, visiting his elderly, widowed, and very lonely father, the father suddenly collapsed with an arrested heart. The son began external cardiac massage—and then he stopped. It seemed to him that it was the right time for his father to die. My friend had the perspective of which I speak" (p. 750).

24. G. B. Giertz, "Ethical Problems in Medical Procedures in Sweden," in Wolstenholme and O'Connor, *Ethics in Medical Progress*, p. 145.

feel any compunction at all about not doing thoracenteses daily, keeping intravenous therapy going, etc. All we did was give her adequate sedation, and I think she rather peacefully slept away." In saying this, Dr. Toch expressed the general and continuous consensus of Western medical ethics.[25]

However, the ethics of only caring for the dying which, as we have seen, was our traditional medical ethics, and which is still promulgated by theological moralists and many doctors, will be opposed, trivialized, and ridiculed by two opposite extremes. One of these extremes is the medical and moral opinion that there is never any reason not to use or to stop using any and all available life-sustaining procedures. The other extreme is that of those, including a few theological ethicists, who favor the adoption of active schemes of positive euthanasia which justify, under certain circumstances, the direct killing of terminal patients. The case for either of these points of view can be made only by discounting and rejecting the arguments for saving life qualifiedly but not always. In both cases, an ethics of only caring for the dying is reduced to the moral equivalent of euthanasia —in the one case, to oppose this ever; in the other case, to endorse it. Thus, the extremes meet, both medical scrupulosity and euthanasia, in rejecting the discriminating concepts of traditional medical ethics.

Proponents of euthanasia agree with advocates of relentless efforts to save life in reducing an ethics of omitting life-sustaining treatments to a distinction without a difference from directly killing the dying. Thus D. C. S. Cameron, former medical and scientific director of the American Cancer Society, writes that "actually the difference between euthanasia and letting the patient die by omitting life-sustaining treatment is a moral quibble."[26] Dr. David A. Karnofsky, of the Sloan-Kettering Institute for Cancer Research, also vigorously defends continuous "aggressive or extraordinary means of

25. Rudolf Toch, "Management of the Child with a Fatal Disease," *Clinical Pediatrics* 3/7 (July 1964): 423. A sampling of articles by other medical writers in support of this point of view includes Naomi Mitchison, "The Right to Die," *Medical World* 85/2 (August 1956): 159–63; John J. Farrell, "The Right of a Patient to Die," *Journal of the South Carolina Medical Association* 54/7 (July 1958): 231–33; Frank J. Ayd, Jr., "The Hopeless Case: Medical and Moral Considerations," *Journal of the American Medical Association* 181/13 (Sept. 29, 1962): 1099–1102; Eugene G. Laforet, "The 'Hopeless' Case," *Archives of Internal Medicine* 112 (1963): 314–26; William P. Williamson, "Life or Death—Whose Decision," *Journal of the American Medical Association* 197/10 (Sept. 5, 1966): 139–41; Aring, "Intimations of Mortality," pp. 137–52.

26. D. C. S. Cameron: *The Truth about Cancer* (Englewood Cliffs, N.J.: Prentice-Hall, 1956), p. 116.

treatment" to prolong life. Karnofsky acknowledges that "the state of dying" may often be protracted only by "expensive and desperate supportive measures," and the patient may be "rescued from one life-threatening situation only to face another." He has heard the pleas of those who, "contemplating this dismal scene," beg the doctor to "let the patient go quickly, with dignity and without pain." This strikes him as the same as getting rid of the dying by any means: "Withholding of aggressive or extraordinary treatment can be urged and supported by state planners, efficiency experts, social workers, philosophers, theologians, economists, and humanitarians. For here is one means of ensuring an efficient, productive, orderly and pain-free society, by sweeping out each day the inevitable debris of life."[27]

The medical imperative, in Katnofsky's opinion, is to apply one temporary relief after another, stretching the life of a patient with cancer of the large bowel to ten months, who would have died within weeks if any one massive remedy had not been used. To the question, "When should the physician stop treating the patient?" there can be but one answer: "He must carry on until the issue is taken out of his hands."[28] From the point of view of this medical ethics of univocal and relentless life prolonging, the moralists' notion of imperative and elective means is bound to seem a moral quibble, and such an outlook will be exceedingly suspicious of all talk of allowing patients to die

27. *Time*, Nov. 3, 1961, p. 60.

28. Ibid. One reason Karnofsky comes to this conclusion is that it is, for him, a function of medicine's scientific mission in fighting *disease:* "The sense of mission . . . is diminished . . . [by] the view that the fight against cancer should not be continuously waged on all sectors. The achievements and triumphs that may occur in the fight against cancer will come from doctors who do too much—who continue to treat the patient when the odds may appear overwhelming—and not from those who do too little. The physicians . . . can learn a great deal from the study of these patients. . . . In facing every challenge, even if doctors usually fail, they are kept in training to handle the remediable situations more effectively" ("Why Prolong the Life of a Patient with Advanced Cancer?" *Cancer Journal for Clinicians* 10 [January–February 1960], p. 10). There is strength in this argument, if it is not possible for the physician to combine both resolves: care for the *patient* and his struggle against the *disease.* The practice of patient-centered medicine must surely cut across Karnofsky's concerns, or at least dethrone them. Follows is an extreme statement of the opposing principle: "A physician-counselor . . . cannot be a good personal and confidential adviser representing the patient's best interests if his own allegiance is divided between the patient's good and the general good of medical science or the welfare of the race at large" (John C. Ford, S. J., and J. E. Drew, M. D., "Advising Radical Surgery: A Problem of Medical Morality," *Journal of the American Medical Association* 151 [Feb. 28, 1953]: 714). Another medical article generally in support of never stopping treatment, however extraordinary, is Louis P. Pertschuk and Albert S. Heyman, "The Physician's Responsibility in 'Hopeless Cases,'" *American Osteopathic Association* 64 (February 1965): 618–19.

and only caring for them. There are moralists who agree with this point of view, and who, in order to protect human life at all costs, would be very suspicious of vesting physicians with the right to make the balancing sorts of medical and moral judgments expounded in this chapter.

On the other hand, precisely the same objection will be brought against the flexibly wise categories of traditional medical ethics from the opposite quarter. This time the objection is raised by proponents of schemes of euthanasia or the direct killing of dying or of untreatable patients. Tribute should be paid to Professor Joseph Fletcher for in season and out of season having kept open the question of allowing to die in the minds and consciences of the public beyond the limits of the medical profession. Still, the fact that he is himself a proponent of euthanasia—he "almost" says "honest" or "straightforward" euthanasia[29]—has meant on his part a serious misunderstanding of the ethics of only attending the dying. He subscribes to this ethics, of course, in moments when he seems compelled to acknowledge that euthanasia is a nonproblem in our present society, and when he wants provisionally to endorse the more commonly shared ethics of allowing to die. But because this is for him a halfway house, he seriously misunderstands the positive quality of the nonconsequential "action" put forth in attending and caring for the dying, and he introduces some confusion by his use of the carefully wrought categories of this ethics.

There is a terminological problem to be settled one way or another at the outset. It is possible to use the term *euthanasia* with the meaning of the two Greek words of which it is composed: a "good death." Dr. Wasserman uses the word in this sense when he says, "The inevitability of death suggests that medicine's greatest gift to mankind could be that of euthanasia in its literal meaning, i.e., death without suffering."[30] By this he meant the practice of only caring for the dying, and he proposed the establishment of a program of "premortem care," and training medical students not only as invincible conquerers who unhappily fail, but also in this positive aspect of their profession. While this is the literal and the original meaning of the term *euthanasia*, it has since and in modern times acquired a quite different meaning. This meaning, I suggest, is now unreformably the

29. Bernard Bard and Joseph Fletcher, "The Right to Die," *Atlantic Monthly* 221 (April 1968): 63.

30. H. P. Wasserman, "Problematic Aspects of the Phenomenon of Death," *World Medical Journal* 14 (1967): 148.

meaning or part of the meaning the term will have in current usage. It is better to invent terms of art such as *agathanasia* or *bene mori*[31] or *pre-mortem care* to convey the ethics and practice of only caring for the dying, if this is what is meant.

Of course, we can agree to use either convention. But there is evidence that efforts to use the term *euthanasia* with any other sense than the one it has in current usage, i.e., direct killing, do not fully succeed. If this is true, our terminological problem has substantive import for ethical analysis and the moral life. The writings of Joseph Fletcher are an instance. He wishes to subscribe both to an ethics of caring, but only caring, for the dying, and to euthanasia in its current meaning. He calls both these practices by the name of euthanasia. He then must attach to the term qualifying predicates. This leads to confusion and inaccuracy in his use of the carefully wrought categories of traditional medical ethics, which he uses as these qualifiers, and to a failure to grasp the positive quality of only caring for the dying.

Thus Fletcher permits himself to speak of a decision to only care for the dying as *indirect euthanasia*. We cannot move forward without flatly denying this concept to be true. There is only one procedure in caring for the dying that need invoke what moralists call the "indirectly voluntary." This is the use of pain-relieving drugs that may also debilitate a patient's strength and shorten his life, or his dying. In this case, the justification is that relief of his pain is the "directly voluntary" action, while the administration of the drug shortens the dying process in only an "indirectly voluntary" way. What ones does directly and immediately is to help the patient in his insufferable pain. That he dies sooner is not the primary result. This case is a prism in which we can see the ingredients that must be present in a case for which the language of "direct" or "indirect" is at all appropriate. There must be two effects caused by the same action, whether these effects are relieving pain and shortening life, or, in conflict-of-life cases, unavoidably and foreknowingly causing the death of a fetus as the "indirectly voluntary" effect of action whose directly voluntary end is the saving of a mother's life.

Incidentally, the life-shortening effect of using pain-relieving drugs is not quite as clear as moralists sometimes assert. Prolonged suffering from extreme pain is also exceedingly debilitating; and it is not always clear whether to keep pain at bay or not to do so would be

31. Cavanagh, "Bene Mori."

more effective in hastening the dying man to realms beyond our love and care. In any case, drugs are not given for that consequence. They rather express in objective service to the dying that we still care for them, and are affirmatively doing so.

It may be entirely appropriate to use the expression *indirect euthanasia* in the case of death-hastening pain-killers. But it is not at all appropriate to use these words to describe cases of ceasing treatments that prolong the patient's life, or withholding life-sustaining treatments altogether, which Fletcher lumps together under this rubric with positive acts of administering drugs which cause the double effect we have described.[32] This he does on the grounds that in these cases "death occurs through omission rather than directly by commission"; it is "not induced but only permitted." Fletcher calls this concept *"indirect* euthanasia" and his warrant for doing so, he says, is because "in some kinds of Christian ethics and moral theology, an action of this kind is called 'indirect voluntary.'"[33] This usage is entirely mistaken. Fletcher's is a *persuasive* use of language, not a convincing one. Writing primarily as a proponent of euthanasia (current usage), he subscribes along the way to an ethics of only caring for the dying. By calling the latter "indirect euthanasia" his words, at least, gain the force of suggesting that this point of view is not quite as honest or forthright as "direct" euthanasia.

To insist that this usage confuses the carefully fashioned categories of medical ethics is no mere logomachy, since it is of first importance, in the characterization or description of actions to be morally evaluated, to make clear precisely this distinction between acts of omission and acts of commission.[34] The difference between only car-

32. Fletcher, "The Patient's Right to Die," *Harper's*, October 1960: 141–42.

33. Fletcher, "Dysthanasia: The Problem of Prolonging Death," *Tufts Folia Medica* 8 (January–March 1962): 30. This article and the one cited in the previous footnote are now reprinted as "Euthanasia and Anti-Dysthanasia," chap. 9 of Joseph Fletcher, *Moral Responsibility* (Philadelphia: Westminster, 1967), pp. 141–60.

34. On the need for accurate characterization or description of actions before evaluating them, see Paul Ramsey, *Deeds and Rules in Christian Ethics* (New York: Scribner's, 1967), pp. 192–225. In his essay "Elective Death," in Torrey, *Ethical Issues*, p. 147, Prof. Fletcher further multiplies the concepts he uses in ethical analysis. He speaks of four sorts of euthanasia: direct voluntary, indirect voluntary, indirect involuntary, and direct involuntary. Under the last pair of terms, one allows to die or kills without the consent of the dying or by construing their consent. Under the first pair of terms, with the patient's consent he is killed or allowed to die. These may be better and more illuminating terms to use in ethical analysis; but it must be pointed out that by means of them one can say little or nothing about past moral reflection and cannot enter into helpful discourse with the meanings in past medical ethics. Fletcher's are *replacing* definitions.

ing for the dying and acts of euthanasia is not a choice between indirectly and directly willing and doing something. It is rather the important choice between doing something and doing nothing, or
(better said) ceasing to do something that was begun in order to do
something that is better because now more fitting. In omission no
human agent causes the patient's death, directly or indirectly. He dies
his own death from causes that it is no longer merciful or reasonable
to fight by means of possible medical interventions. Indeed, it is not
quite right to say that we only care for the dying by an omission, by
"doing nothing" directly or indirectly. Instead, we cease doing what
was once called for and begin to do precisely what is called for now.
We attend and company with him in this, his very own dying, render-
ing it as comfortable and dignified as possible.

In any case, doing something and omitting something in order to
do something else are different sorts of acts. To do or not to do something may, then, be subject to different moral evaluations. One may
be wrong and the other may be right, even if these decisions and
actions are followed by the same end result, namely, the death of a
patient. One need not deny that in the moral life commission and
omission may sometimes be morally equivalent. Still, before we
reach the individual case or the sort of cases in which to do and not to
do are judged to be the same, we need to explore the possibility that to
omit and to do may not at all be equivalent actions, and to ascertain
the pertinence of this possibility for medical practice.[35]

What Fletcher has gained by an improper characterization of actions that allow a patient to die while caring for him—by calling
them indirect voluntary euthanasia—is that, without abandoning
the case he and many other moralists have made for only caring for
the dying, he can the more readily succeed in apparently reducing the
warrants for omitting medical interventions to the moral equivalent
of the alleged warrants for acts of direct euthanasia. Here it is that he
mounts the very same objection against an ethics of only caring for
the dying as the one also affirmed by defenders of medical scrupulosity in the unending use of all available means. Many teachers,
Fletcher writes, Roman Catholics and others, "claim to see a moral
difference between deciding to end a life by deliberately doing something and deciding to end a life by deliberately *not* doing something."

35. For a discussion of the law on acts and omissions, see an article by George P.
Fletcher of the University of Seattle Law School, "Legal Aspects of the Decision Not to
Prolong Life," *Journal of the American Medical Association* 203/1 (Jan. 1, 1968): 65–
68.

This, Fletcher writes, "seems a very cloudy distinction"; and he asks rhetorically, "What, morally, is the difference between doing nothing to keep a patient alive and giving a fatal dose of a pain-killing or other lethal drug?" Of course, as Fletcher goes on to say, the decision to do or not to do are both "morally deliberate." Who ever said they were not? Of course, "the intention is the same, either way"—meaning the end in view (and not bothering here to introduce the usage of the word *intention* in a considerable number of ethical writings where its meaning is *not* restricted to the end in view). Fletcher's whole case depends, then, on his next statement: "As Kant said, if we will the end we will the means."[36]

That, I suppose, is a statement from Kant's analysis of hypothetical imperatives, which are dependent on consequences; and it might be pointed out that Kant did not believe conditional imperatives to be at all constitutive of a truly moral life. One could argue that if one wills the end he wills the means—but not just any old means. One could argue that it is ethical to will the end we have here in mind; for the strictest religious ethics "the desire for death can be licit."[37] One could say that there are different means—and differences between action and omissions that make room for properly caring actions—that may let the patient have the death he not improperly or even quite rightly desires. While it might be argued that the Kantian maxim applies to means necessary to secure a desired and desirable end, still where there are more than one means to this same end, to will that end leaves open the choice among means. A means may be right, another wrong, to the same end.

But to respond in this way would exhibit a considerable misunderstanding of the positive quality and proper purpose intended in only caring for the dying. It is true that death is now accepted; and it is no longer opposed. This makes room for appropriate caring actions which are means to no future consequence. These actions are fulfillments of the *categorical* imperative: Never abandon care! Perhaps they should not be called means at all, since they effectuate or hasten the coming of no end at all. Upon ceasing to try to rescue the perishing, one then is free to care for the dying. Acts of caring for the dying are deeds done bodily for them which serve solely to manifest that they are not lost from human attention, that they are not alone, that mankind generally and their loved ones take note of their dying and

36. Fletcher, "Patient's Right to Die," p. 143.
37. Kelly, "Using Artificial Means," p. 217.

mean to company with them in accepting this unique instance of the acceptable death of all flesh. An attitude toward the dying premised upon mature and profoundly religious convictions will display an indefectable charity that never ceases to go about the business of caring for the dying neighbor. If we seriously mean to align our wills with God's care here and now for them, there can never be any reason to hasten them from the here and now in which they still claim a faithful presence from us—into the there and then in which they, of course, cannot pass beyond God's love and care. This is the ultimate ground for saying that a religious outlook that goes with grace among the dying can never be compatible with euthanasiac acts or sentiments.

. . . Before concluding the present discussion, reference should be made to the "special ethics" of Karl Barth. Barth provides us with an example of a theological moralist who, because of the great weight he places upon the sanctity of each human life and upon our human duty to respect and protect any life that God has valued, initially defends the practice of medical scrupulosity in never ceasing to try to save the dying. From this point of view he brings the same objection against main-line Western medical ethics as comes from the opposite extreme: it is a muddle and a quibble, and moreover, for Barth, a dangerous quibble. In the end, however, Barth breaks away from this extreme and, because his mind is bent on following the lineaments of grace among the dying, he is driven to an understanding of care for the dying which at first he opposed. It is fitting to conclude with Barth because what he says in this brief section in his special ethics is enough to show that always caring and only caring for the dying arises from within the heart and soul of Christian ethics. This is not the property of Roman Catholic moralists alone—unless we mean to deny our common moral heritage which measures every requirement upon men by a relentless charity.

No theologian in the twentieth century has prosecuted more vigorously the meaning of respect for life and the protection of life than the Protestant, Karl Barth. The motif powerfully at work in Barth's analysis is that of a man who understands our fellow humanity in terms of Christ, who was the man with and for other men with indefectable charity. Barth seeks in his "special ethics" to form and inform his thoughts by the degree to which God has from all eternity surrounded with sanctity all these nascent and dying lives of ours and alone knows their secret and destiny. In this outlook and according to this measure of cleaving to the life of a fellow man, it seems to Barth clear that one can "give up" the life of a sick or useless or horribly deformed person *no less* by "letting his life ebb away" than by "encompassing his death."[38] For this reason, the attempted distinction between directly intending the death and allowing to die completely collapses in Barth's view, because both are "deliberate killing." He seems therefore to agree with medical scrupulosity and proponents of euthanasia that this is a muddled distinction that cannot be maintained. But it is in the face of divine charity seeking always to save life that it cannot be maintained, and so Barth's own view is at the opposite pole from euthanasiacs who are allied with him in ridiculing what he rejects.

It can hardly be said that this form of deliberate killing ("letting life ebb away") "can ever seem to be commanded in any emergency, and therefore to be anything but murder." The suggestion that a patient could be "helped to die," not directly but only in the form of mercifully not applying means for artificial prolongation of his life, seems to him to raise "tempting questions" which "contain too much sophistry" to be a form of obedience to the command to respect, protect, and save life. "The same truth" applies to "passive failure to apply the stimulants" in heart cases as to cases of "active killing."[39]

In all this, Barth mistakes the proposal of past moralists to depend on an ethics of "the well-meaning humanitarianism of underlying motive"—i.e., only on consequences subjectively, well-meaningly aimed at—and he correctly believes that "respect for life" knows more than that about right and wrong. He also fails to distinguish between declaring another life to be useless, and declaring a treatment to be useless. Then Barth comes to a breaking point, out of the same powerful respect for the dying man. Out of an unremitting effort to probe the ways in which human life may be sanctified, protected, and served, Barth's analysis brings him to this breaking point. This very concern raises the question

> whether this kind of artificial prolongation of life does not amount to human arrogance in the opposite direction, whether the fulfillment of medical duty does not threaten to become fanaticism, reason folly; and the required assisting of human life a forbidden torturing of it. A case is at least conceivable in which a doctor might have to recoil from his prolongation of life no less than from its arbitrary shortening. . . . It may well be that in this special sphere we do have a kind of exceptional case. For it is not a question of arbitrary euthanasia; it is a

38. *Church Dogmatics* (Edinburgh: T. & T. Clark, 1961), vol. 3, part 4, p. 426.
39. Ibid., pp. 427, 425, 427.

question of a respect which can be claimed by even the dying life as such.[40]

There comes a time when "letting life ebb away" is *not* the same as "actively encompassing" a patient's death.

Thus love's casuistry brings Barth finally to the distinction between allowing to die and arrogantly using all the resources of medical science artificially to prolong dying. Out of respect for the dying life as such, there arises a fresh understanding of the forbidden torturing of it; and, of course, from this same source springs the awesome understanding of the forbidden taking of life.

It may be that only in an age of faith when men know that the dying cannot pass beyond God's love and care will men have the courage to apply these limits to medical practice. It may be that only upon the basis of faith in God can there be a conscionable category of "ceasing to oppose death," making room for caring for the dying. It may also be that only an age of faith is productive of absolute limits upon the taking of the lives of terminal patients, because of the alignment of many a human will with God's care for them here and now, and not only in the there and then of His providence.

It may be that it is quite natural that in an atheistic and secular age the best morality men can think of is to make an absolute of saving life for yet a bit more spatio-temporal existence, even when this is worked massively upon the dying as if death were only and always an unmitigated evil. It may also be that, paradoxically, a secular age is productive of equally powerful currents of thought toward the arbitrary taking of life for the sake of earthly good to come. If this has to be the conclusion of a secular age, then it is the root of many problems, since this would mean, as Barth suggested, that medical duty has become fanaticism. Or, alternatively, that medical duty becomes the engineering of the future of the species. Together, medical men and moralists need most urgently to renew the search for a way to express both moral recoil from any arbitrary shortening of life, and moral recoil from any arbitrary prolongation of dying. This was in fact the morality of the Western world until a scientific ethic inspired by a secular humanism took over and for the first time in our heritage began to draw the conclusion that whatever can be done should be done to ward off death. Since Christians believe that death and dying are a part of life and like birth no less a gift of God, they have not to wrestle with the Almightly with no holds barred for the dying man.

40. Ibid., pp. 425, 423, 427.

16

THE INDIGNITY OF "DEATH WITH DIGNITY"

This essay, published four years after *The Patient as Person*, signals a changed emphasis in Ramsey's work on medical care for the sick and dying. Where he focused in the previous selection on the problem of overtreatment, he here criticizes a stance that could endorse medical undertreatment in the name of giving patients a "good death." The stance in question takes death to be merely "natural," or "a part of life," or perhaps as something "beautiful." Ramsey, in contrast, argues that the Christian vision includes an awareness that death is a deep affront to the individual. His or her world of value and relationship is decisively threatened by death. To fail to acknowledge this risks abandonment of the ill and dying through cheery neglect, or evasion, or premature termination of medical measures that still respond to human need. (*Hastings Center Studies* 2/2 [1974]: 47–62)

Never one am I to use an ordinary title when an extraordinary one will do as well! Besides, I mean to suggest that there is an additional insult besides death itself heaped upon the dying by our ordinary talk about "death with dignity." Sometimes that is said even to be a human "right"; and what should a decent citizen do but insist on enjoying his rights? That might be his duty (if there is any such right), to the commonwealth, to the human race or some other collective entity; or at least, embracing that "right" and dying rationally would exhibit a proper respect for the going concept of a rational man. So "The Indignity of Death" would not suffice for my purposes, even though all I shall say depends on understanding the contradiction death poses to the unique worth of an individual human life.

The genesis of the following reflections may be worth noting. A few years ago,[1] I embraced what I characterized as the oldest morality there is (no "new morality") concerning responsibility toward the dying: the acceptance of death, stopping our medical interventions for all sorts of good, human reasons, *only* companying with the dying in their final passage. Then suddenly it appeared that altogether too many people were agreeing with me. That caused qualms. As a Southerner born addicted to lost causes, it seemed I now was caught up in a triumphal social trend. As a controversialist in ethics, I found agreement from too many sides. As a generally happy prophet of the doom facing the modern age, unless there is a sea-change in norms of action, it was clear from these premises that anything divers people agree to must necessarily be superficial if not wrong.

Today, when divers people draw the same warm blanket of "allowing to die" or "death with dignity" close up around their shoulders against the dread of that cold night, their various feet are showing. Exposed beneath our growing agreement to that "philosophy of death and dying" may be significantly different "philosophies of life"; and in the present age that agreement may reveal that these interpretations of human life are increasingly mundane, naturalistic, antihumanistic when measured by *any* genuinely "humanistic" esteem for the individual human being.

These "philosophical" ingredients of any view of death and dying I want to make prominent by speaking of "The Indignity of 'Death with Dignity.'" Whatever practical agreement there may be, or "guidelines" proposed to govern contemporary choice or practice, these are bound to be dehumanizing unless at the same time we bring to bear great summit points and sources of insight in mankind's understanding of mankind (be it Christian or other religious humanism, or religiously-dependent but not explicitly religious humanism, or, if it is possible, a true humanism that is neither systematically nor historically dependent on any religious outlook).

DEATH-WITH-DIGNITY IDEOLOGIES

There is nobility and dignity in caring for the dying, but not in dying itself. "To be a therapist to a dying patient makes us aware of the uniqueness of each individual in this vast sea of humanity."[2] It is

1. "On (Only) Caring for the Dying," *The Patient as Person* (New Haven: Yale Univ. Press, 1971).

2. Elisabeth Kübler-Ross, *On Death and Dying* (New York: Macmillan, 1969), p. 247.

more correct to say that a therapist brings to the event, from some other source, an awareness of the uniqueness, the once-for-allness of an individual lifespan as part of an "outlook" and "onlook" upon the vast sea of humanity. In any case, that is the reflected glory and dignity of caring for the dying, that we are or become aware of the unique life here ending. The humanity of such human caring is apt to be more sensitive and mature if we do not lightly suppose that it is an easy thing to convey dignity to the dying. That certainly cannot be done simply by withdrawing tubes and stopping respirators or not thumping hearts. At most, those omissions can only be prelude to companying with the dying in their final passage, if we are fortunate enough to share with them—they in moderate comfort—those interchanges that are in accord with the dignity and nobility of mankind. Still, however noble the manifestations of caring called for, however unique the individual life, we finally must come to the reality of death, and must ask, What can possibly be the meaning of "death with dignity"?

At most we convey only the liberty to die with human dignity; we can provide some of the necessary but not sufficient conditions. If the dying die with a degree of nobility it will be mostly their doing in doing their own dying. I fancy their task was easier when death as a human event meant that special note was taken of the last words of the dying—even humorous ones, as in the case of the Roman emperor who said as he expired, "I deify." A human countenance may be discerned in death accepted with serenity. So also there is a human countenance behind death with defiance. . . . But the human countenance has been removed from most modern understandings of death.

We do not begin to keep human community with the dying if we interpose between them and us most of the current notions of "death with dignity." Rather do we draw closer to them if and only if our conception of "dying with dignity" encompasses—nakedly and without dilution—the final indignity of death itself, whether accepted or raged against. So I think it may be profitable to explore "the indignity of 'death with dignity.'" "Good death" (euthanasia) and "Good grief!" are ultimately contradictions in terms, even if superficially, and before we reach the heart of the matter, there are distinctions to be made; even if, that is to say, the adjective "good" still is applicable in both cases in contrast to worse ways to die and worse ways to grieve or not to grieve.

"Death is simply a part of life," we are told, as a first move to persuade us to accept the ideology of the entire dignity of dying with dignity. A singularly unpersuasive proposition, since we are not told what sort of part of life death is. Disease, injury, congenital defects are also a part of life, and as well murder, rapine, and pillage.[3] Yet there is no campaign for accepting or doing those things with dignity. Nor, for that matter, for the contemporary mentality which would enshrine "death with dignity" is there an equal emphasis on "suffering with dignity," suffering as a "natural" part of life, etc. All those things, it seems, are enemies and violations of human nobility while death is not, or (with a few changes) need not be. Doctors did not invent the fact that death is an enemy, although they may sometimes use disproportionate means to avoid final surrender. Neither did they invent the fact that pain and suffering are enemies and often indignities, although suffering accepted may also be ennobling or may manifest the nobility of the human spirit of any ordinary person.

But, then, it is said, death is an evolutionary necessity and in that further sense a part of life not to be denied. Socially and biologically, one generation follows another. So there must be death, else social history would have no room for creative novelty and planet earth would be glutted with humankind. True enough, no doubt, from the point of view of evolution (which—so far—never dies). But the man who is dying happens not to be evolution. He is a part of evolution, no doubt: but not to the whole extent of his being or his dying. A crucial testimony to the individual's transcendence over the species is man's problem and his dis-ease in dying. Death is a natural fact of life, yet no man dies "naturally," nor do we have occasions in which to practice doing so in order to learn how. Not unless the pursuit of philosophy is a practice of dying (as Plato's *Phaedo* teaches); and that I take to be an understanding of the human being we moderns do not mean to embrace when we embrace "death with dignity."

It is small consolation to tell mortal men that as long as you are, the death you contribute to evolution is not yet; and when death is, you are not—so why fear death? That is the modern equivalent to the recipe offered by the ancient Epicureans (and some Stoics) to undercut fear of death and devotion to the gods: as long as you are, death is not; when death is, you are not; there's never a direct encounter between you and death; so why dread death? Indeed, contrary to modern parlance, those ancient philosophers declared that death is *not a part of life*; so, why worry?

3. Schopenhauer's characterization of human history: If you've read one page, you've read it all.

So "death is not a part of life" is another declaration designed to quiet fear of death. This can be better understood in terms of a terse comment by Wittgenstein: "Our life has no limit in just the way in which our visual field has no limit."[4] We cannot see beyond the boundary of our visual field; it is more correct to say that beyond the boundary of our visual field *we do not see*. Not only so. Also, we do not see the boundary, the limit itself. There is no seeable bound to the visual field. *Death is not a part of life* in the same way that the boundary is not a part of our visual field. Commenting on this remark by Wittgenstein, James Van Evra writes: "Pressing the analogy, then, if my life has no end in *just the way* that my visual field has no limit, then it must be in the sense that I can have no experience of death, conceived as the complete cessation of experience and thought. That is, if life is considered to be a series of experiences and thoughts, then it is impossible for me to experience death, for to experience something is to be alive, and hence is to be inside the bound formed by death."[5] This is why death itself steadfastly resists conceptualization.

Still, I think the disanalogy ought also to be pressed, against both ancient and contemporary analytical philosophers. That notion of death as a limit makes use of a visual or spatial metaphor. Good basketball players are often men naturally endowed with an unusually wide visual field; this is true, for example, of Bill Bradley. Perhaps basketball players, among other things, strive to enlarge their visual fields, or their habitual use of what powers of sight they have, if that is possible. But ordinarily, everyone of us is perfectly happy within the unseeable limits of sight's reach.

Transfer this notion of death as a limit from space to time as the form of human perception, from sight to an individual's inward desire, effort and hope, and I suggest that one gets a different result. Then death as the temporal limit of a lifespan is something we live toward. That limit still can never be experienced or conceptualized; indeed death is *never* a part of life. Moreover, neither is the boundary. Still it is a limit we conative human beings know we live *up against* during our lifespans. We do not live toward or up against the side-limits of our visual span. Instead, within that acceptable visual limit (and other limits as well) as channels we live toward yet another limit which is death.

4. Wittgenstein, *Tractatus* 6.4311.
5. "On Death as a Limit," *Analysis* 31/5 (April 1971): 170–76.

Nor is the following analogy for death as a limit of much help in deepening understanding. "The importance of the limit and virtually *all* of its significance," writes Van Evra, "derives from the fact that the limit serves as an ordering device"—just as absolute zero serves for ordering a series; it is not *just* a limit, although nothing can exist at such a temperature. The analogy is valid so far as it suggests that we conceive of death not in itself but as it bears on us while still alive. As I shall suggest below, death teaches us to "number our days."

But that may not be its only ordering function for conative creatures. Having placed death "out of our league" by showing that it is not a "something," or never a part of life, and while understanding awareness of death as awareness of a limit bearing upon us only while still alive, one ought not forthwith to conclude that this understanding of it "exonerates death as the purported snake in our garden." Death as a limit can disorder no less than order the series. Only a disembodied reason can say, as Van Evra does, that "the bound, not being a member of the series, cannot defile it. The series is what it is, happy or unhappy, good or bad, quite independently of any bound as such." An Eric Erikson knows better than that when writing of the "despair and often unconscious fear of death" which results when "the one and only life cycle is not accepted as the ultimate life." Despair, he observes, "expresses the feeling that the time is short, too short for the attempt to start another life and to try out alternate roads to integrity."[6]

It is the temporal flight of the series that is grievous (not death as an evil "something" within life's span to be balanced, optimistically or pessimistically, against other things that are good). The reminder that death is *not a part of life*, or that it is only a boundary never encountered, is an ancient recipe that can only increase the threat of death on any profound understanding of human life. The dread of death is the dread of oblivion, of there being only empty room in one's stead. Kübler-Ross writes that for the dying, death means the loss of every loved one, total loss of everything that constituted the self in its world, separation from every experience, even from future possible, replacing experiences—nothingness beyond. Therefore, life is a time-intensive activity and not only a goods-intensive or quality-intensive activity. No matter how many "goods" we store up in barns, like the man in Jesus' parable we know that this night our soul may be re-

6. "Identity and the Life Cycle," *Psychological Issues*, vol. 1, no. 1 (New York: International Univ. Press, 1959).

quired of us (Luke 12:13–21). No matter what "quality of life" our lives have, we must take into account the opportunity-costs of used time. Death means the conquest of the time of our lives—even though we never experience the experience of the nothingness which is natural death.

"Awareness of dying" means awareness of *that*; and awareness of that constitutes an experience of ultimate indignity in and to the awareness of the self who is dying.

We are often reminded of Koheleth's litany: "For everything there is a season, and a time for every matter under heaven: a time to be born and a time to die; a time to plant, and a time to pluck up what is planted," etc. (Eccles. 3:1,2). Across those words of the narrator of Ecclesiastes the view gains entrance that only an "untimely" death should be regretted or mourned. Yet we know better how to specify an untimely death than to define or describe a "timely" one. The author of Genesis tells us that, at 180 years of age, the patriarch Isaac "breathed his last; and he died and was gathered to his people, old and full of years" (Gen. 35:29). Even in face of sacred scripture, we are permitted to wonder what Isaac thought about it; whether he too knew how to apply the category "fullness of years" *to himself* and agreed his death was nothing but timely.

We do Koheleth one better and say that death cannot only be timely; it may also be "beautiful." Whether such an opinion is to be ascribed to David Hendin or not (a "fact of life" man he surely is, who also unambiguously subtitled his chapter on euthanasia "Let There Be Death"),[7] that opinion seems to be the outlook of the legislator and physician Walter Sackett, Jr., who proposed the Florida "death with dignity" statute. All his mature life his philosophy has been, "Death, like birth, is glorious—let it come easy."[8] Such was by no means Koheleth's opinion when he wrote (and *wrote* beautifully) about a time to be born and a time to die. Dr. Sackett also suggests that up to 90 percent of the 1,800 patients in state hospitals for the mentally retarded should be allowed to die. Five billion dollars could be saved in the next half century if the state's mongoloids were permitted to succumb to pneumonia, a disease to which they are highly suscepti-ble.[9] I suggest that the physician in Dr. Sackett has atrophied. He has become a public functionary, treating taxpayers' pocketbooks under

7. *Death as a Fact of Life* (New York: W. W. Norton, 1973).
8. Reported in ibid., p. 89.
9. *Florida Times-Union*, Jan. 11, 1973.

the general anesthesia of a continuous daytime soap opera entitled "Death Can Be Beautiful!"

"Death for an older person should be a beautiful event. There is beauty in birth, growth, fullness of life and then, equally so, in the tapering off and final end. There are analogies all about us. What is more beautiful than the spring budding of small leaves; then the fully-leaved tree in summer; and then in the beautiful brightly colored autumn leaves gliding gracefully to the ground? So it is with humans." Those are words from a study document on euthanasia drafted in 1972 by the Council for Christian Social Action of the United Church of Christ. An astonishing footnote at this point states that "the naturalness of dying" is suggested in funeral services when the minister says, "God has called" the deceased, or says he has "gone to his reward," recites the "dust to dust" passage, or notes that the deceased led a full life or ran a full course!

Before that statement was adopted by that council on February 17, 1973, more orthodox wording was inserted: "Transformation from life on earth to life in the hereafter of the Lord is a fulfillment. The acceptance of death is our witness to faith in the resurrection of Jesus Christ (Rom. 8). We can rejoice." The subdued words "we can rejoice" indicate a conviction that *something* has been subdued. The words "acceptance of death" take the whole matter out of the context of romantic naturalism and set it in a proper religious context—based on the particular Christian tenet that death is a conquered enemy, to be accepted in the name of its Conqueror. More than a relic of the nature mysticism that was so luxurient in the original paragraph, however, remains in the words "Death for an older person should be a beautiful event. There is beauty in birth, growth, fullness of life and then, *equally so*, in the tapering off and final end." I know no Christian teaching that assures us that our "final end" is "equally" beautiful as birth, growth, and fullness of life. Moreover, if revelation disclosed any such thing it would be contrary to reason and to the human reality and experience of death. The views of our "pre-death morticians" are simply discordant with the experienced reality they attempt to beautify. So, in her recent book, Marya Mannes writes "the name of the oratorio is euthanasia." And her statement that "dying is merely suspension within a mystery" seems calculated to induce vertigo in face of a fascinating abyss in prospect.[10]

No exception can be taken to one line in the letter people are being

10. *Last Rights* (New York: Morrow, 1973), p. 6 (cf., pp. 80, 133).

encouraged to write and sign by the Euthanasia Societies of Great Britain and America. That line states: "I do not fear death as much as I fear the indignity of deterioration, dependence and hopeless pain." Such an exercise in analyzing *comparative indignities* should be given approval. But the preceding sentence states: "Death is as much a reality as birth, growth, maturity, and old age—it is the one certainty." That logically leaves open the question what sort of "reality," what sort of "certainty," death is. But by placing death on a parity with birth, growth, maturity—and old age in many of its aspects—the letter beautifies death by association. To be written long before death when one is thinking "generally" (i.e., "rationally"?) about the topic, the letter tempts us to suppose that men can think generally about their own deaths. Hendin observes in another connection that "there is barely any relation between what people think that they think about death and the way they actually feel about it when it must be faced."[11] Then it may be that "the heart has its reasons that reason cannot know" (Pascal)—beforehand—and among those "reasons," I suggest, will be an apprehension of the ultimate (noncomparative) indignity of death. Talk about death as a fact or a reality seasonally recurring in life with birth or planting, maturity and growth, may after all not be very rational. It smacks more of whistling before the darkness descends, and an attempt to brainwash one's contemporaries to accept a very feeble philosophy of life and death.

Birth and death (our terminus ad quo and our terminus ad quem) are not to be equated with any of the qualities or experiences, the grandeur and the misery, in between, which constitutes "parts" of our lives. While we live toward death and can encompass our own dying in awareness, no one in the same way is aware of his own birth. We know that we were born in the same way we know *that* we die. Explanations of whence we came do not establish conscious contact with our individual origin; and among explanations, that God called us from the womb out of nothing is as good as any other; and better than most. But awareness of dying is quite another matter. That we may have, but not awareness of our births. And while awareness of birth might conceivably be the great original individuating experience (if we had it), among the race of men it is awareness of dying that is uniquely individuating. To encompass one's own death in the living and dying of one's life is more of a task than it is a part of life. And there is something of indignity to be faced when engaging in that final

11. *Death*, p. 103.

act of life. Members of the caring human community (doctors, nurses, family) are apt to keep closer company with the dying if we acknowledge the loss of all worth by the loss of him in whom inhered all worth in his world. Yet ordinary men may sometimes nobly suffer the ignobility of death.

By way of contrast with the "Living Will" framed by the Euthanasia Society, the Judicial Council of the American Medical Association in its recent action on the physician and the dying patient had before it two similar letters. One was composed by the Connecticut delegation:

> To my Family, my Physician,
> my Clergyman, my Lawyer—
> If the time comes when I can no longer actively take part in decisions for my own future, I wish this statement to stand as the testament of my wishes. If there is no reasonable expectation of my recovery from physical or mental and spiritual disability, I, _____, request that I be allowed to die and not be kept alive by artificial means or heroic measures. I ask also that drugs be mercifully administered to me for terminal suffering even if in relieving pain they may hasten the moment of death. I value life and the dignity of life, so that I am not asking that my life be directly taken, but that my dying not be unreasonably prolonged nor the dignity of life be destroyed. This request is made, after careful reflection, while I am in good health and spirits. Although this document is not legally binding, you who care for me will, I hope, feel morally bound to take it into account. I recognize that it places a heavy burden of responsibility upon you, and it is with the intention of sharing this responsibility that this statement is made.

A second letter had been composed by a physician to express his own wishes, in quite simple language:

> To my Family, To my Physician—
> Should the occasion arise in my lifetime when death is imminent and a decision is to be made about the nature and the extent of the care to be given to me and I am not able at that time to express my desires, let this statement serve to express my deep, sincere, and considered wish and hope that my physician will administer to me simple, ordinary medical treatment. I ask that he not administer heroic, extraordinary, expensive, or useless medical care or treatment which in the final analysis will merely delay, not change, the ultimate outcome of my terminal condition.

A comparison of these declarations with "A Living Will" circulated by the Euthanasia Society reveals the following signal differences: neither of the AMA submissions engages in any superfluous calculus of "comparative indignities";[12] neither associates the reality of death with such things as birth or maturation; both allow death to be simply what it is in human experience; both are in a general sense "prolife" statements, in that death is neither reified as one fact among others nor beautified even comparatively.[13]

Everyone concerned takes the wrong turn in trying either to "thing-ify" death or to beautify it. The dying have at least this advantage, that in these projects for dehumanizing death by naturalizing it the dying finally cannot succeed, and death makes its threatening visage known to them before ever there are any societal or evolutionary replacement values or the everlasting arms or Abraham's bosom to rest on. Death means *finis*, not in itself *telos*. Certainly not a telos to be engineered, or to be accomplished by reducing both human life and death to the level of natural events.

"Thing-ifying" death reaches its highest pitch in the stated preference of many people in the present age for *sudden* death,[14] for death from unanticipated internal collapse, from the abrupt intrusion of violent outside forces, from some chance occurrence due to the natural law governing the operation of automobiles. While for a comparative calculus of indignities sudden *unknowing* death may be preferred to suffering knowingly or unknowingly the indignity of deterioration, abject dependence, and hopeless pain, how ought we to assess in human terms the present-day absolute (noncomparative) preference for sudden death? Nothing reveals more the meaning we assign to human "dignity" than the view that sudden death, death as an eruptive natural event, could be a prismatic case of death with

12. What, after all, is the point of promoting, as if it were a line of reasoning, observations such as that said to be inscribed on W. C. Fields's tombstone: "On the whole I'd rather be here than in Philadelphia"?

13. I may add that while the AMA's House of Delegates did not endorse any particular form to express an individual's wishes relating prospectively to his final illness, it recognized that individuals have a right to express them. While it encouraged physicians to discuss such matters with patients and attend to their wishes, the House nevertheless maintained a place for the conscience and judgment of a physician in determining indicated treatment. It did not subsume every consideration under the rubric of the patient's right to refuse treatment (or to have refused treatment). That sole action-guide can find no medical or logical reason for distinguishing, in physician actions, between the dying and those who simply have a terminal illness (or have this "dying life," Augustine's description of all of us). It would also entail a belief that wishing or autonomous choice makes the moral difference between life and death decisions which then are to be imposed on the physician-technician; and that, to say the least, is an ethics that can find no place for either reason or sensibility.

14. Cf. the report of a Swedish survey by Gunnar Biörck, M.D., in *Archives of Internal Medicine*, October 1973; cited in *New York Times*, Oct. 31, 1973.

dignity or at least one without indignity. Human society seems about to rise to the moral level of the "humane" societies in their treatment of animals. What is the principled difference between their view and ours about the meaning of dying "humanely"? By way of contrast, consider the prayer in the Anglican prayer book: "From perils by night and perils by day, perils by land and perils by sea, and *from sudden death*, Lord, deliver us." Such a petition bespeaks an age in which dying with dignity was a gift and a task (*Gaube und Aufgaube*), a liberty to encompass dying as a final act among the actions of life, to enfold awareness of dying as an ingredient into awareness of one's self dying as the finale of the self's relationships in this life to God or to fellow man—in any case to everything that was worthy.

MAN KNOWS THAT HE DIES

Before letting Koheleth's "a time to be born and a time to die" creep as a gloss into *our* texts, perhaps we ought to pay more attention to the outlook on life and death expressed in the enchantment and frail beauty of those words,[15] and ask whether that philosophy can possibly be a proper foundation for the practice of medicine or for the exercise of the most sensitive care for the dying.

That litany on the times for every matter under heaven concludes with the words "What gain has the worker from his toil?" (Eccles. 3:9). In general, the author of Ecclesiastes voices an unrelieved pessimism. He has "seen everything that is done under the sun," in season

---

15. In the whole literature on death and dying, there is no more misquoted sentence, or statement taken out of context, than Koheleth's "time to be born and a time to die"—unless it be "Nor strive officiously to keep alive." The latter line is from an ironic poem by the nineteenth-century poet Arthur Hugh Clough, entitled "The Latest Decalogue":

> Thou shalt not kill; but need'st not strive
> Officiously to keep alive.
> Do not adultery commit;
> Advantage rarely comes of it:
> Thou shalt not steal; an empty feat,
> When it's so lucrative to cheat:
> Bear not false witness; let the lie
> Have time on its own wings to fly:
> Thou shall not covet; but tradition
> Approves all forms of competition.
> The sum of all is, thou shalt love
> If anybody, God above:
> At any rate, shalt never labor
> More than thyself to love thy neighbor.

and out of season. It is altogether "an unhappy business that God has given to the sons of men to be busy with"—this birthing and dying, planting and uprooting; "all is vanity and seeking after wind" (Eccles. 1:3b,14). So, he writes with words of strongest revulsion, "I hated life, because what is done under the sun was grievous to me"; "I hated all my toil and gave myself up to despair" (Eccles. 2:17,18a,20).

After that comes the litany "for everything there is a season"— proving, as Kierkegaard said, that a poet is a man whose heart is full of pain but whose lips are so formed that when he gives utterance to that pain he makes beautiful sounds. Koheleth knew, as later did Nietzsche, that the eternal recurrence of birth and death and all things else was simply "the spirit of melancholy" unrelieved, even though there is nothing else to believe since God died.[16] (The pope knows: he was at the bedside.)

"Death with dignity" because death is a "part" of life, one only of its seasonal realities? If so, then the acceptable death of all flesh means death with the same signal indignity that brackets the whole of life and its striving. Dying is worth as much as the rest; it is no more fruitless.

"For the fate of the sons of men and the fate of the beasts is the same; as one dies so dies the other. They all have the same breath, and man has no advantage over the beasts; for all is vanity" (Eccles. 3:19). "Death with dignity" or death a part of life based on an equilibration of the death of a man with the death of a dog? I think that is not a concept to be chosen as the foundation of modern medicine, even though both dogs and men are enabled to die "humanely."

Or to go deeper still: "death with dignity" because the dead are better off than the living? "I thought the dead who are already dead," Koheleth writes in unrelieved sorrow over existence, "more fortunate than the living who are still alive; and better than both is he who has not yet been, and has not seen the evil deeds that are done under the sun" (Eccles. 4:2,3). Thus the book of Ecclesiastes is the source of the famous interchange between two pessimistic philosophers, each trying to exceed the other in gloom: First philosopher: More blessed are the dead than the living. Second philosopher: Yes, what you say is true; but more blessed still are those who have never been born. First philosopher: Yes, wretched life; but few there be who attain to that condition!

But Koheleth thinks he knows some who have attained to the

16. Nietzsche, *Thus Spake Zarathustra*, esp. XLVI and LXVI.

blessed goal of disentrapment from the cycles in which there is a time for every matter under heaven. "An untimely birth [a miscarriage] is better off [than a living man], for it [a miscarriage] comes into vanity and goes into darkness, and in darkness its name is covered, moreover it has not seen the sun or known anything; yet it finds rest rather than he [the living]" (Eccles. 6:3b,4,5). So we might say that death can have its cosmic dignity if untormented by officious physicians, because the dying go to the darkness, to Limbo where nameless miscarriages dwell, having never seen the sun or known anything. Thus, if dying with dignity as a part of life's natural, undulating seasons seems not to be a thought with much consolation in it (being roughly equivalent to the indignity besetting everything men do and every other natural time), still the dying may find rest as part of cosmic order, from which, once upon a time, the race of men arose to do the unhappy business God has given them to be busy with, and to which peaceful darkness the dying return.

Hardly a conception that explains the rise of Western medicine, the energy of its care of the dying, or its war against the indignity of suffering and death—or a conception on which to base its reformation! . . .

There is finally in Ecclesiastes, however, a deeper strand than those which locate men living and dying as simply parts of some malignly or benignly neglectful natural or cosmic order. From these more surface outlooks, the unambiguous injunction follows: Be a part; let there be death—in its time and place, of course (whatever that means). Expressing a deeper strand, however, Koheleth seems to say: Let the natural or cosmic order be whatever it is; men are different. His practical advice is: Be what you are, in human awareness apart and not a part. Within this deeper understanding of the transcendent, threatened nobility of a human life, the uniqueness of the individual human subject, there is ground for awareness of death as an indignity yet freedom to encompass it with dignity.

Now it is that Koheleth reverses the previous judgments he decreed over all he had seen under the sun. Before, the vale of the sunless not-knowing of a miscarriage having its name covered by darkness seemed preferable to living; and all man's works a seeking after wind. So, of course, there was "a time for dying." But now Koheleth writes, "There is no work or thought or knowledge or wisdom in Sheol, to which you are going" (Eccles. 9:10b). While the fate of the sons of men and the fate of the beasts are the same, still "a living dog is better than a dead lion"; and to be a living man is better than either, because of what Koheleth means by "living." "He who is joined with all the living has hope" (Eccles. 9:4), and that is hardly a way to describe dogs or lions. Koheleth, however, identifies the grandeur of man not so much with hope as with awareness, even awareness of dying, and the misery of man with the indignity of dying of which he, in his nobility, is aware. "For the living know that they will die," he writes, "but the dead know nothing" (Eccles. 9:5). Before, the dead or those who never lived had superiority; now, it is the living who are superior precisely by virtue of their awareness of dying and of its indignity to the knowing human spirit.

Therefore, I suggest that Koheleth probed the human condition to a depth to which more than twenty centuries later Blaise Pascal came. "Man is but a reed, the feeblest in nature, but he is a thinking reed. . . . A vapour, a drop of water, is sufficient to slay him. But were the universe to crush him, man would still be nobler than that which kills him, for *he knows that he dies*, while the universe knows nothing of the advantage it has over him. Thus our whole dignity consists in thought" (italics added).[17]

So the grandeur and misery of man are fused together in the human reality and experience of death. To deny the indignity of death requires that the dignity of man be refused also. The more acceptable in itself death is, the less the worth or uniqueness ascribed to the dying life.

TRUE HUMANISM AND THE DREAD OF DEATH

I always write as the ethicist I am, namely, a Christian ethicist, and not as some hypothetical common denominator. On common concrete problems I, of course, try to elaborate analysis at the point or on a terrain where there may be convergence of vectors that began in other ethical outlooks and onlooks. Still one should not pant for agreement as the hart pants for the water-brooks, lest the substance of one's ethics dissolve into vapidity. So in this section I want, among other things, to exhibit some of the meaning of "Christian humanism" in regard to death and dying, in the confidence that this will prove tolerable to my colleagues for a time, if not finally instructive to them.

In this connection, there are two counterpoised verses in the First Epistle of St. John that are worth pondering. The first reads: "Perfect

17. Pascal, *Pensées*, no. 347.

love casts out fear" (which being interpreted means: Perfect care of the dying casts out fear of one's own death or rejection of their dying because of fear of ours). The second verse reads: "Where fear is, love is not perfected" (which being interpreted means: Where fear of death and dying remains, medical and human care of the dying is not perfected). That states nothing so much as the enduring dubiety and ambiguity of any mortal man's care of another through his dying. At the same time there is here applied without modification a standard for unflinching care of a dying fellow man, or short of that of any fellow mortal any time. That standard is cut to the measure of the perfection in benevolence believed to be that of our Father in Heaven in His dealings with mankind. So there is "faith-ing" in an ultimate righteousness beyond the perceptible human condition presupposed by those verses that immediately have to do simply with loving and caring.

Whatever non-Christians may think about the *theology* here entailed, or about similar foundations in any religious ethics, I ask that the notation upon or penetration of the human condition be attended to. Where and insofar as fear is, love and care for the dying cannot be perfected in moral agents or the helping professions. The religious traditions have one way of addressing that problematic. In the modern age the problematic itself is avoided by various forms and degrees of denial of the tragedy of death which proceeds first to reduce the unique worth and once-for-allness of the individual lifespan that dies.

Perhaps one can apprehend the threat posed to the dignity of man (i.e., in an easy and ready dignifying of death) by many modern viewpoints, especially those dominating the scientific community, and their superficial equivalents in our culture generally, by bringing into view three states of consciousness in the Western past.

The burden of the Hebrew Scriptures was man's obedience or disobedience to covenant, to Torah. Thus sin was the problem, and death came in only as a subordinate theme; and, as one focus for the problematic of the human condition, this was a late development. In contrast, righteousness and disobedience (sin) were a subordinate theme in Greek religion. The central theme of Greek religious thought and practice was the problem of death—a problem whose solution was found either by initiation into religious cults that promised to extricate the soul from its corruptible shroud or by belief in the native power of the soul to outlast any number of bodies. Alongside these, death was at the heart of the pathos of life depicted in Greek tragical drama, against which, and against the flaws of finitude in general, the major character manifested his heroic transcendence. So sin was determinative for the Hebrew consciousness; death for the Greek consciousness.

Consciousness III was Christianity, and by this, sin and death were tied together in Western man's awareness of personal existence. These two foci of man's misery and of his need for redemption—sin and death—were inseparably fused. This new dimension of man's awareness of himself was originally probed most profoundly by St. Paul's Letter to the Romans (5–7). Those opaque reflections, I opine, were once understood not so much by the intellect as along the pulses of ordinary people in great numbers, in taverns and marketplaces; and it represents a cultural breakdown without parallel that these reflections are scarcely understandable to the greatest intelligences today. A simple night-school lesson in them may be gained by simply pondering a while the two verses quoted above from St. John's Epistle.

The point is that according to the Christian saga the Messiah did not come to bring boors into culture. Nor did he bear epilepsy or psychosomatic disorders to gain victory over them in the flesh before the interventions of psychoneurosurgery. Rather is he said to have been born *mortal* flesh to gain for us a foretaste of victory over sin and death where those twin enemies had taken up apparently secure citadel.

Again, the point for our purposes is not to be drawn into agreement or disagreement with those theological affirmations, and it is certainly not to be tempted into endless speculation about an afterlife. Crucial instead is to attend to the notation on the human condition implied in all that. Death is an enemy even if it is the last enemy to be fully conquered in the Fulfillment, the eschaton; meanwhile, the sting of death is sin. Such was the new consciousness raising that Christianity brought into the Western world. And the question is whether in doing so it has not grasped some important experiential human realities better than most philosophies, whether it was not attuned to essential ingredients of the human condition vis-à-vis death—whatever the truth or falsity of its theological address to that condition.

The foregoing, I grant, may be an oversimplification; and I am aware of needed corrections more in the case of Hebrew humanism than in the case of Greek humanism. The New Testament word "He will wipe away every tear from their eyes, and death shall be no more, neither shall there be mourning nor crying nor pain any more, for the former things have passed away," (Rev. 21:3,4) has its parallel in the

Hebrew Bible: "He will swallow up death forever, and the Lord God will wipe away tears from all faces" (Isa. 25:8). Again, since contemplating the Lord God may be too much for us, I ask only that we attend to the doctrine of death implied in these passages: it is an enemy, surely, and not simply an acceptable part of the natural order of things. And the connection between dread of death and sin, made most prominent in Christian consciousness, was nowhere better stated than in Ecclesiastes: "This is the root of the evil in all that happens under the sun, that one fate comes to all. Therefore, men's minds are filled with evil and there is madness in their hearts while they live, for they know that afterward—they are off to the dead!"

One can, indeed, ponder that verse about the source of all evil in the apprehended evil of death together with another verse in Ecclesiastes which reads: "Teach us so to number our days that we may apply our hearts unto wisdom." The first says that death is an evil evil: it is experienced as a threatening limit that begets evil. The second says that death is a good evil: that experience also begets good. Without death, and death perceived as a threat, we would also have no reason to "number our days" so as to ransom the time allotted us, to receive life as a precious gift, to drink the wine of gladness in toast to every successive present moment. Instead, life would be an endless boredom and boring because endless; there would be no reason to probe its depths while there is still time. Some there are who number their days so as to apply their hearts unto eating, drinking, and being merry—for tomorrow we die. Some there are who number their days so as to apply their hearts unto wisdom—for tomorrow we die. Both are lifespans enhanced in importance and in individuation under the stimulus of the perceived evil of death. Knowledge of human good or of human evil that is in the slightest degree above the level of the beasts of the field are both enhanced because of death, the horizon of human existence. So, debarment from access to the tree of life was on the horizon and a sequence of the events in the Garden of Paradise; the temptation in eating the fruit of the tree of knowledge of good and evil was because that seemed a way for mortal creatures to become like gods. The punishment of that is said to have been death; and no governor uses as a penalty something that anyone can simply choose to believe to be a good or simply receive as a neutral or dignified, even ennobling, part of life. So I say death may be a good evil or an evil evil, but it is perceived as an evil or experienced indignity in either case. Existential anxiety or general anxiety (distinguishable from particular fears or removable anxieties) means anxiety over death toward which we live. That paradoxically, as Reinhold Neibuhr said, is the source of all human creativity and of all human sinfulness.

Of course, the sages of old could and did engage in a calculus of comparative indignities. "O death, your sentence is welcome," wrote Ben Sira, "to a man worn out with age, worried about everything, disaffected and beyond endurance" (Eccles. 41:2,3). Still death was a "sentence," not a natural event acceptable in itself. Moreover, not every man grows old gracefully in the Psalms; instead, one complains:

> Take pity on me, Yahweh,
> I am in trouble now.
> Grief wastes away my eye,
> My throat, my inmost parts.
> For my life is worn out with sorrow,
> My years with sighs;
> My strength yields under misery,
> My bones are wasting away.
> To every one of my oppressors
> I am contemptible,
> Loathsome to my neighbors,
> To my friends a thing of fear.
> Those who see me in the street
> Hurry past me.
> I am forgotten, as good as dead, in their hearts,
> Something discarded. (Ps. 31:9–12)

What else is to be expected if it be true that the madness in men's hearts while they live, and the root of all evil in all that happens under the sun, lie in the simple fact that every man consciously lives toward his own death, knowing that afterward he too is off to the dead? Where fear is—fear of the properly dreadful—love and care for the dying cannot be perfected.

Unless one has some grounds for respecting the shadow of death upon every human countenance—grounds more ultimate than perceptible realities—then it makes good sense as a policy of life simply to try to outlast one's neighbors. One can, for example, *generalize*, and so attenuate our neighbors' irreplaceability. "If I must grieve whenever the bell tolls," writes Wilson Carey McWilliams, "I am never bereft: some of my kinsmen will remain. Indeed, I need not grieve much—even, lest I suggest some preference among my brethren, should not grieve much—for each loss is small compared to what remains."[18] But that solace, we know, is denied the dead who have

18. *The Idea of Fraternity in America* (Berkeley: Univ. of California Press, 1973), p. 48.

lost everything making for worth in this their world. Realistic love for another irreplaceable, noninterchangeable individual human being means, as Unamuno wrote, care for another "doomed soul."

In this setting, let us now bring into consideration some empirical findings that in this day are commonly supposed to be more confirmatory than wisdom meditated from the heart.

In the second-year anatomy course, medical students clothe with "gallows humor" their encounter with the cadaver which once was a human being alive. That defense is not to be despised; nor does it necessarily indicate socialization in shallowness on the students' part. Even when dealing with the remains of the long since dead, there is special tension involved . . . when performing investigatory medical actions involving the face, the hands, and the genitalia. This thing-in-the-world that was once a man alive we still encounter as once a communicating being, not quite as an object of research or instruction. Face and hands, yes; but why the genitalia? Those reactions must seem incongruous to a resolutely biologizing age. For a beginning of an explanation, one might take up the expression "carnal knowledge"—which was the best thing about the movie bearing that title—and behind that go to the expression "carnal *conversation*," an old, legal term for adultery, and back of both to the biblical word "knew" in "And Adam *knew* his wife and begat. . . ." Here we have an entire anthropology impacted in a word, not a squeamish euphemism. In short, in those reactions of medical students can be discerned a sensed relic of the human being bodily experiencing and communicating, and the body itself uniquely speaking.

Notably, however, there's no gallows humor used when doing or observing one's first autopsy, or in the emergency room when a DOA (dead on arrival) is brought in with his skull cleaved open. With regard to the "newly dead" we come as close as we possibly can to experiencing the incommensurable contrast between life and death. Yet those sequential realities—life and death—here juxtaposed never *meet* in direct encounter. So we never have an impression or experience of the measure and meaning of the two different worlds before which we stand in the autopsy and the emergency room. A cadaver has over time become almost a thing-in-the-world from which to gain knowledge of the human body. While *there* a little humor helps, to go about acquiring medical knowledge from autopsies requires a different sort of inward effort to face down or live with our near-experience of the boundary of life and death. The cleavage in the brain may be quite enough and more than enough to *explain* rationally why this man was DOA. But, I suggest, there can be no gash deep enough, no physical event destructive enough to account for the felt difference between life and death that we face here. The physician or medical student may be a confirmed materialist. For him the material explanation of this death may be quite sufficient rationally. Still the heart has its reasons that the reason knows not of; and, I suggest, the awakening of these feelings of awe and dread should not be repressed in anyone whose calling is to the human dignity of caring for the dying.

In any case, from these empirical observations, if they be true, let us return to a great example of theological anthropology in order to try to comprehend why death was thought to be the assault of an enemy. According to some readings, Christians in all ages should be going about bestowing the gift of immortality on one another posthaste. A distinguished Catholic physician, beset by what he regarded as the incorrigible problems of medical ethics today, once shook his head in my presence and wondered out loud why the people who most believe in an afterlife should have established so many hospitals! That seems to require explanation, at least as against silly interpretations of "otherworldliness." The answer is that none of the facts or outlooks cited ever denied the reality of death, or affirmed that death ever presents a friendly face (except comparatively). The explanation lies in the vicinity of Christian anthropology and the biblical view that death is an enemy. That foundation of Western medicine ought not lightly to be discarded, even if we need to enliven again the sense that there are limits to man's struggle against that alien power.

Far from the otherworldliness or body-soul dualism with which he is often charged, St. Augustine went so far as to say that "the body is not an extraneous ornament or aid, but a part of man's very nature."[19] Upon that understanding of the human being, Augustine could then express a quite realistic account of "the dying process":

> Wherefore, as regards bodily death, that is, the separation of the soul from the body, it is good to none while it is being endured by those whom we say are in the article of death [dying]. For the very violence with which the body and soul are wrenched asunder, which in the living are conjoined and closely intertwined, brings with it a harsh experience, jarring horribly on nature as long as it continues, till there comes a total loss of sensation, which arose from the very interpenetration of flesh and spirit.[20]

19. Augustine, *City of God*, bk. 1, chap. 13.
20. Ibid., bk. 13, chap. 6.

From this Augustine correctly concludes: "Wherefore death is indeed . . . good to none while it is actually suffered, and while it is subduing the dying to its power." His ultimate justifications attenuate not at all the harshness of that alien power's triumph. Death, he only says, is "meritoriously endured for the sake of winning what *is* good. And regarding what happens after death, it is no absurdity to say that death is good to the good, and evil to the evil."[21] But that is not to say that death as endured in this life, or as life's terminus, is itself in any way good. He even goes so far as to say:

> For though there can be no manner of doubt that the souls of the just and holy lead lives in peaceful rest, yet so much better would it be for them to be alive in healthy, well-conditioned bodies, that even those who hold the tenet that it is most blessed to be quit of every kind of body, condemn this opinion in spite of themselves.[22]

Thus, for biblical or later Christian anthropology, the only possible form which human life in any true and proper sense can take here or hereafter is "somatic." That is the Pauline word; we today say "psychosomatic." Therefore, for Christian theology death may be a "conquered enemy"; still it was in the natural order—and as long as the generations of mankind endure will remain—an enemy still. To pretend otherwise adds insult to injury—or, at least, carelessness.

There are two ways, so far as I can see, to reduce the dreadful visage of death to a level of inherently acceptable indifference. One way is to subscribe to an interpretation of "bodily life" that reduces it to an acceptable level of indifference to the person long before his dying. That—if anyone can believe it today, or if it is not a false account of human nature—was the way taken by Plato in his idealized account of the death of Socrates. (It should be remembered that we know not whether Socrates' hands trembled as he yet bravely drank the hemlock, no more than we know how Isaac experienced dying when "fullness of years" came upon him. Secondary accounts of these matters are fairly untrustworthy.)

Plato's dialogue *The Phaedo* may not "work" as a proof of the immortality of the soul. Still it decisively raises the question of immortality by its thorough representation of the incommensurability between mental processes and bodily processes. Few philosophers today accept the demonstration of the mind's power to outlast bodies because the mind itself is not material, or because the mind "plays"

21. Ibid., bk. 13, chap. 8.
22. Ibid., bk. 13, chap. 29.

the body like a musician the lyre. But most of them are still wrestling with the mind-body problem, and many speak of two separate languages, a language for mental events isomorphic with our language for brain events. That's rather like saying the same thing as Socrates (Plato) while claiming to have gone beyond him (Søren Kierkegaard).

I cite *The Phaedo* for another purpose: to manifest one way to render death incomparably welcomed. Those who most have mature manhood in exercise—the lovers of wisdom—have desired death and dying all their life long, in the sense that they seek "in every sort of way to dissever the soul from the communion of the body"; "thought is best when the mind is gathered into herself and none of these things trouble her—neither sounds nor sights nor pain nor any pleasure—when she takes leave of the body." That life is best and has nothing to fear that has "the habit of the soul gathering and collecting herself into herself from all sides out of the body." (Feminists, note the pronouns.)

Granted, Socrates' insight is valid concerning the self's transcendence, when he says: "I am inclined to think that these muscles and bones of mine would have gone off long ago to Megara and Boeotia—by the dog, they would, if they had been moved only by their own idea of what was best." Still, Crito had a point when he feared that the impending dread event had more to do with "the same Socrates who has been talking and conducting the argument" than Socrates is represented to have believed. To fear the loss of Socrates, Crito had not to fancy, as Socrates charged, "that I am the other Socrates whom he will soon see, a dead body." Crito had only to apprehend, however faintly, that there is not an entire otherness between those two Socrates *now,* in this living being; that there was unity between, let us say, Socrates the conductor of arguments and Socrates the gesticulator or the man who stretched *himself* because his muscles and bones grew weary from confinement.

The other way to reduce the dreadful visage of death is to subscribe to a philosophy of "human life" that reduces the stature, the worth, and the irreplaceable uniqueness of the individual person (long before his dying) to a level of acceptable transiency or interchangeability. True, modern culture is going this way. But there have been other and better ways of stipulating that the image of death across the human countenance is no shadow. One was that of Aristotelian philosophy. According to its form-matter distinction, reason, the formal principle, is definitive of essential humanity. That is universal, eternal as logic. Matter, however, is the individuating factor. So when a man who bears a particular name dies, only the individuation disintegrates—to provide matter for other forms. Humanity goes on in other instances. Anything unique or precious about mankind is not individual. There are parallels to this outlook in Eastern religions and philosophies, in which the individual has only transiency, and should seek only that, disappearing in the Fulfillment into the Divine pool.

These then are two ways of denying the dread of death. Whenever these two escapes are *simultaneously* rejected—i.e., if the "bodily life" is neither an ornament nor a drag but a part of man's very nature; and if the "personal life" of an individual in his unique lifespan is accorded unrepeatable, noninterchangeable value—then it is that Death the Enemy again comes into view. Conquered or Unconquerable. A true humanism and the dread of death seem to be dependent variables. I suggest that it is better to have the indignity of death on our hands and in our outlooks than to "dignify" it in either of these two possible ways. Then we ought to be much more circumspect in speaking of death with dignity, and hesitant to—I almost said—thrust that upon the dying! Surely, a proper care for them needs not only to know the pain of dying which human agency may hold at bay, but also to acknowledge that there is grief over death which no human agency can alleviate.

17

JUSTICE AND EQUAL TREATMENT

Worries about undertreatment carry forward in this moral analysis of what Ramsey called the "benign neglect of defective infants." Both a "true humanism" and the Christian gospel demand that social, economic, and cognitive criteria of human worth play no role in determining whether or not to treat children born with serious illness. Ramsey hopes that physicians, should they play God, will "play God as God plays God" and be "no respecter of persons of good quality." (From *Ethics at the Edges of Life*, pp. 201–08)

There is still another moral aspect of the practice of neglect: this is a question of justice. Some physicians who have reported that they let some babies die (perhaps hasten their dying) also report that they make such life-or-death decisions not only on the basis of the newborn's medical condition and prognosis, but on the basis of familial, social, and economic factors as well. If the marriage seems to be a strong one, an infant impaired to x degree may be treated, while an infant with the same impairment may not be treated if the marriage seems about to fall apart. Treatment may be given if the parents are wealthy; not, if they are poor.[1] Now, life may be unfair, as John Ken-

---

1. In a published interview, Dr. Raymond S. Duff seems to me to be ambiguous on these points, even contradictory. On the one hand he says, "My guess is that neither social nor economic considerations influence the decisions we are talking about to any significant degree. I never felt that a troubled marriage or the economics of the family has really had a major influence. Parents may fight with one another but they still adhere to what they both consider is fair to the child." Yet two or three paragraphs later he reported the case of a couple who had to decide "how many lives would be wrecked: one of dubious value plus four others, *or* the one of dubious value. There was no real choice the family felt" primarily because of space, money, time, and personal re-

nedy said; but to deliberately make medical care a function of ineq-
uities that exist at birth is evidently to add injustice to injury and fate.

Wiser and more righteous is the practice of Dr. Chester A.
Swinyard of the New York University medical school's rehabilitation
center. Upon the presentation to him of a defective newborn, he
immediately tries to make clear to the mother the distinction between the question of ultimate custody of the child and questions
concerning the care it needs. The mother must consent to operations,
of course. But she is asked only to make judgments about the baby's
care, while she is working through the problem of whether to accept
the defective child as a substitute for her "lost child," i.e., the perfect
baby she wanted. In the prism of the case, when the question is, Shall
this open spine be closed? Shall a shunt be used to prevent further
mental impairment? the mothers can usually answer correctly. In the
case of spina bifida babies, Dr. Swinyard also reports very infrequent
need of institutionalization or foster parents. That results from concentrating the mother's attention on what medical care requires, and
not on lifelong burdens of custody.[2] One must entirely reject the

---

sources. That couple of modest means noted that the wealthy can "buy out" of the
choice. Yet, again, a few paragraphs later, when asked whether there would be "a
substantiative difference in the number of infants allowed to die" if society was
equipped with uniformly excellent, well-staffed custodial institutions, Dr. Duff replied, "I doubt it," citing "several parents who felt it is not right for their child to exist
primarily to provide employment for others." He also distinguished the decision to
"let die" in Yale–New Haven Hospital from the treatment accorded defective children
in Nazi Germany by saying that in the current cases "family and physicians took into
account not only the child's right (to live or to die) but the needs of the family and
society, and, to some extent, future generations," protesting that "if we cannot trust
these persons to do justice here, can anyone be trusted?" (Beverly Kelsey, "Shall These
Children Live?"; repr. in the Hastings Center Report 5/2).

The more technical and presumably well considered article by Duff and A. G. M.
Campbell is quite clear on these points ("Moral and Ethical Dilemmas in the Special-
Care Nursery," New England Journal of Medicine 289/17). There, the references to
"the family economy," "siblings' rights to relief from the seemingly pointless, crush-
ing burden," "the strains of the illness . . . believed to be threatening the marriage
bonds and to be causing sibling behavioral disturbances," "fear that they and their
other children would become socially enslaved, economically deprived, and permanently stigmatized, . . . [in] a state of 'chronic sorrow,'" stand without modulation, or
without the claim that the family-physician decision was made simply for the sake of
the defective child.

2. Swinyard's practice, as I understand it, is quite different from withholding
prognosis of the child's condition. The parents of a child with meaningomyelocele are
not "simply told that the child needed an operation on the back as the first step in
correcting several defects . . . while the activities of care proceeded at a brisk pace"
(Duff and Campbell, "Moral and Ethical Dilemmas").

contention of Duff and Campbell that parents, facing the prospect of oppressive burdens of care, are capable of making the most morally sensible decisions about the needs and rights of defective newborns. There is a Jewish teaching to the effect that only disinterested parties may, by even so innocuous a method as prayer, take any action which may lead to premature termination of life. Husband, children, family, and those charged with the care of the patient may not pray for death.[3]

One can understand—even appreciate—the motives of a physician who considers an unhappy marriage or family poverty when weighing the tragedy facing one child against that facing another, and rations his help accordingly. Nevertheless, that surely is a species of injustice. Physicians are not appointed to remove all life's tragedy, least of all by lessening medical care now and letting infants die who for social reasons seem fated to have less care in the future than others. That's one way to remove every evening the human debris that has accumulated since morning.

There is a story that is going around—in fact I'm going around telling it—about how the pope, the chief rabbi of Jerusalem, and the general secretary of the World Council of Churches arrived in heaven the same day. Since they had been spiritual leaders here below and ecclesiastical figures to take notice of, they had some difficulty adjusting. Such was the equality there that everyone had to take his place and turn in the cafeteria line. After some muttering protest they fell into the customs of the place, until one day a little man dressed in a white coat came in and rushed to the head of the line. "Who's that?" asked the pope resentfully. "Oh, that's God," came the reply. "He thinks He's a doctor!"

If physicians are going to play God under the pretense of providing relief for the human condition, let us hope they play God as God plays God. Our God is no respecter of persons of good quality. Nor does He curtail his care for us because our parents are poor or have unhappy marriages, or because we are most in need of help. Again, a true humanism also leads to an "equality of life" standard.

A policy of selectively not treating severely defective infants appeals ultimately, it is true, to whatever constitutes the greatness and glory of humankind to give us a standard by which to determine the bottom line of life to be deemed worth living. Thus Joseph Fletcher proposed fifteen "positive human criteria" and five "negative human

<hr/>

3. R. Chaim Palaggi, Chikekei Lev., I, Yoreh De'ah, no. 50.

criteria" as an ensemble quality-of-life index.[4] Then he reduced the number in an article entitled "Four Indicators of Humanhood—the Enquiry Matures."[5] There is no need for us to examine Fletcher's criteria—three of which seem to declare anyone who does not have a Western sense of time to be a nonperson. Fletcher is simply a sign of our times. Many, more serious ethicists have joined in the search for "indicators of personhood." The fundamental question to be faced is whether the practice of medicine should be based on any such set of criteria (presuming they can be discovered and agreed upon).

To that question I want first to say that that's no way to play God as God plays God. That was not the bottom line of His providential care. When the prophet Jeremiah tells us, "Before I formed thee in the belly I knew thee; and before thou camest forth out of the womb I sanctified thee; and I ordained thee" (1:5), he does not mean to start us on a search for the "indicators of personhood" God was using or should have used before calling us by name. Neither did the psalmist when he cried, "Behold . . . the darkness and the light are both alike to thee. For thou hast possessed my reins: thou hast covered me in my mother's womb. I will praise thee; for I am fearfully and wonderfully made: marvelous are thy works; and that my soul knoweth right well" (139:12b,13,14). No more did God, at the outset of His Egyptian rescue operation, look around for "indicators of peoplehood," choosing only those best qualified for national existence. "The Lord did not set his love upon you, nor choose you, because you were more in number than any people; for you were the fewest of all people. But because the Lord loved you, and because He would keep the oath he had sworn unto your fathers, hath the Lord brought you out with a mighty hand" (Deut. 7:7,8a).

4. "Medicine and the Nature of Man," in *The Teaching of Medical Ethics*, ed. Robert M. Veatch, Willard Gaylin, and Councilman Morgan; *Hastings Center Report* 2/5 (November 1972): 1–4. See also the correspondence in ibid. 1/1 (February 1973): 13.

5. *Hastings Center Report* 4/6 (December 1974): 4–7. These accordion concepts of "meaningful/meaningless," "humanhood," "relationships that can be considered human," and "man's ability to relate" (called, incorrectly, "minimal" criteria) are used throughout *Dying: Considerations Concerning the Passage from Life to Death*, Interim Report by the Task Force on Human Life of the Anglican Church of Canada (Toronto, June 1977; presented to the 1977 session of the Synod on Aug. 11–18). Representing no official or authoritative views of the Anglican church of Canada, the report proceeds to address our duties toward defective newborns as if they are "human-looking shapes" or at most "sentient" creatures: "The only way to treat such defective infants humanly is not to treat them as human" (p. 14). A widening controversy over the report was reported in the *New York Times*, July 28, 1977. The Synod sent the report back to committee.

Many of God's life-and-death decisions are inscrutable to us. People are born and die. Nations rise and fall. Doubtless God in His official governance does—or at least permits—lots of things (as the Irishman said) which He would never think of doing in a private capacity. Nor should we, who are not given dominion or coregency over humankind. But there is no indication at all that God is a rationalist whose care is a function of indicators of our personhood, or of our achievement within those capacities. He makes his rain to fall upon the just and the unjust alike, and His sun to rise on the abnormal as well as the normal. Indeed, He has special care for the weak and the vulnerable among us earth people. He cares according to need, not capacity or merit.

These images and shadows of divine things are the foundation of Western medical care, together with that "Pythagorean manifesto,"[6] the Hippocratic oath. As *John* Fletcher has written:

> If we choose to be shaped by Judeo-Christian visions of the "createdness" of life within which every creature bears the image of God, we ought to care for the defective newborn as if our relation with the Creator depended on the outcome. If we choose to be shaped by visions of the inherent dignity of each member of the human family, no matter what his or her predicament, we ought to care for this defenseless person as if the basis of our own dignity depended on the outcome. Care cannot fall short of universal equality.[7]

Indicators of personhood may be of use in psychology, in educational theory, and in moral nurture, but to use such indices in the practice of medicine is a grave mistake. Even the search for such guidelines on which to base the care of defective newborn infants would launch neonatal medicine upon a trackless ocean of uncertainty, directly into arbitrary winds. Thus, one of the physicians at Yale–New Haven Hospital, explaining on television the newly announced policy of benign neglect of defective infants in that medical center, said that to have a life worth living a baby must be "lovable."[8]

6. *Roe v. Wade*, 410, U.S. 113.
7. John Fletcher, "Abortion, Euthanasia, and Care of Defective Newborns," *New England Journal of Medicine* 292 (Jan. 9, 1975): 75–78.
8. *CBS News*, Jan. 2, 1973. In their landmark article ("Moral and Ethical Dilemmas") Drs. Raymond S. Duff and A. G. M. Campbell used the expression "meaningful humanhood." Dr. Duff in a subsequently published interview explained that criteria to mean "the capacity to love and be loved, to be independent, and to understand and plan for the future" (Kelsey, "Shall These Children Live?"). Asked whether a mongoloid child may have "meaningful humanhood," Dr. Duff seemed to hedge, leaving the decision to parents who "pay the fiddler to call the tune," while the physician and hospital policy need only sometimes decide "whether the family's God is fair to the child."

Millard S. Everett, in his book *Ideals of Life*, writes that "no child should be admitted into the society of the living" who suffers "any physical or mental defect that would prevent marriage or would make others tolerate his company only from a sense of mercy."[9] Mercy me, to that we must say no. Medical criteria for care should remain physiological, as should also the signs by which physicians declare that a patient has died. Decisions to treat or not to treat should be the same for the normal and the abnormal alike. Searching for an index of personhood to use (comparing patient-persons, not treatments or treatment with no treatment) is rather like founding medical care on theological judgments about when God infuses the soul into the human organism.

In face of the slipperiness of such criteria as "lovable" or capacity to live without the mercy of others, some doctors suggest that the defective themselves be consulted. They should be asked whether they themselves should have been assisted to live or allowed to die; or whether medical aid should be extended if they have a child afflicted as they are. That, it is suggested, would be a realistic way for us to tell the difference between a life worth living and one that is not. But who does not realize that answers to such questions would be a comparison of normal life with defective life—the same as a mother's initial reaction to such a tragedy—and not a comparison of life with no life? No one can weigh life against nothingness; and, of course, an abnormal person saved by modern medicine will say he wants no *affliction* such as his to be the fate of others. Faced with the question, he may very well say that he *wants no child* afflicted as he is. That will be his manner of speaking. Still, no one can look into the chasm between life and death and weigh the difference—not without first being alive, which makes quite a difference. Such speculations are rather like the "wrongful life" cases that have been brought to our courts:[10] suing one's parents for having been born illegitimate, or of parents with borderline intelligence, or in unhappy surroundings. The courts have held that the petitioner would not be there to sue if he had never been born. Likewise, no one has "standing" in the moral universe to tell

9. Cited by Daniel C. Maguire, *Death by Choice* (New York: Doubleday, 1974), p. 7. Here Maguire indicates no disagreement with such criteria.

10. A convenient reference and discussion of these cases is in *The Problem of Abortion*, ed. Joel Feinberg (Belmont, Calif.: Wadsworth, 1973), pp. 161–80. At one point Duff and Campbell expressly claim they are enabling infants "to escape 'wrongful life,' a fate rated as worse than death." We need to know, by whose ratings? The suicide rate among normal people is *higher* than among so-called defective people. That's one way to "consult" them.

whether he should ever have been or not. Life is not a good; it is an inexplicable gift. When we speak of *good* we speak of *life's* well-being. It is a duty of parents and physicians and the human community in general to sustain the life of a defective infant—who is not born dying and who cannot refuse treatment—and to insure that its life shall be as good and as free from disability as possible.

The proper treatment of defective newborns, especially proper care in the paradigmatic case of spina bifida babies, cannot be determined without a more radical rethinking than is usually proposed of the meaning of traditional medical ethical concepts. I have suggested that the distinction between ordinary and extraordinary measures in the case of patients who are not dying (and who cannot themselves refuse treatment) means discrimination between indicated and non-indicated treatments. It requires choice among beneficial treatments and simple refusal to use medically nonbeneficial measures. The question to be asked concerning nondying patients incapable of consent is, What will help? What will ease?

Failure to take this route entails treating defective newborns who are not dying *as if* they were competent conscious patients refusing treatment. To continue discussion of these crucial cases under the alternative "to save or let die" forces an ethicist or a physician to move from consultation about beneficial and nonbeneficial treatments to consultation about conditions of life that are beneficial to the possessor thereof. This obscures the distinction between voluntary and involuntary euthanasia, or at least erodes the moral grounds for making that distinction. It also erodes the moral reasons for distinguishing between letting die and actively dispatching defective newborns, or hastening their deaths. Comparison of human lives and not comparison of treatments (including only palliative treatment) becomes the issue.

A Paul Ramsey Bibliography

BOOKS

Basic Christian Ethics. New York: Scribner's, 1950. Repr. Louisville: Westminster/John Knox Press, 1993.

Faith and Ethics: The Theology of H. Richard Neibuhr (editor and contributor). New York: Harper and Brothers, 1957.

Freedom of the Will (editor, with critical introduction). Vol. 1 of *The Works of Jonathan Edwards.* New Haven: Yale University Press, 1957.

Christian Ethics and the Sit-In. New York: Association Press, 1961.

War and the Christian Conscience: How Shall Modern War Be Conducted Justly? Durham, N.C.: Duke University Press, 1961. Published for the Lilly Endowment Research Program in Christianity and Politics.

Nine Modern Moralists. Englewood Cliffs, N.J.: Prentice-Hall, 1962. Also published as *Nueve Moralistas modernos* (Mexico: Herrero Hermanos Sucesores, 1965) and as *Gendaiteki Jitsuzon to Rinri,* trans. Kuniyasu Take (Kyoto: Sekai Shiso sha, 1970).

The Limits of Nuclear War: Thinking about the Do-Able and the Un-Do-Able. New York: Council on Religion and International Affairs, 1963. An Occasional Paper in the Ethics and Foreign Policy Series.

Again, the Justice of Deterrence. New York: Council on Religion and International Affairs, 1965. An Occasional Paper in the Ethics and Foreign Policy Series.

Deeds and Rules in Christian Ethics. Edinburgh and London: Oliver and Boyd. *Scottish Journal of Theology* Occasional Papers no. 11, 1965. American edition published by Scribner's [New York, 1967]).

Religion (editor). *The Princeton Studies: Humanistic Scholarship in America.* Englewood Cliffs, N.J.: Prentice-Hall, 1965.

Who Speaks for the Church? A Critique of the 1966 Geneva Conference on Church and Society. Nashville and New York: Abingdon, 1967; Edinburgh: St. Andrew's, 1970.

The Just War: Force and Political Responsibility. New York: Scribner's, 1968.

Norm and Context in Christian Ethics (edited with Gene H. Outka). New York: Scribner's, 1968.

Fabricated Man: The Ethics of Genetic Control. New Haven and London: Yale University Press, 1970. Also published as *El Hombre fabricado,* trans. Julian Rubio (Madrid: Guadarrama, 1973).

The Patient as Person: Explorations in Medical Ethics. New Haven and London: Yale University Press, 1970.

The Study of Religion in Colleges and Universities (edited with John F. Wilson). Princeton: Princeton University Press, 1970.

One Flesh: A Christian View of Sex Within, Outside, and Before Marriage. Grove Booklets on Ethics no. 8. Nottingham, England: Grove, 1975.

The Ethics of Fetal Research. New Haven and London: Yale University Press, 1975.

Ethics at the Edges of Life: Medical and Legal Intersections. New Haven and London: Yale University Press, 1978.

Doing Evil to Achieve Good: Moral Choice in Conflict Situations (edited with Richard A. McCormick, S. J.). Chicago: Loyola University Press, 1978.

Three on Abortion (reprint booklet series). *Child and Family* (Oak Park, Ill.), 1978. (Contains "Feticide/Infanticide Upon Request" [1970], "Abortion: A Review Article" [1973], and "Protecting the Unborn" [1974].)

Speak Up for Just War or Pacifism (with epilogue by Stanley Hauerwas). State College: Pennsylvania State University Press, 1988.

Ethical Writings (editor, with critical introduction). Vol. 8 of *The Works of Jonathan Edwards.* New Haven and London: Yale University Press, 1989.

ARTICLES AND CHAPTERS

(listed alphabetically by year)

"Christianity and War." *The Christian Advocate* 110, no. 4 (Feb. 15, 1935): 202–03.

"The Great Commandment." *Christianity and Society* 8, no. 4 (Fall 1943): 29–35.

"The Manger, the Cross, and the Resurrection." *Christianity and Crisis* 3, no. 6 (April 19, 1943): 2–5.

"Natural Law and the Nature of Man." *Christendom* 9, no. 3 (Summer 1944): 369–81.

"A Social Policy for Liberal Religion." *Religion in Life* 13, no. 4 (Autumn 1944): 495–507.

"The Idealistic View for Moral Evil: Josiah Royce and Bernard Bosanquet." *Philosophy and Phenomenological Research* 6, no. 4 (June 1946): 554–89.

"Religious Instruction Problematically Christian." *Journal of Religion* 26, no. 4 (October 1946): 243–62.

"A Theology of Social Action." *Social Action* 12, no. 8 (Oct. 15, 1946): 4–34.

"The Theory of Democracy: Idealistic or Christian?" *Ethics* 56, no. 4 (July 1946): 251–66.

"Beyond the Question of Tongues." *Theology Today* 3, no. 4 (January 1947): 446–58.

"Religion at Princeton" (with Robert E. Wick and Burton A. MacLean). *Religious Education* 42, no. 2 (March–April 1947): 65–69.

"A Theory of Virtue According to the Principles of the Reformation." *Journal of Religion* 27, no. 3 (July 1947): 178–96.

"*Existenz* and the Existence of God: A Study of Kierkegaard and Hegel." *Journal of Religion* 28, no. 3 (July 1948): 157–76.

"Elements of a Biblical Political Theory." *Journal of Religion* 29, no. 4 (October 1949): 258–83.

"*Non Solum in Memoriam Sed in Intentionem:* A Tribute to the Late Rev. John W. Ramsey." *Mississippi Methodist Advocate*, o.s. 95 (n.s. 2), no. 40 (March 23, 1949): 8, 9, 12.

"In This Is Love. . . ." *Motive* 11, no. 1 (October 1950): 21–23.

"God's Grace and Man's Guilt." *Journal of Religion* 31, no. 1 (January 1951): 21–37.

"The Revealer of Many Hearts." *Adult Teacher* 4, no. 6 (June 1951): 7–9.

"God and the Family." Sunday School Lesson for May 18. *Crossroads*, April–June, 1952: 59–61.

"God's Estimate of Human Life." Sunday School Lesson for May 25. *Crossroads*, April–June, 1952: 62–64.

"Paul and Some of His Letters." A series of seven Sunday school lessons for adult classes, May 17–June 28. *Crossroads*, April–June, 1953: 77–79; together with the exegesis of scripture and instruction for teachers, *Westminster Teacher*, April–June 1953.

"God and the Family." A series of five adult lessons. *Crossroads*, July

1955: 13–30; together with instructions to teachers, *Westminster Teacher*, July–September 1955: 5–14.

"Freedom and Responsibility in Medical and Sex Ethics: A Protestant View." *New York University Law Review* 31, no. 7 (November 1956): 1189–1204.

"Love and Law." Pp. 80–123 in Charles W. Kegley and Robert W. Bretall, eds., *Reinhold Niebuhr: His Religious, Social, and Political Thought.* New York: Macmillan, 1956.

"Marriage and the Kingdom of God." *Crossroads*, January 1956: 13–16, 19.

"No Morality Without Immortality: Dostoevski and the Meaning of Atheism." *Journal of Religion* 36, no. 2 (April 1956): 90–108.

"Christian Ethics." *Collier's Encyclopedia*, 5: 227. New York: Collier, 1957.

"The Church Is You." *Growing*, October–December, 1957: 14–16; also in *Victory*, October–December, 1957: 4–6.

"The Transformation of Ethics." Pp. 140–72 in Paul Ramsey, ed., *Faith and Ethics: The Theology of H. Richard Niebuhr.* New York: Harper and Brothers, 1957.

"Mysticism." *Collier's Encylcopedia*, 14: 343. New York: Collier, 1957.

"A Fable." *Chaplain* 15, no. 5 (October 1958): 27–28. Repr. in *Motive* 19, no. 7 (April 1959): cover; and in *Christian Advocate* 5, no. 1 (Jan. 5, 1961): 11.

"Freedom and Responsibility in Medical and Sex Ethics: A Protestant View." Pp. 284–99 in Burke Shartel and B. J. George, Jr., eds., *Readings in Legal Methods.* Ann Arbor, Mich.: Overbeck, 1959.

"The Legal Imputation of Religion to an Infant in Adoption Proceedings." *New York University Law Review* 34, no. 4 (April 1959): 649–90.

"Religious Aspects of Marxism." *Canadian Journal of Theology* 5, no. 3 (July 1959): 143–55.

"Right and Wrong Calculation." *worldview* 2, no. 12 (December 1959): 6–9.

"Faith Effective through In-Principled Love." *Christianity and Crisis* 20, no. 9 (May 30, 1960): 76–78.

"Male and Female He Created Them." *Victory*, January–March 1960: 1–4.

"Marriage of Adam and Eve." *Moravian Theological School Bulletin* 1960: 35–56.

"Reinhold Niebuhr: Leader in Social, Political and Religious Thought." *New York Herald-Tribune Book Review*, June 19, 1960: 4.

"Religious Aspects of Marxism." *Moravian Theological School Bulletin* 1960: 57–75.

"Sex and People: A Critical Review." *Religion in Life* 30, no. 1 (Winter 1960–61): 53–70.

"The Case for Just or Counterforces Warfare." *Pittsburgh [Theological Seminary] Perspective* 2, no. 3 (September 1961): 7–20.

"Dream and Reality in Deterrence and Defense." *Christianity and Crisis* 21, no. 22 (December 25, 1961): 228–32.

"The New Papal Encyclical—I." *Christian Century* 78, no. 36 (Sept. 6, 1961): 1047–1050.

"The New Papal Encyclical—II." *Christian Century* 78, no. 37 (Sept. 13, 1961): 1077–1079.

"The Nuclear Dilemma." Pp. 108–34 in U. S. Allers and W. V. O'Brien, eds., *Christian Ethics and Nuclear Warfare*. Washington: Georgetown Univ. Institute of World Polity, 1961.

Preface to Gabriel Vahanian, *The Death of God: The Culture of Our Post-Christian Era*. New York: Braziller, 1961.

"Right and Wrong Calculation." Pp. 47–54 in William Clancy, ed., *The Moral Dilemma of Nuclear Weapons*. New York: Church Peace Union, 1961.

"Shelter Morality." *Presbyterian Life* 14 (Nov. 15, 1961): 7–8, 41–42; discussion, ibid., 15 (Jan. 1, 1962): 4–5, 42.

"Theological Studies in College and Seminary." *Theology Today* 17, no. 4 (January 1961): 466–84.

"The Case for Making 'Just War' Possible." Pp. 143–70 in John C. Bennett, ed., *Nuclear Weapons and the Conflict of Conscience*. New York: Scribner's, 1962.

"Community of Two." *Crossroads*, 12, no. 3 (April–June 1962): 92–94.

"Death's Duel." *Motive* 22, no. 7 (April 1962): 2–5. Repr., abridged, in *Pulpit* 38, no. 3 (March 1967): 16–19.

"Life, Death, and the Law." *Journal of Public Law* 11 (1962): 377–93.

"Porcupines in Winter." *Motive* 22, no. 8 (May 1962): 6–11.

"Princeton University's Graduate Program in Religion." *Journal of Bible and Religion* 30, no. 4 (October 1962): 291–98.

"Turn Toward Just War." *worldview* 5, nos. 7–8 (July–August 1962): 8–13.

"U.S. Military Policy and 'Shelter Morality.'" *worldview* 5, no. 1 (January 1962): 6–9; discussion, ibid., vol. 5, no. 3 (March 1962): 6–9.

"Church and Academy: A Tension in Theological Education." *Garrett Tower* 39, no. 1 (December 1963): 8–15.

"The Just War Theory on Trial." *Cross Currents* 13, no. 4 (Fall 1963): 477–90.

"Marriage Law and Biblical Covenant." Pp. 41–77 in D. A. Giannella, ed., *Religion and the Public Order, 1963*. Chicago: Univ. of Chicago Press, 1964.

"Morgenthau on Nuclear War." *Commonweal* 78, no. 21 (Sept. 20, 1963): 554–57.

"On Taking Sex Seriously Enough." *Christianity and Crisis* 23, no. 19 (Nov. 11, 1963): 204–06.

"*Pacem in Terris.*" *Religion in Life* 33, no. 1 (Winter 1963–64): 116–35.

"Protestant Casuistry Today." *Christianity and Crisis* 23, no. 3 (March 4, 1963): 24–28.

"Review of St. John-Stevas's 'Life, Death and the Law.'" *Journal of Public Law* 11, no. 2 (1963): 77–93.

"Teaching 'Virtue' in the Public Schools." Pp. 336–38 in D. A. Giannella, ed., *Religion and the Public Order, 1963*. Chicago: University of Chicago Press, 1964.

"Toward a Test-Ban Treaty: Is Nothing Better than On-Sight Inspection?" *worldview* 6, nos. 7–8 (July–August 1963): 4–10.

"How Shall We Sing the Lord's Song in a Pluralistic Land? The Prayer Decisions." *Journal of Public Law* 13, no. 2 (1964): 353–400.

"Is God Mute in the Goldwater Candidacy?" *Christianity and Crisis* 24, no. 15 (Sept. 21, 1964): 175–78.

"Justice in War." *New Wine: A Christian Journal of Opinion* 2, no. 3 (Spring 1964): 21–25.

"Morals and Nuclear Weapons." Pp. 23–41 in *A Study of Morals and the Nuclear Program*. Albuquerque: Headquarters Field Command, Defense Atomic Support Agency, Sandria Base, 1964.

"On Taking Sexual Responsibility Seriously Enough." *Christianity and Crisis* 23, no. 23 (Jan. 6, 1964): 247–51.

"The Status and Advancement of Theological Scholarship in America." *Christian Scholar* 47 (Spring 1964): 7–23.

"Theological Studies in College and Seminary." Pp. 21–114 in K. R. Bridgston and D. W. Culver, eds., *The Making of Ministers*. Minneapolis: Augsburg, 1964.

"The Uses of Power." *Perkins [School of Theology] Journal* 18, no. 1 (Fall 1964): 13–24.

"A Christian Approach to the Question of Sexual Relations Outside Marriage." *Journal of Religion* 45, no. 2 (April 1965): 100–118.

"The Church and the Magistrate." *Christianity and Crisis* 25, no. 11 (June 28, 1965): 136–40.

"The Ethics of Intervention." *Review of Politics* 27, no. 3 (July 1965): 287–310.

"Lehmann's Contextual Ethics and the Problem of Truth-Telling." *Theology Today* 21, no. 4 (January 1965): 466–75.

"Modern Papal Social Teachings." Pp. 220–38 in Robert E. Cushman and

Egil Grislis, eds., *The Heritage of Christian Thought* (festschrift for R. L. Calhoun). New York: Harper and Brothers, 1965.

"More Unsolicited Advice to Vatican Council II." Pp. 37–66 in James Finn, ed., *Peace, the Churches and the Bomb*. New York: Council on Religion and International Affairs, 1965.

"The Uses of Power." *Catholic Mind* 63, no. 1196 (October 1965): 11–23.

"Farewell to Christian Realism." *America* 114, no. 18 (April 30, 1966): 618–22.

"A Letter from Canon Rhymes to John of Patmos." *Religion in Life* 35, no. 2 (Spring 1966): 218–29.

"Living with Yourself." *Pulpit* 37, no. 7 (July–August 1966): 4–8.

"Moral and Religious Implications of Genetic Control." Pp. 107–69 in John D. Roslansky, ed., *Genetics and the Future of Man*. Amsterdam: North-Holland, 1966.

"Nuclear War and Vatican Council II." *Theology Today* 23, no. 2 (July 1966): 244–63.

"Responsible Parenthood: A Response to Fr. Bernard Häring." In *The Vatican Council and the World of Today*. Providence: Office of the Secretary, Brown University, 1966.

"Tucker's *Bellum contra Bellum Justum*." Pp. 67–101 in Robert W. Tucker, *Just War and Vatican Council II: A Critique*. New York: Council on Religion and International Affairs, 1966.

"Two Concepts of General Rules in Christian Ethics." *Ethics* 76, no. 3 (April 1966): 192–207.

"The Vatican Council on Modern War." *Theological Studies* 27, no. 2 (June 1966): 179–203.

"Vietnam: Dissent from Dissent." *Christian Century* 83, no. 29 (July 20, 1966): 909–13.

"Counting the Costs." Pp. 24–44 in Michael B. Hamilton, ed., *The Vietnam War: Christian Perspectives*. Grand Rapids: Eerdmans, 1967.

"Discretionary Armed Service." *worldview* 10, no. 2 (February 1967): 8–11.

"From Princeton with Love." *Reflection* 64, no. 1 (January 1967): 5–6.

"Is Vietnam a Just War?" *Dialog* 6, no. 1 (Winter 1967): 19–29.

"On Sexual Responsibility." *Catholic World* 205, no. 1128 (July 1967): 210–16.

"Over the Slope to Total War?" *Catholic World* 205, no. 1127 (June 1967): 166–68.

"Responsible Parenthood: An Essay in Ecumenical Ethics." *Religion in Life* 36, no. 3 (Autumn 1967): 343–54.

"The Sanctity of Life—In the First of It." *Dublin Review* 241, no. 511 (Spring 1967): 3–23.

"Two Extremes: Ramsey Replies to the Critics." *Dialog* 6, no. 3 (Summer 1967): 218–19.

"The Case of Curious Exception." Pp. 67–135 in Gene H. Outka and Paul Ramsey, eds., *Norm and Context in Christian Ethics.* New York: Scribner's, 1968.

"Christian Ethics Today." *Rockford College Alumni Magazine* 45, no. 2, Spring 1968: 3–6, 23.

"Christianity and Modern War." *Theology Digest* 16, no. 1 (Spring 1968): 47–53.

"Dissent, Democracy and Foreign Policy: A Symposium." *Headline Series* 190 (August 1968): 40–44. New York: Foreign Policy Association.

"Commentary on 'Election Issues 1968.'" *Social Action* 35, no. 2 (October 1968) and *Social Progress* 59, no. 1 (September–October 1968): 19–28.

"Election 1968, and Beyond." *worldview* 11, no. 12 (December 1968): 16–19.

"The Morality of Abortion." Pp. 60–93 in Daniel Labby, ed., *Life or Death: Ethics and Options.* Seattle: University of Washington Press, 1968.

"Naturrecht und christliche Ethik bei N. H. Søe." *Zeitschrift für Evangelische Ethik* 12, no. 2 (March 1968): 80–98.

"On Taking Sexual Responsibility Seriously Enough." Pp. 44–54 in Gibson Winter, ed., *Social Ethics.* New York: Harper and Row; London, SCM, 1968.

"Political Repentance Now!" *Christianity and Crisis* 28, no. 18 (Oct. 28, 1968): 247–52.

"Politics as Science, Not Prophecy." *worldview* 11, no. 1 (January 1968): 18–21.

"A Proposal to the New Moralists." *Motive* 28, no. 7 (April 1968): 38–44.

"A Reaction to 'Black Power and the Shock of Recognition' by James Luther Adams." *Action/Reaction,* Summer 1968: 5–6.

"Selective Conscientious Objection: Warrants and Reservations in the Just War Doctrine." Pp. 31–77 in James Finn, ed., *Conflict of Loyalties: Selective Conscientious Objection.* New York: Pegasus, 1968.

"War and the New Morality." *Reformed Journal* 18, no. 2 (February 1968): 25–28, with subsequent discussion.

Introduction to William V. O'Brien, *War and/or Survival.* Garden City, N.Y.: Doubleday, 1969.

"Medical Ethics: A Joint Venture." *Reflection* 66, no. 3 (March 1969): 4–5.

"On Up-Dating Death." Pp. 253–75 in Donald R. Cutler, ed., *The Religious Situation, 1969.* Boston: Beacon, 1969. Also (as "On Updating

Death") pp. 31–54 in Donald R. Cutler, ed., *Updating Life and Death: Essays in Ethics and Medicine.* Boston: Beacon, 1969.

"Abortion: A Theologian's View." *AORN* (Journal of the Association of Operating Room Nurses), November 1970: 55–62. Also pp. 112–20 in Valerie Vance Dillon, ed., *In Defense of Life.* Trenton: New Jersey Right to Life Committee, 1970.

"The Biblical Norm of Righteousness." *Interpretation* 24, no. 4 (October 1970): 419–29.

"Christian Love in Search of a Social Policy." Pp. 184–96 in Harmon L. Smith and Louis W. Hodges, eds., *The Christian and His Decisions.* Nashville and New York: Abingdon, 1969.

"Christianity and Modern War." Pp. 275–85 in Everett J. Morgan, S. J., ed., *Christian Witness in the Secular City.* Chicago: Loyola University Press, 1970.

"Feticide/Infanticide Upon Request." *Child and Family* 9, no. 3 (Summer 1970): 257–72; *Religion in Life* 39, no. 2 (Summer 1970): 170–86.

"Panel Discussion." *Annals of the New York Academy of Sciences* 169, no. 2 (Jan. 21, 1970): 576–83.

"Reference Points in Deciding about Abortion." Pp. 60–100 in John T. Noonan, *The Morality of Abortion: Legal and Historical Perspectives.* Cambridge: Harvard University Press, 1970.

"Shall We Clone a Man?" Pp. 78–113 in Kenneth Vaux, ed., *Who Shall Live? Medicine, Technology, Ethics.* Philadelphia: Fortress, 1970.

"The Betrayal of Language." *worldview* 14, no. 2 (February 1971): 7–10.

"Christian Ethics and the Future of Humanism." Pp. 83–91 in Carl W. Grindell, ed., *God, Man and Philosophy.* New York: St. John's University Press, 1971.

"Church Stand Should Be Withdrawn" [response to Albert C. Outler]. *The Christian Advocate* 15, no. 21 (Nov. 11, 1971): 11–12.

"The Ethics of a Cottage Industry in an Age of Community and Research Medicine." *New England Journal of Medicine* 284, no. 13 (April 1, 1971): 700–706.

"The Morality of Abortion." Pp. 1–27 in James Rachels, ed., *Moral Problems: A Collection of Philosophical Essays.* New York: Harper and Row, 1971.

"A Proposal to the New Moralists." Pp. 112–25 in Paul T. Jersild and Dale A. Johnson, eds., *Moral Issues and Christian Response.* New York: Holt, Rinehart and Winston, 1971.

"Some Moral Problems Arising in Genetic Medicine." *Linacre Quarterly* 38, no. 1 (February 1971): 15–20.

"The Wedge: Not So Simple." *Hastings Center Report* 1, no. 3 (December 1971): 11–12.

"Who Speaks for the Church?" Pp. 47–54 in Paul T. Jersild and Dale A. Johnson, eds., *Moral Issues and Christian Response*. New York: Holt, Rinehart and Winston, 1971.

"Author-Reviewer Symposia" [on *Fabricated Man*]. *Philosophy Forum* 12 (1972): 149–64.

"Does the Church Have Any Political Wisdom for the 70's?" *Perkins [School of Theology] Journal* 26, no. 1 (Fall 1972): 29–40.

"Force and Political Responsibility." Pp. 43–73 in Ernest W. Lefever, ed., *Ethics and World Politics*. Baltimore: Johns Hopkins University Press, 1972.

"Genetic Engineering." *Bulletin of the Atomic Scientists* 28, no. 10 (December 1972): 14–17.

"Genetic Therapy: A Theologian's Response." Pp. 157–75 in Michael Hamilton, ed., *The New Genetics and the Future of Man*. Grand Rapids: Eeerdmans, 1972.

"The MAD Nuclear Policy." *worldview* 15, no. 11 (November 1972): 16–20.

"The Morality of Manipulation." *Worcester Polytechnic Institute Journal* 76, no. 1 (August 1972): 11–13.

"Shall We 'Reproduce'? I. The Medical Ethics of *In Vitro* Fertilization." *Journal of the American Medical Association* 220, no. 10 (June 5, 1972): 1346–1350.

"Shall We 'Reproduce'? II. Rejoinders and Future Forecast." *Journal of the American Medical Association* 220, no. 11 (June 12, 1972): 1480–1485.

"Abortion: A Review Article." *Thomist* 37, no. 1 (January 1973): 174–226.

"The Abstractness of Concrete Advice." Pp. 335–45 in Norbert Brockman and Nicholas Piediscalzi, eds., *Contemporary Religion and Social Responsibility*. New York: Alba House, 1973.

"The Just Revolution." *worldview* 16, no. 10 (October 1973): 37–40.

"Medical Progress and Canons of Loyalty to Experimental Subjects." *Proceedings* (Institute for Theological Encounter with Science and Technology) 1973: 51–77.

"Military Service as a Moral System." *Military Chaplains' Review* 2, no. 1 (January 1973): 8–21.

"The Moral and Religious Implications of Genetic Control." Pp. 364–82 in Adela S. Baer, ed., *Heredity and Society: Readings in Social Genetics*. New York: Macmillan, 1973.

"Morals and the Practice of Genetic Medicine." Pp. 71–84 in Joseph Papin, ed., *The Pilgrim People: A Vision with Hope*. Villanova, Pa.: Villanova University Press, 1970.

"The Nature of Medical Ethics." Pp. 14–28 in Robert M. Veatch, Willard Gaylin, and Councilman Morgan, eds., *The Teaching of Medical Ethics.* Hastings-on-Hudson, N.Y.: Hastings Center, Institute of Society, Ethics, and the Life Sciences, 1973.

"Should Medicine Today Be Taught Without Medical Ethics?" *Connecticut Medicine* 37, no. 8 (August 1973): 420–21.

"A Political Ethics Context for Strategic Thinking." Pp. 101–47 in Morton A. Kaplan, ed., *Strategic Thinking and Its Moral Implications.* Chicago: University of Chicago Center for Policy Study, 1973.

"Screening: An Ethicist's View." Pp. 147–67 in Bruce Hilton et al., eds., *Ethical Issues in Human Genetics: Genetic Counseling and the Use of Genetic Knowledge.* New York: Plenum, 1973.

"Shall We 'Reproduce'?" Pp. 87–120 in Martin E. Marty and Dean G. Peerman, eds., *New Theology,* no. 10. New York: Macmillan, 1973.

"Beyond Relief and Liberation." *worldview* 17, no. 12 (1974): 12–13.

"Conceptual Foundations for an Ethics of Medical Care: A Response." In *Ethics and Health Care: Proceedings of the Conference on Health Care and Changing Values.* Washington, D.C.: National Academy of Sciences, 1974.

"Death's Pedagogy: The Assault on the Last Taboo." *Commonweal,* Sept. 20, 1974: 497–502.

"The Indignity of 'Death with Dignity.'" With Response by Leon R. Kass and Robert Morison. *Hastings Center Studies* 2, no. 2 (May 1974): 47–62; repr. in P. Steinfels and R. M. Veatch, eds., *Death Inside Out.* New York: Harper and Row, 1975.

"Models For Decision Making." *Thesis Theological Cassettes* 5, no. 2 (March 1974).

"Protecting the Unborn" [testimony before Senate Judiciary Subcommittee, March 8, 1974]. *Commonweal,* May 31, 1974: 308–14; *Linacre Quarterly* 41 (1974): 269–80; *Blackacre* 3, no. 5 (1974): 3–4.

"Taxonomy." *worldview* 17, no. 8 (August 1974): 6.

"The Bicentennial Began Last August"; "The Church's Role to Celebrate"; "'Unfound' Theologians." *Theology Today* 31, no. 4 (January 1975): 331–36.

"Moral Issues in Fetal Research." Statement submitted to the National Commission for the Protection of Human Subjects in Biomedical and Behavioral Research. Pp. 1–21 of transcript of the meeting proceedings, March 14, 1975. Springfield, Va.: National Technical Information Service, 1975.

"Some Ethical Reflections on Prospective Studies of Families at High Risk of Schizophrenia." In *Proceedings of Conference, World Health Organization.* Copenhagen, May 28, 1975.

"Death as an Ethical Issue for the Professions." Columbia University Seminar Reports, vol. 3, no. 8: 150–52. New York: Columbia University 1975–76.

"Abortion After the Law." *Journal of the Christian Medical Society* 7, no. 3 (Summer 1976): 10–17.

"Conceptual Foundations for an Ethics of Medical Care: A Response." Pp. 35–55 in R. M. Veatch and R. Branson, eds., *Ethics and Health Policy.* Cambridge, Mass.: Ballinger, 1976.

"The Enforcement of Morals: Nontherapeutic Research on Children." *Hastings Center Report* 6, no. 4 (August 1976): 21–30.

"Prolonged Dying: Not Medically Indicated." *Hastings Center Report* 6, no. 1 (February 1976): 14–17.

"The Right Care of Karen Quinlan." *Crucible,* April–June 1976: 66–71.

"Some Rejoinders." *Journal of Religious Ethics* 4, no. 2 (Fall 1976): 185–237.

"Abortion: Last Resort." Pp. 61–75 in R. Abelson and M. L. Frequegnon, eds., *Ethics for Modern Life.* New York: St. Martin's, 1977.

"Children as Research Subjects: A Reply [to Richard A. McCormick, S. J.]." *Hastings Center Report* 7, no. 2 (April 1977): 40–41.

"Consider the Morning Glory." *worldview* 20, no. 12 (December 1977): 41–44.

"Death's Pedagogy." Pp. 331–43 in D. J. Horan and D. Hall, eds., *Death, Dying and Euthanasia.* Washington, D.C.: University Publications of America, 1977.

"'Euthanasia' and Dying Well Enough." *Linacre Quarterly* 44, no. 1 (February 1977): 331–43.

"Korean Creeds and the Rejection of Old Heresies." *worldview* 20, no. 11 (November 1977): 27–28.

"A Human Lottery?" Pp. 444–51 in R. Hunt and J. Arras, eds., *Ethical Issues in Modern Medicine.* Palo Alto, Calif.: Mayfield, 1977.

"The Indignity of 'Death with Dignity.'" Pp. 305–31 in D. J. Horan and D. Hall, eds., *Death, Dying and Euthanasia.* Washington, D.C.: University Publications of America, 1977.

"Kant's Moral Philosophy or a Religious Ethics? A Response to Alasdair MacIntyre." Pp. 44–74 in H. T. Engelhardt, Jr., and D. Callahan, eds., *Knowledge, Value and Belief.* Hastings-on-Hudson, N.Y.: Hastings Center, 1977.

"The Dade County Vote and Our Crisis of Community." *worldview* 20, no. 10 (October 1977): 32–34.

"Protecting the Unborn." Pp. 143–50 in J. Feinberg and H. Gross, eds., *Liberty: Selected Readings.* Belmont, Calif.: Dickenson, 1977.

"Research Involving Children or Incompetents." Pp. 297–304 in R. Hunt and J. Arras, eds., *Ethical Issues in Modern Medicine*. Palo Alto, Calif.: Mayfield, 1977.

"The Same Old Illusions." *worldview* 20, no. 9 (September 1977): 42–43.

"Screening: An Ethicist's View." Pp. 110–17 in R. Hunt and J. Arras, eds., *Ethical Issues in Modern Medicine*. Palo Alto, Calif.: Mayfield, 1977.

"Can the 1973 Abortion Decisions Be Justly Hedged?" *Human Life Review* 4, no. 3 (Summer 1978): 77–110.

"'The Cruise Missile and the Neutron Bomb': Some Critical Reflections [on James T. Johnson]." *worldview* 21, no. 4 (April 1978): 2, 56–57.

"Ethical Dimensions of Experimental Research on Children." Pp. 57–68 in J. van Eys, ed., *Research on Children: Medical Imperatives, Ethical Quandaries, and Legal Constraints*. Baltimore: University Park Press, 1978.

"Incommensurability and Indeterminacy in Moral Choice." Pp. 69–144 in Richard A. McCormick, S. J., and Paul Ramsey, eds., *Doing Evil to Achieve Good*. Chicago: Loyola University Press, 1978.

On In Vitro Fertilization. Studies in Law and Medicine, no. 3. Chicago: Americans United for Life, 1978.

"In Vitro Fertilization: Four Commentaries" [with Stephen Toulmin, Mark Lappe, and John Robertson]. *Hastings Center Report* 8, no. 5 (October 1978): 7–14.

"The *Saikewicz* Precedent: What's Good for an Incompetent Patient?" *Hastings Center Report* 8, no. 6 (December 1978): 36–42.

"Self-Conflict in Ethical Decisions: Response to Eric Cassell." Pp. 234–46 in H. T. Englehardt, Jr., and D. Callahan, eds., *Morals, Science and Sociality*. Hastings-on-Hudson, N.Y.: Hastings Center, 1978.

"The Background Music" [in "Symposium on Civil Defense"]. *worldview* 22, nos. 1–2 (January–February 1979): 46–48.

"Do You Know Where Your Children Are?" *Theology Today* 36, no. 1 (April 1979): 10–21.

"Liturgy and Ethics." *Journal of Religious Ethics* 7, no. 2 (Fall 1979): 139–71.

"Washington Knows?" *Theology Today* 35, no. 4 (January 1979): 428–37.

"The Essentials of Just War Theory." *New Oxford Review*, 1979: 23–24.

"The Vietnam War: Is It Time to Forgive and Forget? Three Views" [with Patrick Dobel and Stanley Hauerwas]. *worldview* 23, nos. 1–2 (January–February 1980): 14.

"Medical Paternity and 'Wrongful Life'" [response to G. Annas]. *Hastings Center Report* 10, no. 1 (February 1980): 4.

"On In Vitro Fertilizations." *Crucible*, 1981: 175–84. London: Board of Social Responsibility, Church of England.

"The Two-Step Fantastic: The Continuing Case of Brother Fox." *Theological Studies* 42, no. 1 (March 1981): 122–34.

"Adolescent Morality—A Theologian's Viewpoint." *Post-Graduate Medicine* 72, no. 1 (July 1982): 233–36.

"Tradition and Reflection in Christian Life." *Perkins [School of Theology] Journal* 35, no. 2 (Winter–Spring 1982): 46–56.

"Do You Know Where Your Children Are?" *Journal of Psychiatry and Christianity* 1, no. 4 (Winter 1982): 7–16.

Foreword (with William F. May). Pp. 7–15 in Arthur C. McGill, *Suffering: A Test of Theological Method*. Philadelphia: Westminster, 1982.

Introduction. Pp. vii–xvi in Dennis J. Horan and Melinda Delahoyde, eds., *Infanticide and the Handicapped Newborn*. Provo, Utah: Brigham Young Univ. Press, 1982.

"Response to Richard John Neuhaus." Pp. 17–24 in *Speaking to the World: Four Protestant Perspectives*. Washington, D.C.: Ethics and Public Policy Center, 1983.

"Testimony." Hearings before the Subcommittee on Family and Human Services of the Committee on Labor and Human Resources, U.S. Senate, April 6, 1983. Washington: Government Printing Office, 1983. Pp. 94–110, 120–21.

"The Issues Facing Mankind." Pp. 19–45 in *The Question of In Vitro Fertilization: Studies in Medicine, Law and Ethics*. London: Society for the Protection of Unborn Children Educational Trust, 1984. Testimony to the Warnock Committee.

"A Letter to James Gustafson." *Journal of Religious Ethics* 13, no. 1 (Spring 1985): 71–100.

"Sexuality in the History of Redemption." *Journal of Religious Ethics* 16, no. 1 (Spring 1988): 56–86.

Index